DATE DUE

N

A

SOVIET POLICY TOWARD TURKEY, IRAN, AND AFGHANISTAN

STUDIES OF INFLUENCE IN INTERNATIONAL RELATIONS

Alvin Z. Rubinstein, *General Editor*

SOUTH AFRICA AND THE UNITED STATES
The Erosion of an Influence Relationship
Richard E. Bissell

SOVIET-INDIAN RELATIONS
Issues and Influence
Robert C. Horn

SOVIET INFLUENCE IN EASTERN EUROPE
Political Autonomy and the Warsaw Pact
Christopher D. Jones

U.S. POLICY TOWARD JAPAN AND KOREA
A Changing Influence
Chae-Jin Lee and Hideo Sato

**SOVIET AND AMERICAN INFLUENCE IN
THE HORN OF AFRICA**
Marina S. Ottaway

THE UNITED STATES AND IRAN
The Patterns of Influence
R. K. Ramazani

**SOVIET POLICY TOWARD TURKEY, IRAN
AND AFGHANISTAN**
The Dynamics of Influence
Alvin Z. Rubinstein

THE UNITED STATES AND PAKISTAN
The Evolution of an Influence Relationship
Shirin Tahir-Kheli

THE UNITED STATES AND BRAZIL
Limits of Influence
Robert Wesson

SOVIET POLICY TOWARD TURKEY, IRAN, AND AFGHANISTAN

The Dynamics of Influence

Alvin Z. Rubinstein

PRAEGER

PRAEGER SPECIAL STUDIES • PRAEGER SCIENTIFIC

Library of Congress Cataloging in Publication Data

Rubinstein, Alvin Z.
  Soviet policy toward Turkey, Iran, and
Afghanistan.

  (Studies of influence in international relations)
  Bibliography: p.
  Includes index.
  1. Soviet Union—Foreign relations—Turkey.
2. Turkey—Foreign relations—Soviet Union.
3. Soviet Union—Foreign relations—Iran.   4. Iran
—Foreign relations—Soviet Union.   5. Soviet
Union—Foreign relations—Afghanistan.   6. Afghan-
istan—Foreign relations—Soviet Union.   I. Title.
II. Series.
DK68.7.T9R83   327.4705   82-7513
ISBN 0-03-052506-3,   AACR2
ISBN 0-03-052511-X (pbk.)

Published in 1982 by Praeger Publishers
CBS Educational and Professional Publishing
a Division of CBS, Inc.
521 Fifth Avenue, New York, New York 10175 U.S.A.

©1982 by Praeger Publishers

23456789   052   987654321

Printed in the United States of America

To Frankie

PREFACE

When this study was conceived, Turkey was in trouble economically, at odds with the United States over Greece, and receptive to improved relations with the Soviet Union; a stable Iran was riding the crest of rising oil prices, growing in military strength and assertiveness in the Persian Gulf/Indian Ocean region, and expanding its ties with the USSR; and Afghanistan was ruled by a patrician-turned-plebian, who, after seizing power in 1973, was bent on maintaining the country's independence, nonaligned character, and close, though guarded, relationship with the Soviet Union, its principal benefactor. By the end of the 1970s, this belt of non-Arab Muslim states on the southern border of the Soviet Union was in turmoil. Turkey's internal derangement resulted in a military takeover in September 1980; Iran's Islamic revolution that toppled the pro-Western Shah transferred the mantle of absolute power to a religious zealot who quickly antagonized all the countries in the region; and Afghanistan had experienced a communist revolution and a Soviet occupation to boot. These very different internal upheavals wrought a fundamental change in the regional environment and in the relationship that each country now has with the communist colossus to the north.

After more than a generation of courting countries in the Third World, the USSR has undoubtedly achieved its greatest strategic-political triumphs in this diplomatic arena, in the changed policies of Turkey, Iran, and Afghanistan. Turkey, though still formerly allied with the West, is groping for alternatives, as it continues its détente with the Soviet Union; Iran, until 1979 securely in the Western camp, is now an adversary of the United States and in the midst of a revolution whose long term consequences for Soviet-Iranian, U.S.-Iranian, and Arab-Iranian relations have not yet emerged; and Afghanistan, until 1978 a nonaligned and independent country, is being brutally decimated by Soviet military power, as Moscow seeks to turn it into a compliant satellite.

The purpose of this study is twofold: first, to provide an assessment of Soviet policy under Khrushchev and Brezhnev toward Turkey, Iran, and Afghanistan, thus filling a glaring gap in the scholarly literature on Soviet foreign policy toward the Third World; and second, to illumine as precisely and concretely as possible the actual influence relationship between the Soviet Union, on the one hand, and Turkey, Iran, and Afghanistan, on the other. By using the concept of influence to evaluate

Moscow's payoffs for its inputs into these three targeted Third World countries, we hope to contribute to the modest body of international relations theory on the subject of who influences whom, and on what issues and in what ways, in relations between a superpower and a Third World country. Special attention has been given to the following questions: What was the USSR's actual effect on the foreign policy and domestic behavior of the courted country? How was the Soviet Union able to translate its largesse and presence into tangible political influence? How did Soviet policy/behavior change as result of its courtship of the country in question?

Influence is easier to identify than evaluate. It is different from power in that it cannot be quantified or measured; and it is not synonymous with a presence, which may or may not bring the tangible outcome that is the focus of our investigation. As a working definition we shall use the following: Influence is manifested when country A affects, through nonmilitary means, directly or indirectly, the behavior of country B so that it redounds to the advantage of A. There is a semantic problem immediately evident, because the phenomenon of influence is clearly both a process and a product. Admittedly no wording can completely free us of this problem, but this is more a complexity for the theorist than an impediment for the policy analyst, who looks primarily for the concrete manifestations of the process.

A number of assumptions underlie our exploration of the phenomenon of influence.° First, every nation seeks to exercise influence through the varied noncoercive means that are available to it. Influence-building is a multidimensional and continuous process that is at the heart of all diplomacy. Second, the concept of influence should be used as precisely as possible, for the purpose of singling out and evaluating achievements, and not for speculation about aims, though the latter may be inferred from the former. Third, changes in behavior or attitude are the stuff of which assessments of any influence relationship are made, and the place to look for them is generally in the interaction of the two parties within the country that is the target. Thus Soviet influence in Turkey, Iran, or Afghanistan must be sought in the political system and behavior of these countries. Fourth, influence is most readily apparent in the principal issues that are at the heart of the bilateral relationship at a given time. Since there are only a few serious policy issues at any one time, instances of influence will be relatively few and can therefore be carefully studied. Fifth, the donor is not unaffected by his courtship of the donee or

---

° These are developed in detail in the author's, *Red Star on the Nile: The Soviet-Egyptian Influence Relationship Since the June War* (Princeton, N.J.: Princeton University Press, 1977), pp. xii–xxiii.

target, albeit the effects are asymmetrical; a feedback appertains to all influence relationships. Finally, an influence relationship is always changing and is never a mere reflection of disparities in power. Indeed, it is precisely because neither power nor inputs necessarily bring influence on the main issues that dominate bilateral relationships between a super-power and a Third World country that this study—and the series of which it is a part—has been undertaken.

A number of prevalent hypotheses in the social sciences that seek to shed light on possible correlations between inputs and influence will be examined in the course of analyzing the three bilateral relationships: Soviet-Turkish, Soviet-Iranian, and Soviet-Afghan.°

The interaction hypothesis: The greater the political, economic, military, and cultural interaction between A and B, the greater will be A's influence. (Rationale: An intensified interaction process between a super-power and a Third World country will, inevitably, be asymmetrical, bringing more goods and services from A to B; create a measure of dependency; and therefore enable A to exercise influence over B.)

The presence hypothesis: The greater the presence of A in B, the more likely A is to exercise influence over B. (Rationale: Access is a prerequisite for influence; the more A funnels goods and services into B's domestic system, the more will be its dealings with B's decision-making elite; since B is unable to fend for itself, A's greater involvement will result in its greater presence and greater influence.)

The notables hypothesis: The larger the relative number of B's missions to A, the greater will be A's influence. (Rationale: According to the literature on small groups and organizational theory, and the traditional diplomatic lore that over the long term the more influential of two actors will be the recipient of the disproportionate number of visits, the influencer is considered to be the party that receives the larger number of missions.)

The diminishing returns hypothesis: The political use of aid diminishes over time. (Rationale: Aid is useful primarily in establishing an initial presence; its utility in bringing influence wanes with institutionalization, because A's propensity to continue existing programs and levels is greater than B's fear of deprivation; indeed, any substantial diminution of aid by A is apt to entail political costs that are greater for A than B.)

Foreign policy is a function of many considerations, among which historical consciousness and patterns are extremely important to leaders of countries whose animosities and perceptions of threat go back deep in

---

° *Ibid.*, pp. xxii-xxiii.

time. In looking at the interactions between Moscow—both czarist and communist—and Turkey, Iran, and Afghanistan, I therefore paid considerable attention to the historical dimension.

I would like to express my deep appreciation to the Earhart Foundation for its receptivity to a cross-regional foreign policy study and for its generous support. The secretaries in the Department of Political Science of the University of Pennsylvania and at the Foreign Policy Research Institute typed the manuscript. My wife, as always, was a keen and demanding reader and a constant source of encouragement.

CONTENTS

SOVIET POLICY TOWARD TURKEY, IRAN, AND AFGHANISTAN

SOVIET-TURKISH RELATIONS: THE ORIGINS AND EVOLUTION OF COEXISTENCE

The modern era of Soviet-Turkish relations originated in the changed circumstances of the two historic enemies at the end of World War I. The new Soviet state was sorely threatened by the Western powers and Japan, which were trying, as Winston Churchill observed, to strangle the infant communism in its cradle; at the same time, the nascent Turkish nation-state was struggling to emerge from the ruins of the Ottoman empire, to avoid the partitioning of its Anatolian heartland by the victorious Entente powers (Great Britain, France, Greece, Italy, and, to a lesser extent, the United States) and to cast off the degrading Treaty of Sevres (1920) that they had imposed on the feckless Ottoman Sultan. For the first time, Russia and Turkey found themselves looking to each other for support against a common threat. Their preoccupation with survival temporarily overshadowed the enmity of the past, and their commitment to revolutionary transformation gave rise to cooperation in the world of unfriendly status quo powers.

ANTECEDENT ANIMOSITY

The hostility between the Russian and Ottoman Empires had a long and violent history. Over the course of four centuries they had battled each other 13 times: the first was in the period between 1676 and 1681, the last in the years 1914 to 1918. In its heyday, Ottoman rule extended deep into southern Russia, the Balkans, and the Caucasus, as well as the Arab East. However, in the eighteenth century the tide turned, and the Russians expanded at the expense of the Ottomans. It was Czar Peter the Great who intensified Russian pressure on the Ottoman and Persian

Empires in earnest. Two generations later, under the humiliating Treaty of Kuchuk-Kainarji that ended the Russo-Turkish War of 1768 to 1774, Russia became the dominant power in the rivalry. The Ottoman Turks ceded the Crimea and the northern coast of the Black Sea, and accorded privileged treatment to Russian subjects in the Ottoman Empire and open access for Russian merchant ships through the Bosporus and Dardenelles (the Straits). Russia coveted Constantinople (renamed Istanbul after World War I) and control of the Straits, gateway to the eastern Mediterranean. Then as now, Russia's impetus was generated by a combination of religious–ideological and strategic considerations. The Russian-Turkish relationship was shaped by the inexorable dictates of geographic determinism, at the heart of which was a struggle for control of the Straits.

By the beginning of the nineteenth century, the only bar to Russia's supremacy was Great Britain. Determined to prevent any great power from dominating the land route from the Mediterranean to the Persian Gulf and thereby threatening its empire in India, Britain assumed the role of ultimate guarantor of continued Ottoman rule. It wanted the Straits kept in Ottoman hands, and throughout the century the Straits question centered on "British efforts to prevent the Russian fleet from gaining free access to the Mediterranean."[1] The Ottoman Empire became hostage to Russo-British imperial rivalry and British policy; it survived, barely, because Britain wanted to keep Russia from becoming a Mediterranean power.

Russia's expansion continued. In 1801 Georgia was annexed; in 1828 Azerbaijan. Suspicious of British and French designs on the tottering Ottoman Empire, Russian leaders carried on an endless discussion of possible actions in the event of its dissolution. According to one plan presented by Count Capo d'Istria (a pro–Russian Greek, who had attended the Congress of Vienna in 1815 as a representative of Russia and sought Russian assistance for Greek independence from the Ottomans), Constantinople would be made a free city:

> Its territory was to be limited to strips of land along the Black Sea and the Sea of Marmara, the island of Tenedos [in the Aegean Sea, guarding the entry into the Dardenelles] and two fortified positions on the Asiatic shore of the Bosporus. All the other fortifications in this area, as well as along the Dardenelles, were to be dismantled.[2]

Another proposal called for Russia to fortify the Asian shore of both Straits, annex Constantinople, and acquire military bases on both sides of the Bosporous. What these and other plans had in common was to prevent the Straits from falling into the hands of any other powerful state. Thus, if Russia could not control the Straits, it preferred continued Ottoman custodianship.

There was a continual tug in czarist circles between those who argued against further territorial expansion and for preservation of a compliant Ottoman neighbor, and those who believed that Russia's national and religious destiny required domination of the strategic Straits. This nineteenth-century debate had its counterpart in Soviet policy toward Turkey in the periods after the two world wars.

In 1854 Turkish weakness proved too great a temptation for Russian leaders, a temptation they were to succumb to again in 1876, in 1914, and still again in 1945—each time with unanticipated and adverse consequences. Russia was defeated in the Crimean War (1853-56) by Britain and France, which allied with the Ottoman Empire to forestall Russia's seizure of the Straits. Defeat gave impetus to further expansion in Central Asia, adding plausibility to the hoary proposition that when frustrated in one area Russia expands in another, though the opportunity factor may be a more accurate explanation. Russia annexed the feudal khanates of Khiva, Bokhara, and Samarkand, completing its conquest of Muslim Central Asia and advancing to the border of Afghanistan, and to a new confrontation with the British.

In 1876-77 Russia severely defeated the Turks—its advance forces had reached San Stefano, not far from Constantinople and the Straits—and was well on the way to realizing its historic ambitions. Again the British brought their military power to bear, and at the Congress of Berlin (1878) Disraeli pressured the Czar to accept more modest spoils: Bulgaria was detached from the Ottoman Empire and granted independence; Russia settled for the Turkish districts of Kars, Ardahan, and Batum; while Britain took Cyprus, thus strengthening its dominance over the eastern Mediterranean. The "sick man of Europe"—a phrase coined by Czar Nicholas I in 1844— was given a final lease on life.

World War I opened the way for maximalist Russian aggrandizement at Ottoman expense, this time with reluctant British acquiescence. In an aide-memoire to the British and French governments on March 4, 1915, the Russian foreign minister presented the price tag for Russia's participation in the war:

> The course of recent events leads His Majesty Emperor Nicholas to think that the question of Constantinople and of the Straits must be definitively solved, according to the time-honored aspirations of Russia.
>
> Every solution will be inadequate and precarious if the city of Constantinople, the western bank of the Bosporus, of the Sea of Marmara and of the Dardenelles, as well as southern Thrace to the Enez–Midye line, should henceforth not be incorporated into the Russian Empire.
>
> Similarly, and by strategic necessity, that part of the Asiatic shore that lies between the Bosporus, the Sakarya River and a point to be

determined on the Gulf of Izmit, and the islands of the Sea of Marmara, the Imbros Islands and the Tenedos Islands must be incorporated into the [Russian] Empire.[3]

Britain and France accepted Russia's terms in the secret agreement that came to be known as the Constantinople Agreement, the first of a series among the European members of the Entente for partitioning the Ottoman Empire. However, victory found a communist not a Czar ruling in Russia, and Britain and France felt no obligation to uphold this particular accord; on the contrary, fear of Bolshevism prompted extensive moves to truncate the Soviet state. As for the Bolshevik leaders, the fears for their own survival gave rise to a line of thinking that was the counterpart of the Czars' policy to uphold the independence of a weak Turkey rather than permit a hostile great power to entrench itself on the Straits and threaten Russia itself.

THE FRIENDLY INTERREGNUM: 1920-38

The Soviet-Turkish accommodation that started in the early 1920s was triggered by a number of convergent considerations: fear of foreign intervention; a commitment to antiimperialism; a desire to overthrow the Versailles peace settlement imposed by the victorious Western powers; a preference that the Straits remain under Turkish control; and a suspicion of the League of Nations, which neither country was initially invited to join. The Russian and Turkish revolutions also shared a commitment to secularism, modernization, and radical social transformation. They differed, though, in important respects: whereas the Russian revolution was internationalist in its outreach, the Turkish was nationalistic and introspective; whereas the Soviet quest for modernization was doctrinally rooted, the Turkish model was West European; and whereas the Soviet Union aspired to an activist foreign policy, Turkey cultivated an isolationist course.

The Bolsheviks had come to power in November 1917. After the defeat of the Central powers in November 1918, the Entente mounted an intervention in support of former Czarist groups who, however, failed in their bid to topple the Soviet regime. Turkey was equally beset: Greek forces landed to annex the Aegean and Mediterranean littoral; France occupied Alexandretta; Britain controlled Constantinople and the Sultan, who was only nominally the Ottoman ruler, and intrigued to establish an independent Armenia in the Caucasus. In the bleakest moment of defeat in 1918, Turkish resistance revived under the leadership of one of the country's genuine war heroes, Mustafa Kemal, soon to be known as

Ataturk. Intent on expelling all foreign invaders and creating a secular and Turkish state, Kemal quickly perceived the advantages of relations with the Soviet government. As early as September 1919, he sent a mission to the Bolsheviks in Baku, seeking military and financial assistance. Matters moved slowly, in part because the communist regime was also sorely beleaguered and going through a period of maximum danger. A year later, however, Soviet assistance began to reach Ataturk, who was rebuilding the Turkish army. By the end of 1920, Soviet and Turkish offensives squashed the fledgling Republic of Armenia, and the two revolutionary regimes normalized their relationship.

The treaty of friendship, signed by the Soviet Union and Turkey, on March 16, 1921, was the first major international treaty for each. It delineated their frontiers in the Caucasus, thus avoiding possible friction; renounced all former treaties between the Czarist and Ottoman rulers; and wiped the political slate clean. Under the treaty, the districts (sanjaks) of Kars and Ardahan, annexed by Russia in 1878, were recognized as Turkey's, while Batum remained part of the Soviet Union. Article V was particularly important to Turkey: It left the final determination of regulations governing the Straits to a conference "of the littoral States, on condition that the decisions of the above–mentioned conference shall not be of such a nature as to diminish the full sovereignty of Turkey or the security of Constantinople, her captital."[4]

The constraints on closer relations came primarily from the Turkish side. First, there was geography. The borders had been successfully delineated, and Moscow acknowledged Turkey's control of the Straits. Indeed, in 1923, when Turkey agreed at the Lausanne conference to the establishment of an International Straits Commission and freedom of passage for all ships, Moscow was disappointed, preferring exclusive Turkish control and closing of the Straits to all warships except those of Turkey. However, political situations change and no small nation can ever be fully at ease when it is situated in the shadow of a big neighbor. In the past Turkey had maintained control over the Straits by playing off rival powers against each other. Whereas Britain had formerly been Turkey's protector against Russia, now Russia was important in offsetting Western pressures—but how permanent was Russia's newly manifested benignity and friendship?

This gnawing concern kept alive a second reservation against too intimate an embrace with the bear to the north: the historic dimension of their relationship. Turkey's new friend was an old and formidable enemy, and the former enmity

> was almost bound to revive with a revival of the geographical situation in which Russia held the house and Turkey the entrance–hall. Moreover,

Russia was very close, very large, and above all very alien—at least as alien in the guise of a socialist Soviet Republic as when she had been an Orthodox Christian Czardom. In either form, the Turks found Russian culture unattractive.[5]

Ataturk, however, was shrewd enough not permit these residual reservations to restrict his immediate diplomatic behavior. Annoyed by Britain's opposition to Turkey's claim to the oil-rich province of Mosul, which was awarded by the British-influenced Council of the League of Nations to newly created, British-controlled Iraq, he signed a treaty of nonaggression and neutrality with the Soviet Union on December 17, 1925—the day after the League's decision was made public. (Similar friendship treaties were signed by Moscow with Afghanistan and Persia, in 1926 and 1927, respectively, as part of its policy to ensure the safety of its southern border.) Security considerations prompted Turkey to sign a variety of treaties with the Soviet Union, but the desire to create a modern and secular democratic state made Ataturk look to the West. It was there, and not to Soviet communism, that he turned for ideas, institutions, economic and technological expertise, and possible guidelines. This was the third inhibiting factor that put distance between Turkey and the revolutionary regime in Russia.

The fourth was Ataturk's distrust of communism. He never had any illusions about the communists, whom he saw as rivals for power. Early on, he took measures to isolate them, even while using them. For example, in May 1920, when he was still dickering for Soviet gold and arms to organize resistance to the Greeks and British, he created a Turkish Communist Party (TCP) that was staffed by trusted military aides: "It had no connection with the Third International and engaged in no political activity; its sole purpose was to show the Russians how friendly the new Turkey was to the ideas of the new Russia."[6] The pro-Moscow TCP, on the other hand, was organized in the USSR by Mustafa Subhi, a radical who had opposed the Ottoman regime, fled to czarist Russia, been imprisoned as an enemy alien, and converted to communism in prison. He worked closely with Stalin, helped found the so-called Muslim Bureau, and became an effective organizer among the Turks living in the Soviet Union. Eager to return to Turkey, he pledged his support to Ataturk, though the TCP in Baku continued to criticize the Kemalists. Subhi and 15 other communists entered Turkey in late 1920; on January 28, 1921, while crossing to Trabzon, they were murdered. This incident did not alter Lenin's policy of friendship with Ataturk:

On the one hand, Moscow was coming to appreciate the services of the Anatolian nationalist movement in diverting resources which the

Entente might otherwise have thrown against the Soviet regime. At the same time, the Soviets felt keenly their diplomatic isolation. The overtures of the Ankara government were the first to hold out the prospect of recognition. Moreover, the Kremlin leaders nourished the hope that Turkey's prestige in the Muslim world might lead large sections of the East, if not into the Soviet orbit, at least into revolt against the Great Powers of Europe. Finally, Lenin's doctrine on "national liberation" movements dictated active efforts to woo the Kemalists. And these larger considerations perforce took precedence over the luxury of openly sponsoring movements to overthrow Ataturk's regime.[7]

Ataturk sensed, and exploited, this ambivalence and dilemma in Soviet policy. He moved prudently and effectively to counter the pro-Moscow communists seeking to infiltrate his nationalist movement. Once firmly in control and enjoying good relations with Britain, he cracked down on the TCP, banning it in 1925—and the TCP has remained illegal ever since. Ataturk's persecution of communists displeased Moscow, and protests were made at world communist gatherings, but it did not hinder the good diplomatic and economic relations that prevailed in the 1920s.

Friendly relations continued on into the 1930s, reinforced by Soviet economic aid and periodic visits by high-ranking officials. In October 1931 the Soviet-Turkish friendship treaty was renewed for five years, and in 1935, for another ten. Soviet economic assistance was important in Turkey's first development plan, and on September 15, 1935, the Kayseri textile plant was opened, the first to be built with Soviet aid.

Disturbed by the failure of disarmament to take hold and by the storm gathering over Europe, on April 10, 1936, Turkey requested revision of the 1923 Lausanne Convention regulating the Straits. With the exception of Italy, the signatory powers responded favorably. In particular, Britain and France were eager to strengthen a friendly country in the eastern Mediterranean; and the Soviet Union preferred to see Turkey "the sole concierge of the Black Sea,"[8] and not bound to an international commission of the League for defense of the Straits. In August 1936 the Montreux Convention (still in effect) gave Turkey permission to remilitarize the Straits and placed stricter limits on the types and tonnage of warships that could navigate them. The result greatly enhanced Turkey's security and strategic importance; and its also assured the USSR of preponderant military power in the Black Sea. Moscow was to reject these optimal conditions in 1945 in its quest for a commanding position in the Straits.

Ataturk died on November 10, 1938. He left Turkey on the eve of World War II in a much better position to resist pressure from the great powers—belligerents and nonbelligerents alike—and to sit out the catastrophic struggle that engulfed the rest of the Eurasian land mass.

THE EFFECT OF THE WAR ON SOVIET AMBITIONS

World War II became inevitable on August 23, 1939, with the signing of the Nazi-Soviet pact that gave Germany the green light to invade Poland. A secret protocol divided Poland and the Baltic states into Soviet and German spheres of influence. The consequences for Soviet-Turkish relations were quickly forthcoming.

Whereas in the spring of 1939 Moscow had urged "Turkey to consolidate her relations with the Balkan states and the Western Allies against a possibility of German aggression," by early September Soviet Foreign Minister V. M. Molotov suggested closing the Straits to British and French fleets and tilting toward Germany.[9] This would have entailed a violation of the Montreux Convention, which allowed the passage of warships through the Straits, provided that Turkey was not a belligerent. In his talks in Moscow in October 1939, Turkish Foreign Minister Sukru Sarcoglu refused to revise the 1936 convention unilaterally or downgrade a newly negotiated treaty with Britain and France. Later Molotov raised Soviet claims to Kars and Ardahan and a priviledged position as regards the Straits—claims that became open demands in 1945. This surfacing of traditional Russian territorial ambitions marked the end of an era in Soviet-Turkish relations.

After two decades of accommodation, of encouraging Turkey's neutralist foreign policy and of championing its custodianship of the Straits, Moscow wanted something more, a partnership that would give it strategic advantages never held by the Czars. In a seemingly commanding position now that Britain and France were locked in struggle with Germany, the Soviet Union reverted to a historic pattern of behavior. Its invasion of Finland in late November 1939 confirmed the Turks' worst fears of Russian expansionist ambitions and led them to mobilize on a wartime footing.

The defeat of France in June 1940 and Britain's glaring weakness exacerbated Turkey's uneasiness. In Berlin in November, German and Soviet leaders bargained over the division of Europe. Molotov was willing to participate in allocating spheres of influence,

> provided that within the next few months the security of the Soviet Union in the Straits is assured by the conclusion of a mutual assistance pact between the Soviet Union and Bulgaria, which geographically is situated inside the security zone of the Black Sea boundaries of the Soviet Union, and by the establishment of a base for land and naval forces of the USSR within range of the Bosphorus and the Dardenelles by means of a long term lease; ...
>
> [and] provided that the area south of Batum and Baku in the general direction of the Persian Gulf is recognized as the center of the aspirations of the Soviet Union.[10]

If Turkey refused to accept the "new order," then appropriate "military and diplomatic measures" were to have been taken. On a number of occasions prior to the German invasion of the Soviet Union on June 22, 1941, Moscow impressed upon Berlin its special interest in the Straits.

The Nazi-Soviet turnabout eased but did not end Turkish fears of the USSR. The hopes of the 1920s for a new era of friendly relations were dashed by Moscow's imperialist demands during its moment of advantage. Anti-Russian feeling was strong, but the pervasive pro-German sentiment did not sway the Turks from a cautious line that assumed security lay in avoiding provocation of the Soviet Union. Throughout the war they walked a diplomatic tightrope, clinging to neutrality and successively resisting, first, the seemingly invincible Germans, then, after 1943, the ascendant Soviet Union and Western powers. What Turkey feared, and took great care to counter, was a U.S.–British green light conceding to the Soviet Union a clear road to fulfill historic Russian ambitions in the Straits. The Turks feared Allied collusion and Western generosity at their expense. During the last two years of the war, they repeatedly fended off pressures from the Allies to enter the war. Their proposal to the Soviet government for "closer political cooperation, which should include security guarantees in the Balkans," foundered on Moscow's insistence that Turkey first break off all relations with Germany and enter the war.[11]

On February 10, 1945, at a meeting of the Big Three at Yalta with victory imminent, Stalin declared the Montreux Convention outmoded and in need of revision, because "it was impossible to accept a situation in which Turkey had a hand on Russia's throat."[12] He added that the "legitimate interests of Turkey" should not be harmed, but this qualifier was also outmoded once Stalin played his hand.

STALIN'S GRAB FOR THE STRAITS

On March 19, 1945, the Soviet government informed the Turkish government that it would not renew the 1925 friendship treaty on its expiration in November. Ankara offered concessions for a new treaty, but soon learned that the price was exorbitant: return of the districts of Kars and Ardahan and bases on the Straits. The Soviet media then suddenly began a vitriolic campaign against Turkey, presumably to create an atmosphere of alarm in which the Western powers would pressure the Turks to compromise and ease the situation—a diplomatic style the Soviets have developed into an art form.

At the Potsdam Conference in late July, Stalin pressed for Turkish concessions to return the borders to pre-1918 lines and for bases on the Straits, invoking 1805 and 1833 treaties with Turkey as the basis for an agreement. Despite the USSR's troop concentrations along the Turkish border, its efforts to gain U.S. and British support, and its courting of overseas Armenian communities as part of the campaign to force Turkey to relinquish Kars and Ardahan (thousands of Armenians in the Middle East responded to Soviet blandishments to resettle in Soviet Armenia, some 86,000 by 1948), the Western powers held firm, agreeing only to a resolution that called for a revision of the Montreux Convention, since it failed "to meet present-day conditions."

The issue simmered, while the problems of Germany and Eastern Europe preoccupied the Western powers, already drifting from allies to adversaries of the Soviet Union. Stalin overplayed a strong hand. Instead of requesting reasonable concessions that might have procured long-term leverage over Turkey and strengthened the domestic position of the sizable sympathetic leftist opposition that was developing, he made a crude bid for domination. Whatever merit inhered in his case for the need to strengthen Soviet security was overshadowed by the scope of the demands. The Turks saw it as merely a rationale for the imperialist ambitions that were openly proclaimed in December 1945 by two members of the Academy of Sciences of the Georgian SSR, who laid claim on historic grounds not only to Kars and Ardahan but to much of the Black Sea coast, including Trebizond (Trabzon).[13] Public opinion in Turkey was alarmed; one immediate consequence was a rupture between the newly formed opposition Democratic Party (DP) and the pro-Soviet left.

Unwilling to go to war to possess the Straits, and realizing that Turkey would not submit "and that she was likely to receive support from both Britain and the United States," Stalin decided to press for a revision of the Montreux Convention, in accordance with the provisions of Article 29.[14] In a note on August 7, 1946, the Soviet government proposed new regulations for the Straits, notably that

> passage through the Straits for warships not belonging to the Black Sea powers shall not be permitted except in cases specifically provided for; [that the regime administering the Straits] should come under the competence of Turkey and other Black Sea powers; [and that] Turkey and the Soviet Union, as the powers most interested and capable of guaranteeing freedom to commercial navigation and security in the Straits, shall organize joint means of defense of the Straits for the prevention of the utilization of the Straits by other countries for aims hostile to the Black Sea powers.[15]

In their responses, the Turkish, U.S., and British governments observed that the regulation of the Straits was an international concern and any revision of the Montreux Convention must be the subject of an international conference, which they were prepared to attend. However, until that time, Turkey as the territorial power directly concerned should continue to be responsible for the security of the Straits.

In its reply to the Turkish government on September 24, 1946 (deserving lengthy quotation because of the detailed strategic arguments that must still loom large in Kremlin calculations), Moscow went beyond previous communications in laying out the Straits' strategic significance for Soviet security.[16] It called attention to "the special situation of the Black Sea as a closed sea," which means that the Straits "represent a seaway leading only to the shores ... of several Black Sea Powers." Accordingly, the USSR and other Black Sea powers have an interest in the Straits that "cannot be compared with that of other powers." Referring back to the 1921 Soviet-Turkish treaty, Moscow said Ankara had then agreed that the international statute regulating access to the Black Sea and the Straits be limited "to a conference composed only of the representatives of riverain countries":

> The refusal of Turkey to assure the defense of the Straits *jointly* with the Soviet Union deprives the Black Sea Powers of the possibility of guaranteeing the necessary security in this region .... It would be unjust to forget that the Soviet Black Sea shores, extending 2100 kilometers, give access to the most important regions of the country, wherefrom the necessity for assuring their security with direct participation of the Soviet Union in the defense of the Straits, has its origin in the vital interests of the U.S.S.R. All this explains the reason why the Soviet Government considers it necessary that the defense of the Straits should be carried out by the *joint* efforts of Turkey and the Soviet Union .... [Italics added.]

Turkey, backed by the United States and Britain, argued that Soviet wishes on the matter of regulating the Straits had to be balanced against the requirements of its own security and independence;[17] and that under the cover of security, the USSR aimed at Turkey's submission and a base on the Mediterranean. One would have to be naive, wrote a Turkish official, to believe that Soviet policy was purely defensive.[18]

By 1947 the onset of the Cold War froze any move to revise the Montreux Convention and brought Turkey friends in the West. Western Europe's economic dislocation and political vulnerability; Washington's conviction that Moscow was responsible for the civil war in Greece; Britain's inability any longer to play the role of guarantor of Turkey's independence; and Soviet pressure on Turkey all served to bring the United States back into the European arena. On March 12, 1947, the Truman Doctrine for Greece and Turkey was enunciated: President Harry S. Truman asked Congress for the wherewithal to safeguard states threatened by "international communism."

The Truman Doctrine imbued the Turks with an upsurge of confidence. At the United Nations, in October 1947, Ambassador Selim Sarper accused the USSR of inciting belligerency; the Turkish press spoke out more openly; and the government—"undeterred by Soviet rhetoric—quietly went ahead to secure American military equipment and to refurbish its communications network, with heavy stress on roads, port facilities, and airports."[19] On the other hand, to the Kremlin,

> the construction of airfields and ports on a scale greater than Turkey had known in the past appeared especially sinister . . . . Indeed, it seems clear that the Truman Doctrine for the first time raised the specter before Soviet eyes that Turkey might present a military danger to the heartland of the U.S.S.R. This concern that Turkey might serve as a base for U.S. operations against the Soviet Union would be a lasting consideration in Soviet policy.[20]

As in the nineteenth century, a weak Turkey turned to the Western powers for security against Russian aggrandizement. Exceedingly backward, both in the economic and military spheres, its leaders wanted U.S. assistance to stimulate the country's modernization. The logical next, and major, step was membership in the North Atlantic Treaty Organization (NATO), established in April 1949 to deter the Soviet threat to Western Europe. Turkey formally applied on August 1, 1950, only to be rebuffed by the British and French on the grounds that it was not a North Atlantic country. However, Turkey's contribution to the Korean War, its readiness to join the British-sponsored Middle East Treaty Organization, and its geographic position that fit into the U.S. strategy of containing Soviet expansion by bringing into alliance with the West all countries situated along the border of the Soviet Union paved the way for Turkey's eventual membership in 1952.

The step from alignment to alliance marked a significant departure from the Ataturk policy of unalignment and moderation toward the Soviet Union. Three possible considerations for the shift in Turkish outlook have been suggested: that Turkish leaders feared exclusion from NATO might "lead to a diminution of U.S. interest and consequently a reduction in American aid," and they wished to demonstrate Turkey's value to the West's defense; that the establishment of NATO, "by barring further encroachment in Western Europe, might induce the Kremlin to increase pressure on such less firmly protected points as Turkey"; and that the ruling Republican People's Party (RPP) wanted to avoid the appearance of having been rebuffed by the Western Powers lest this "be exploited by the DP opposition inside Turkey."[21]

Moscow called Turkey's decision to join NATO an act of hostility. In its blast of November 3, 1951, the Soviet government charged that NATO has "nothing in common with aims of the self-defense of States participating in this bloc whom, as is known, no one intends to attack":

> According to available numerous data, air and naval bases are being set up on Turkish territory under the guidance and with the help of the command and specialists of the United States, with military aerodromes, situated closest of all to the frontiers of the Soviet Union, being built on a broad scale.
>
> Under these conditions it is fully evident that the invitation into the Atlantic bloc of Turkey, which moreover has no relation whatever to the Atlantic, can mean nothing else but a striving of the imperialist States to use Turkish territory for setting up at the frontiers of the Soviet Union military bases for aggressive ends.

Another note warned that the USSR, "being a State neighboring on Turkey, naturally cannot remain indifferent" to Turkey's membership in the "aggressive Atlantic bloc and permitting the utilization of Turkish territory for the setting up of foreign military bases on the borders of the Soviet Union."

None of this affected the decision of Turkey, who on February 18, 1952, officially became a full member of NATO. A year later, Turkey, Greece, and Yugoslavia signed a tripartite treaty of friendship and co-operation, which in August 1954 was developed into a formal treaty of military alliance and political cooperation, for protection against possible Soviet aggression in the Balkans. Scarcely had these security arrangements matured into treaties than the precipitating cause disappeared: Stalin died on March 5, 1953.

The polarization of Soviet relations with Turkey and Iran was Stalin's folly. Though a Georgian, he was as committed to a policy of territorial expansion as the most expansionist-minded Great Russian Czar. His heavy-handed diplomacy and unmistakable territorial designs on these two countries had led them to alliance with the United States. By bungling the handling of the rimland states in the 1940s, Stalin bequeathed to his successors the formidable tasks of unhinging the military alliances that threatened the USSR from the south; promoting Soviet security and easing the deep-rooted fears of the USSR's southern neighbors through accommodation and cooperation; and advancing Soviet ambitions with cunning and the carrot, not threats and the big stick. In the decades after Stalin's death, Soviet diplomacy toward Turkey centered on efforts to undo the harm done by his policy during the 1939 to 1953 period.

THE THAW

After Stalin's death Soviet leaders initiated a number of major foreign policy changes, especially toward the Third World. Nowhere was the new look more evident than in Moscow's attitude toward Turkey, where the new Soviet leadership made its first concrete overture for better relations.

The Soviet note of May 30, 1953, was the first step in a persistent Soviet effort to undo the harm done by Stalin, to reestablish the kind of diplomatic relationship that had prevailed in the 1920s, and to resolve differences by negotiation. It was unusual for two reasons: first, it was a rare instance of public acknowledgment that a previous policy had been a mistake; second, it was an unequivocal renunciation of Soviet territorial claims against Turkey. The note owned that earlier, that is, in 1945 and 1946, there had "figured certain territorial claims" by the Soviet Republics of Armenia and Georgia on Turkey, "and also considerations of the Soviet Government relative to removal of the possible threat to the security of the U.S.S.R. from the side of the Black Sea Straits":

> This was accepted badly by the Government and public circles of Turkey, which could not but in certain degree be reflected in Soviet-Turkish relations. In the name of preserving good neighborly relations and strengthening peace and security, the Governments of Armenia and Georgia have found it possible to renounce their territorial claims on Turkey.
>
> Concerning the question of the Straits the Soviet Government has reconsidered its former opinion on this question and considers possible the provision of security of the USSR from the side of the Straits on conditions acceptable alike to the USSR and to Turkey. Thus the Soviet Government declares that the Soviet Union has not any kind of territorial claims on Turkey.[22]

The Turkish reply of July 18 was cool and to the point: It noted with satisfaction the Soviet declaration "that the USSR has no territorial claims against Turkey whatsoever" and recognized "the question of the Straits ... is regulated by the clauses of the Montreux Convention" and "could not be resolved by bilateral negotiations between the two countries." A few days later the Turkish government rejected Soviet protests regarding visits to Turkish ports by American and British naval vessels, observing that the USSR government, "being regularly informed under Article 24 of the Montreux Convention on the straits regime, cannot but know that the visits referred to in the [Soviet note] are courtesy visits." Ankara saw Moscow's conciliatory tack as an attempt to weaken Turkey's newly embraced commitment to NATO and to forestall the final steps toward the Balkan Pact with Greece and Yugoslavia and the alliance with

Iran, Pakistan, and Iraq, later known as the Baghdad Pact and in 1959 renamed the Central Treaty Organization (CENTO). Moreover, the Turkish government was not comforted by the Soviet renunciation, in particular the expression "found it possible to renounce their territorial claims on Turkey," which implied abandonment of a right whose juridical basis would continue to hold good.[23]

However, Moscow was not deterred; it had only started its courtship. In September 1953, as evidence of good intentions, it agreed to a settlement of a lingering dispute over Turkey's share of the cost and benefits of the Serdarabat Dam, situated on the frontier in northeastern Turkey, and the use of the Arak River waters; and in January 1954 it replaced Ambassador Alexander A. Lavrischev, who had served in Ankara during the worst of the Stalin period, with Boris F. Podtserov, who, in turn, was replaced in 1957 by Nikita S. Ryzhov, the engineer who had supervised the construction of the Kayseri textile mill in the mid-1930s and who, Moscow hoped, would be able to move economic relations off dead center. In April 1956, shortly after an exchange of messages between Presidents Kliment Voroshilov and Celal Bayar commemorating the thirty-fifth anniversary of the first Soviet-Turkish friendship treaty, the Soviet press not only proposed a new treaty of nonaggression, but also declared that "Soviet proposals for better relations carry no stipulations".[24] Turkey need not discard its Western ties.

Soviet-Turkish relations, however, were slow to improve because of conflicting aims in the Middle East and Turkey's decision to permit the United States to station intermediate range ballistic missiles (IRBMs) on its territory. On March 1, 1955, Moscow denounced Turkey's involvement in Western-sponsored military alliances, this time in the Baghdad Pact, which it called "a stab in the back of all Arab nations." By exaggerating the threat, Moscow hoped to demonstrate its support for those Arab countries that preferred a policy of nonalignment, and to entrench its newly acquired footholds in Egypt and Syria During the Suez crisis of October 1956, Khrushchev's rocket-rattling threats and brutal suppression of the Hungarian revolt reinforced the Turks' cynical attitude toward Moscow's off-again, on-again calls for better relations. In early 1957, fearing a possible communist takeover in neighboring Syria, Turkey held military maneuvers near the Syrian border, prompting Soviet admonitions not to engage in "armed intervention against Syria," with which it had developed close ties. In the succeeding months the situation was strained, but by October the minicrisis suddenly dissipated, leading one analyst to the supposition that both Moscow and Ankara had ulterior motives in encouraging the crisis atmosphere: Khrushchev to gain an advantage in his domestic struggle for power and to have a pretext for asserting, as Andrei Gromyko did at the UN General Assembly in September, that the Middle

East, as an area "in direct proximity to the territory of the Soviet Union," was integrally linked to Soviet security; and Prime Minister Adnan Menderes to exploit an external threat to rally the electorate behind his incumbent Democratic Party in what was proving a tough reelection campaign, and perhaps to induce the United States to increase its assistance for the Baghdad Pact.[25]

Though nothing happened to dispel Turkish suspicions of the USSR, Ankara reacted fairly dispassionately to the 1958 Lebanese and Iraqi crises, believing they were caused by intra–Arab discontents, and not by foreign subversion. It adjusted to the duality in Soviet policy, which professed a desire to improve formal government-to-government ties with the very regime it was seeking to undermine through nongovernmental channels, such as the communist radio station Bizim Radyo (Our Radio), established in 1958 and operating out of East Germany.

The Turkish quest for missiles was a reaction to the shift in NATO's strategy from "massive retaliation" to "flexible response." Ankara, fearing "that Turkish territory might be traded against time in the event of Soviet aggression," pressed for deployment of U.S. nuclear-tipped IRBMs and accepted Washington's conditions of "the so-called double key system of activation used in Germany," which provides that though nuclear weapons would be controlled by American crews, in the event of war, they would be launched only after the consent of both governments.[26] In October 1959 the arrangements for implantation were completed.

The Soviets called the missile bases a grave provocation and "threat not only to the Soviet Union and other Socialist countries, but also to India, Afghanistan, and to Iraq and other Arab countries; and even to Turkey itself, which, in the event of a conflict in the Middle East, could not escape "an annihilating counter-blow." One must not forget, noted a Soviet writer, that "what you put into your plate is what you get in your spoon."[27] Turkey's policy, Moscow cautioned, placed it "increasingly in the grip of military and economic dependence on U.S. imperialism." Its dependence grew out of economic difficulties, which stemmed from excessive military expenditures, a vicious circle that "creates a mortal danger for Turkey herself first and foremost."[28] This line of reasoning against the installation of IRBMs became part of the persistent Soviet campaign for the dismantling of all U.S. overseas military bases, which were described as "a dangerous anachronism."

In April 1960, in an atmosphere of incipient détente (Eisenhower and Khrushchev were to meet in Paris in mid-May), Prime Minister Menderes dropped a political bombshell: his intention of visiting the Soviet Union in July and of hosting a return visit by Khrushchev at some future date. Intended as a dramatic gesture to bolster his sagging domestic position, it backfired and, on May 27, 1960, led to an intervention by the Turkish military, which seized power and banned all political parties. Ironically, as events unfolded, it was the military government of General Cemal Gursel that effected a major improvement in relations with the Soviet Union.

DOUBTS AND DETENTE

Four days after the coup Moscow recognized the Gursel government. The media reported the takeover without comment, and for the next six months or so directed their shafts against the deposed Menderes regime; and Bizim Radyo criticized only the new government's internal policies.

Seizing on a promising conversation on June 14 between the Soviet ambassador and General Gursel, Premier Khrushchev extended an olive branch. In a note on June 28 he acknowledged the "complexity" [a favorite Russian word for difficult, seemingly insoluble situations] of the circumstances that had enmeshed Turkey in military pacts with the Western powers:

> ... It is our deep conviction that the most sincere relations between our two countries would develop if Turkey embarked upon the road of neutrality. This would only benefit the country. Turkey would receive an opportunity to use her resources, not for war preparations, on which huge funds have so far been squandered, but for raising the level of the country's national economy and the wellbeing of its people. Military expenditures, Mr. Prime Minister, are a bottomless pit and not every country can endure the burden of them and develop its economy at the same time.

He emphasized that "the road of neutrality" was "not a condition for beginning the improvement of our relations," and that immediate steps should be taken without waiting "until all the major problems" were resolved.[29] On July 8 Gursel's response reaffirmed Turkey's loyalty to its alliances and international commitments, which are in "conformity with the United Nations Charter" and are "purely defensive," but held the door open for Soviet overtures.

Moscow was enthusiastic, offering a $500 million loan as a measure of its friendly intentions.[30] To facilitate a shift by the new regime, the Soviet press placed responsibility on the previous government for the poor state of Soviet-Turkish relations. On October 29, 1960, Turkey's independence day, *Pravda* hailed Menderes's treason trial, describing him as "the American henchman" responsible for leading Turkey into NATO and CENTO. (Menderes was executed on September 17, 1961.)

Soviet commentaries on Turkish politics grew more sophisticated but dwelt on only a few themes: the military was a "progressive" force intent on reform and on overcoming the legacy of its corrupt, reactionary predecessor; Turkey's high level of military spending and misdirected foreign aid from the West did not promote the desired development or assure security; membership in NATO and CENTO had outlived its usefulness since new weapons and the general drift toward détente diminished the West's real interest in Turkey; and, as a consequence of changed strategic doctrines and priorities, Turkey's allies sought excuses to reduce their military and economic assistance. After 1964, with the erosion of NATO's cohesion in the eastern Mediterranean, the strains in U.S.–Turkish relations arising out of the Cyprus issue, and growing (especially after 1973) economic troubles, these arguments found more and more receptive listeners. However, the overall impact took time and required other developments, still in the future.

On occasion, Moscow reverted to criticisms of Turkey's military alliances and the existence of foreign bases on its territory. The IRBM sites were a source of particular concern, as can be seen in Admiral Sergei Gorshkov's warning of February 1962: "I can . . . reliably say that even the nuclear power available to our Black Sea fleet alone is ample to raze to the ground the countries adjacent to the Black Sea which have become NATO military bridge–heads."[31] Despite these objections, Moscow kept its main objective, the dealignment of Turkey, at the center of all it did and said, realizing this was a process that could not be achieved quickly or by direct pressure. There were exchanges of minor missions, some modest increase in trade, an offer of Soviet economic assistance, a railroad agreement, and so on, but after almost a decade of trying, Moscow still had little to show for its efforts and offers.

However, one aftermath of the Cuban missile crisis was the Turkish elite's greater receptivity to Soviet wares. When President John F. Kennedy had taken office he told his aides that the U.S. Jupiter missiles should be removed from Turkey, but he never followed through on the matter. On October 22, 1962, his announcement that the Soviet Union was preparing to place missiles in Cuba brought the superpowers into an "eyeball to eyeball" confrontation. Five days later Kennedy officially rejected Khrushchev's offer to dismantle Soviet missile sites in Cuba in return for removal of the U.S. missiles from Turkey, but it would have been no burden, since they were obsolete, unnecessary for deterrence, and destined for an early phase-out.[32] An agreement was reached soon thereafter, without reference to the missiles in Turkey, whereby the Soviet Union agreed not to implant missiles in Cuba and the United States promised not to invade Cuba. This Soviet-U.S. crisis was over; the U.S.–Turkish crisis was about to begin.

Khrushchev's offer had greatly embarrassed Kennedy and had been rejected because to have done otherwise would have been a staggering blow to U.S. credibility within NATO. On January 23, 1963, however, too soon for a connection not to be assumed by the Turks, Washington announced that the Jupiters were to be removed. The effect on Ankara was nothing less than electrifying, though this was not immediately evident, except to keen observers of the Turkish scene.

What disturbed the Turkish leadership was not just the decision but the high-handed and unilateral way in which it was taken. Nor was Ankara convinced or assuaged by Washington's explanation that the vulnerable land-based IRBMs were being replaced by mobile submarine-launched missiles that would enhance Turkey's security. The American-manned Jupiters had been Turkey's assurance of immediate U.S. involvement in the event of a Soviet attack; but missiles placed on Polaris submarines were no longer an automatic tripwire. Moreover, many Turks came to believe that the United States was less concerned with Turkey's security than with its own superpower game.

Less than a week after Washington exploded its surprise, Ankara dropped one of its own: For the first time since 1932 a high-ranking parliamentary delegation would visit the USSR in late spring. During the next few months, Ankara hosted a Soviet trade mission, concluded a telephone and telegraph agreement with the USSR, and agreed to joint construction of a dam. The June visit of the Turkish parliamentarians was widely and favorably reported in the Soviet press. In October the Turkish newspaper *Cumhuriyet* featured an article by Khrushchev praising the friendship between Lenin and Ataturk and emphasizing that then as now there were "no serious reasons that could prevent the establishment of good-neighbor relations between our two countries. The Soviet people want friendship with their Turkish neighbors. We want our frontiers to be frontiers of good neighbors, we want the Black Sea to be a sea of peaceful navigation, of trade, a sea of resorts."[33] Despite these promising developments, the Turkish government was slow to embark on a new course with the Soviet Union. Cyprus was to be a decisive catalyst.

The island of Cyprus is situated 40 miles off Turkey's southeast coast. It was ceded to Britain in 1878 after more than 300 years of Ottoman rule and was granted independence in 1960. Under the terms of the treaty establishing the Republic of Cyprus (and granting Britain two military bases), Britain, Greece, and Turkey pledged to ensure the island's independence, territorial integrity, and security; and "to prohibit, so far as concerns them, any activity aimed at promoting, directly or indirectly, either union of Cyprus with any other State or partition of the Island." For its part, the government of Cyprus undertook "not to participate, in whole or in part, in any political or economic union with any State whatsoever" and to fulfill the provisions of its Constitution, including the guarantees to the minority Turkish Cypriot population (approximately 20 percent). Finally, in the event that the treaty was violated and "insofar as common or concerted action may not be possible, each of the three guaranteeing Powers reserves the right to take action with the sole aim of reestablishing the state of affairs created by the present Treaty." The prohibitions against *enosis* (union) with Greece disappointed the 80 percent Greek Cypriot population of the binational state.

Communal tension was never far from the surface, and the Turkish minority had reason to fear for its status. In 1963 Archbishop Makarios, Cyprus's president, attempted to change the Constitution and eliminate the political guarantees for the Turkish minority. Widespread communal violence broke out. Turkey warned that it would use force to prevent any change in the status of the island. Makarios rejected the West's proposal of mediation and turned to the UN Security Council, where he hoped to gain support by exploiting his nonaligned status. On March 14, 1964, the Security Council created the United Nations Peacekeeping Force in Cyprus (UNIFCYP) "to prevent a recurrence of fighting and, as necessary, to contribute to the maintenance and restoration of law and order and a return to normal conditions."

The Turkish government several times threatened military intervention—a step that it believed authorized by the 1960 treaty. In early June, to head off a Turkish invasion that was judged imminent, President Lyndon B. Johnson sent a stiff note to the Turks:

> I must call to your attention . . . the obligations of NATO. There can be no question in your mind that a Turkish intervention in Cyprus would lead to military engagement between Turkish and Greek forces . . . . Furthermore, a military intervention in Cyprus could lead to a direct involvement by the Soviet Union. I hope you will understand that your NATO allies have not had a chance to consider whether they have an obligation to protect Turkey against the Soviet Union if Turkey takes a step which results in Soviet intervention without the full consent and understanding of its NATO allies.

Ankara was shocked by the crude implication that it might find itself alone, should the Soviet Union intervene, in a local dispute that it, but clearly not Washington, regarded as impinging on its security and as being quite divorced from East-West considerations. Once again, as in 1956 during the Suez crisis, Washington had shown itself self-righteous in dealing with close allies, insensitive to their regional interests, and indifferent to the domestic consequences for the pro-U.S. governments of these countries, and to the future of the alliance. Turkey's reappraisal of its relationship with the United States and its fresh assessment of prospects for Soviet-Turkish relations may be said to date from the Johnson note.

Neither the Cuban nor Cypriot crises directly involved the Soviet-Turkish relationship, but both were important to its subsequent evolution. Henceforth, the Turkish leadership, regardless of political affiliation, accepted the need to explore all foreign policy options, one of which was certainly better relations with the Soviet Union. A tentative examination into the assumptions underlying Turkey's post-World War II foreign policy began to appear gingerly in the Turkish press, and was actively discussed in private among the elite: Had the departure from Ataturk's antipathy to entangling alliances been really necessary? How valuable was membership in NATO? Could greater flexibility and scope be introduced into Turkey's policy? Was the Soviet threat really serious? The search for options began slowly.[34]

In October 1964 Turkey sent two observers to the Cairo Conference of Nonaligned States—the beginning of a varied attitude toward closer association with the Afro-Asian countries. At the end of the month Foreign Minister Feridun Erkin visited Moscow; and Prime Minister Ismet Inonu turned up with a large entourage at the Soviet Embassy celebration of the Bolshevik Revolution. In January 1965 a delegation from the Supreme Soviet, headed by Politburo member Nikolai Podgorny, returned the June 1963 visit of its Turkish counterpart. While the Soviet delegation was still in Turkey, an intriguing series of developments unfolded: the Turkish government cancelled its decision to participate in the U.S.–proposed multilateral nuclear force (under which several nuclear-armed warships would be manned by crews from all the NATO countries, in order to forestall any German policy to go nuclear); its also cancelled the scheduled visit of the U.S. nuclear-powered merchant ship *Savannah*; and Gromyko came out, for the first time, in favor of the concept of federation on Cyprus, the position preferred by Ankara.[35] Coincidence? Linkage? A revival of peaceful coexistence?

During Soviet Foreign Minister Gromyko's visit in May 1965, the failure to reach agreement on any substantive issue prompted the headline in one Turkish newspaper: "No Divorce from America—Marriage to Moscow Off." Reality was more complex. In August, Suat Hayri Urguplu (who had replaced Inonu in February) became the first Turkish prime minister since 1932 to visit the Soviet Union, and he returned with a Soviet offer of credits to construct a number of industrial projects, but negotiations went slowly, primarily because of Turkish indecisiveness.

In neither country did domestic politics seriously delay the quest for closer ties. Khrushchev's deposal in October 1964 had not caused any visits to be deferred or foreign policy overtures to change. In Turkey, the elections of October 1965 brought the Justice Party, headed by Suleiman Demirel, to power. This successor to the Democratic Party, which had been dissolved by the military after their takeover in 1960, was identified with the more conservative and pro-NATO elements, but it made clear its interest in better relations with the Soviet Union.

Both countries were ready for a new relationship, characterized by significant economic cooperation and a political accommodation that was highly pragmatic, issue-specific, and compartmentalized so as to prevent any one issue from disrupting the essential movement toward a stable bilateral relationship.

NOTES

1. Royal Institute of International Affairs, *Political and Strategic Interests of the United Kingdom: An Outline* (London: Oxford University Press, 1939), 102–03.

2. Sergei Goriainov, *Bosfor i dardanelly* [The Bosporous and the Dardenelles] (St. Petersburg: Tipografiia I.N. Skorokhodova, 1907), 22–23.

3. J. C. Hurewitz, ed., *The Middle East and North Africa in World Politics: A Documentary Record*, 2d ed., vol. 2, *British-French Supremacy, 1914-1945* (New Haven, Conn.: Yale University Press, 1979), 17.

4. Ibid., 252.

5. Arnold J. Toynbee and Kenneth P. Kirkwood, *Turkey* (London: Ernest Benn, 1926), 288.

6. Geoffrey Lewis, *Turkey*, 3rd ed. (London: Ernest Benn, 1965), 115.

7. George S. Harris, *The Origins of Communism in Turkey* (Stanford, Calif.: The Hoover Institution, 1967), 62.

8. Royal Institute of International Affairs, *Survey of International Affairs 1936* (London: Oxford University Press, 1937), 607.

9. Altemur Kilic, *Turkey and the World* (Washington, D.C.: Public Affairs Press, 1959), 77.

10. Raymond J. Sontag and James S. Beddie, eds., *Nazi-Soviet Relations 1939-1941: Documents from the Archives of the German Foreign Office* (Washington, D.C.: Department of State, 1948), 258.

11. Royal Institute of International Affairs, *Survey of International Affairs 1939-1946: The Middle East in the War* (London: Oxford University Press, 1952), 461.

12. *Foreign Relations of the United States: The Conferences at Malta and Yalta 1945* (Washington, D.C.: U.S. Government Printing Office, 1955), 903.

13. Feridun Cemal Erkin, *Les relations turco-soviétiques et la question des Détroits* (Ankara: Basnur Matbaasi, 1968), 323-24. This account by a former head of the Turkish Foreign Office and foreign minister examines the 1945 to 1947 crisis in detail.

14. Ferenc A. Váli, *The Turkish Straits and NATO* (Stanford, Calif.: Hoover Institution Press, 1972), 71.

15. The complete note is given in ibid., 249.

16. Ibid., 269-74.

17. Erkin, 396-404; 418-25.

18. Ibid., 403.

19. George S. Harris, "The Soviet Union and Turkey," in Ivo J. Lederer and Wayne S.

Vucinich, eds., *The Soviet Union and the Middle East: The Post World War II Era* (Stanford, Calif.: Hoover Institution Press, 1974), 30.

20. Ibid.

21. George S. Harris, *Troubled Alliance: Turkish-American Problems in Historical Perspective 1945-1971* (Washington, D.C.: American Enterprise Institute, 1972), 35-36.

22. Royal Institute of International Affairs, *Documents on International Affairs 1953* (London: Oxford University Press, 1956), 277-278.

23. Erkin, 411.

24. For example, Anatoli Miller, "Unfounded Doubts," *New Times*, no. 20 (May 2, 1956), 10-13.

25. Harris, "The Soviet Union and Turkey," 40-41.

26. Ferenc A. Váli, *Bridge Across the Bosporus: The Foreign Policy of Turkey* (Baltimore: Johns Hopkins University Press, 1971), 120.

27. Kh. Grigoryan, "More U.S. Trouble-Making in the Middle East," *International Affairs*, no. 6 (June 1959), 48.

28. Kh. Grigoryan, "Effects of Turkey's Militarization," *International Affairs*, no. 1 (January 1960), 77.

29. Váli, *The Turkish Straits and NATO*, 303-05.

30. This was revealed by General Gursel on June 16, 1962. New York *Times*, June 17, 1962.

31. "A Soviet Warning to Turkey," *Mizan Newsletter* 3, no. 2 (February 1962):6-7.

32. Robert F. Kennedy, *Thirteen Days: A Memoir of the Cuban Missile Crisis* (New York: W. W. Norton, 1969), 94-95.

33. As quoted in *Current Digest of the Soviet Press* 15, no. 46 (December 11, 1963–April 8, 1964):17.

34. Illustrative of the rethinking was the appearance in prestigious journals of articles by Turkish scholars, arguing the "New Left" contention that the United States was responsible for the onset of the Cold War and the Soviet Union did not threaten aggression. See Turkkaya Ataöv, "The Origins of the Cold War: 1945-1949," in the *Turkish Yearbook of International Relations* 7 (1966):28-103. That Soviet-Turkish relations is accorded only one paragraph is an indication of the author's distorted analysis.

35. Washington *Post*, February 16, 1965.

2

THE WARY DETENTE

By the mid-1960s, as East-West détente took root in Europe, Turkish leaders were increasingly disturbed by U.S. priorities and policies. Ever the realists unencumbered by doctrine, they cast about for possible options, especially regarding the Soviet Union. Suppose, one American analyst presciently observed, the Turks decide their national interests do not completely mesh with those of the United States and that (1) Turkey does not impede any vital Soviet interest, as long as it allows Soviet ships easy access through the Straits in periods other than war; (2) Turkey is not apt to be the first target of a Soviet aggression against Europe, particularly if there are no missile sites on its territory; and (3) given the obsolescent weaponry its army possesses, Turkey is most unlikely to have any effect on the outcome of a third World War.[1] It was just such a set of assumptions that shortly thereafter underlay the Turkish response to Soviet overtures, and by the late 1960s led the two countries to an atypical phase of their long contentious relationship. Since this relationship is a function of Turkish-U.S. and Turkish-Greek relations, it will be analyzed within the relevant regional and international contexts, and the determination of who influenced whom on what issues will be developed topically by examination of the key issues.

The Soviets have generally played their hand well—offering large-scale economic assistance without political strings; keeping the border quiet; avoiding bluster or sudden demands; and exploiting the divisions that beset NATO's southern flank. Their aims are strategic and military: to ensure unimpeded and easy access through the Straits in order to reinforce the USSR's expanding role in the Arab world and naval presence in the Mediterranean; to erode Turkey's commitment to U.S.-sponsored alliances; to undermine the U.S. network of military bases; to augment Turkey's reliance on Soviet trade and economic assistance; and to allay traditional Turkish fears of Moscow's imperial ambitions. Soviet methods have been primarily a combination of economic largesse and diplomatic restraint.

ECONOMIC COOPERATION

Except for a sheet-glass factory built in 1959, Turkey had refused repeated post-Stalin Soviet offers of economic assistance. In 1964 trade was minimal, totalling less than $20 million, but on August 31 an agreement was concluded for the first joint Soviet-Turkish project: The construction of a dam and hydroelectric station on the Arpa-Chai (Akhuryan) River, which flows along the border in the Caucasus about 30 miles from the city of Kars. On November 12, 1965, after some last-minute hesitation, Ankara signed a protocol (an announcement of intention) for a Soviet credit of $200 million to be used for various industrial projects; but still it was reluctant to take the plunge.

The turning point was December 1966, when Premier Alexei Kosygin became the first Soviet head of government ever to visit Turkey. He ignored the cool reception and strove to allay his hosts' suspicions. At a dinner in his honor, he declared that the USSR's policy toward states with "a social system that differs from ours" was based on the principles of peaceful coexistence—"equality of rights, respect of sovereignty, independence and territorial integrity, noninterference in domestic affairs, cooperation in accordance with the interests of both countries"; and he reaffirmed Soviet relinquishment of any territorial claims:

> We have managed to remove much of what had formerly stood in the way. Between the Soviet Union and Turkey, there are no territorial or other controversial questions which might hinder the development of relations on the basis of genuinely good-neighborly relations and friendship.[2]

The joint communiqué of December 27, 1966, dealt mostly with political themes—Cyprus, Vietnam, disarmament, European security, and the Middle East—and said little about economic cooperation; however, behind the scenes intense negotiations were going on. Three months later, in March 1967, Turkey signed the most far-reaching industrial assistance agreement it had ever concluded with any country. It accepted a $200 million credit, to be repaid in agricultural exports over a 15-year period at 2.5 percent interest (much more generous terms than provided by Western countries) and intended for use in seven projects: an iron and steel plant with an initial capacity of 1.2 million tons at the Mediterranean port of Iskenderun; an aluminum plant at Seydesehir; a petroleum refinery capable of handling 3 million tons of crude oil a year; a sulfuric acid plant in Bandirma; a fiberboard plant in Artvin; expansion of the glass works at Caylrova; and enlargement of a vodka-producing unit in the alcohol factory in Istanbul. Steps were also taken to institute regular passenger flights and to demarcate the frontier, in accordance with Kosygin's desire that "both on land and sea," there be "a frontier of friendship" that "cannot be changed under the influence of any external factors."

In September 1967 Turkish Prime Minister Suleiman Demirel returned Kosygin's visit, despite some criticism from members of his own Justice Party (JP). He stressed the closeness of Soviet and Turkish views on the need for an independent Cyprus, the importance of economic cooperation, and the improvement of diplomatic ties. The next year, work started on the seven industrial projects and the Arpa-Chai River dam. Notwithstanding the tension in the Middle East stemming from Israel's victory over Egypt, Syria, and Jordan in the June War, the Soviet naval buildup in the Mediterranean, and the invasion of Czechoslovakia in August 1968, Soviet-Turkish relations stayed on a steady course. The ceremony, on October 3, 1970, when Demirel laid the foundation stone for work on the Iskenderun iron and steel complex, was an augur of the expanding and important role that Soviet assistance was to play in Turkey's industrial development and of the political accommodation that accompanied it. By the end of the decade, the Soviet Union had become Turkey's most important source of assistance for public–sector projects, and Turkey was the recipient of more Soviet economic assistance than any other Third World country.

In the early 1970s the economic projects contributed significantly to the promotion of political ties. They received considerable attention in the joint communiqué issued at the conclusion of President Podgorny's visit in April 1972, when a preliminary accord was also reached for doubling the output of the Iskenderun complex, with the USSR providing an additional $288 million in equipment, material, and technical assistance. An agreement signed in Ankara on July 9, 1975, during the visit of Semyon Skachkov, head of the USSR State Committee for Foreign Economic Relations, was another milestone: It called for an additional Soviet credit of $700 million for further expansion of the Iskenderun plant to 4 million tons annually, enlargement of the Seydesehir aluminum works, and construction of two thermal power plants to operate on lignite in the Orhaneli district of Bursa and the Can district of Canakkale. Coming as it did in the wake of the 1974 Cyprus crisis and the strains between Turkey and the United States, seriously aggravated by the U.S. arms embargo, the new Soviet economic package was particularly welcome. Bulent Ecevit, leader of the Republican People's Party, then in opposition, expressed the growing feeling among all Turkish political parties that it was appropriate for Turkey to pursue a more "balanced" foreign policy—meaning better relations with the Soviet Union—noting that "even if the [U.S.] embargo is lifted, we cannot rely on the United States for our security, beyond certain limits . . . ."[3]

In December 1975 Kosygin attended the opening of the Iskenderun complex, which he described as "détente in action." Exuding goodwill, he noted that the Seydisehir aluminum combine, the oil refinery, and the sulfuric acid plant also were operating and expressed confidence that such economic cooperation would continue to develop. Economic interactions did indeed increase significantly in following years (see Appendix 1) and a year later, at the first meeting of the Turkish-Soviet Economic Cooperation Joint Committee, established by the July 1975 agreement, plans for a number of other projects were discussed. A ten-year agreement, totalling $1.3 billion, was drafted in Moscow in March 1977 and formally approved in March 1978.

Thus, Soviet-Turkish economic relations came of age in the decade after the trailblazing 1967 accord: Trade more than quadrupled and Soviet equipment and expertise moved very much into the center of Turkey's public-sector development. Especially important has been the Soviet role in Turkey's energy program. Oil-poor (it produces less than 20 percent of its needs), shaken economically by the escalating costs of oil imports since late 1973, caught in the midst of a major industrialization drive by these costs plus the global recession of the 1974-76 period (a contributing factor in the severe inflation and political extremism that afflicted it from 1975 to 1980), Turkey welcomed the USSR's assistance, which has included the construction of several thermal plants, dams, and a nuclear power plant with a guarantee of fuel for its operation; exploration for oil in southeastern Turkey; the sale of larger quantities of oil; and erection of a second power transmission line that will more than double Turkey's imports of electricity from the USSR.[4] A ten-year agreement concluded in November 1976 for the sale and exchange of electric power, and a $3.8 billion protocol for a variety of energy-related projects, signed on June 5, 1979, highlighted the ongoing and forward-looking relationship.

The Turks have generally been satisfied with the Soviet projects, and the Soviet effort in Turkey has been as good as any it made anywhere in the Third World. Moscow delivered on what it can do best: heavy industrial projects, power plants, and electrical transmission grids. It likes to contrast its easily visible contributions to Turkey's industrialization and economic development with the less conspicuous Western efforts on agricultural and infrastructure-type projects; its investment in the public rather than private sector; and its repayment schedules, which are more advantageous than the West's, because as a rule they are at lower interest rates and accept Turkish goods, thus saving Turkey scarce hard currency. (U.S. officials acknowledge that the USSR has provided Turkey with a great deal of economic assistance, about $2 billion worth through 1980. However, they claim that Soviet projects, which are in the public sector, encourage the worst features of Turkey's economy—the overemployment, inefficiency, and corruption through the award of jobs to the party faithful by the group in power, without regard to economic rationality; and, as a result, these enterprises are unproductive and drain resources from more productive sectors. Many Turkish sources confirm this observation.)

Moscow exploits the guns-will-not-bring-butter theme and criticizes the extent to which Western assistance is tied to the purchase of weapons, as well as to debt repayment; Soviet assistance, on the other hand, is not "dragging Turkey toward militarization and greater military expenditures."[5] Soviet commentaries beamed to Turkish audiences denigrate the efforts of the West to help Turkey out of its economic troubles (like the $3 billion emergency package that was put together in 1980—$1.6 million from the International Monetary Fund and the remainder from Western creditors), saying "the West does not actually want to solve the economic impasse. It only wants to maintain Turkey as a NATO base and to channel the financial aid it extends not to the development of the economy, where it is most needed by the Turkish people, but to various military goals . . . ."[6]

Moscow keeps a watchful eye on the Turkish scene.[7] The political violence and economic dislocation of the 1975-80 period have given way to a tenuous quiet and stability following the coup of the generals in September 1980, but the preoccupation with domestic disequilibrium, the disillusionment with the United States and Western Europe, and the lingering crisis with Greece have all reaffirmed Ankara's belief in the need for good relations with the Soviet Union. It is against this background that the key issues in the Soviet-Turkish relationship will be examined.

CYPRUS: CRISIS AND CATALYST

The 1964 Cyprus crisis had shocked the Turks into reassessing the utility of a heavy reliance on the United States, and had brought a rise in anti-Americanism that was exploited by the RPP and radical splinter groups to weaken Demirel's government. The 1974 Cyprus crisis was even more damaging to Turkish-U.S. and Turkish-Greek ties, and to NATO's position in the eastern Mediterranean; and it gave additional impetus to the Turkish-Soviet accommodation Moscow had been assiduously cultivating.

In the decade after 1964, during which the Cyprus crisis simmered before erupting again with even greater political fallout, the Soviet Union tried not to offend the Greeks, the Cypriot authorities, or the Turks, each of which it had reason to believe was dissatisfied with the United States and receptive to closer ties. However, Moscow discovered it could not play siren to all three, and in the hierarchy of Soviet policy Turkey was the most important. It had expanded economic cooperation, upgraded political exchanges, slowly improved the diplomatic environment, and was eager to follow up these gains.

In Turkey's eyes the Soviets passed the political litmus test by their modified policy on the Cyprus issue. In the period before Cyprus became independent in 1960, the Soviet position that had emerged mirrored that of the local pro-Moscow Communist Party (AKEL), which opposed enosis (union) with Greece. Since AKEL was outlawed in Greece, enosis would have been incompatible with the party's future existence. At that time Moscow also denounced the limitations placed on Cyprus' sovereignty, as set forth in the 1959 Zurich accords between Greece and Turkey. According to the USSR, the island should be fully independent, demilitarized, and empowered to eliminate the clauses in the Constitution granting Britain base rights.[8]

As the 1963-64 crisis mushroomed, Khrushchev at first sided with the Cypriot government of Archbishop Makarios. Thus, in his letter to the heads of state of the United States, Britain, France, Greece, and Turkey in early February 1964, he said the violence was being "whipped up from outside" and used "as a pretext" for dispatching NATO forces to the island, and he warned that

> the Soviet Union, although it has no common boundaries with the Republic of Cyprus, cannot remain indifferent to the situation that is taking shape in the area of the eastern Mediteranean, an area which is not very distant from the southern frontiers of the U.S.S.R., particularly if we take into consideration how our idea of distances has changed in our time.
>
> I should think that abstention from all plans that could aggravate the situation . . . and infringe on the lawful rights of the people of Cyprus to freedom and independence, meets not only the interests of the Cypriots but also our common interests.[9]

Later, after a series of Turkish air attacks on August 8, TASS affirmed that

> in reply to the appeal of the Government of Cyprus and President Makarios personally, the Soviet Government declares that if a foreign armed invasion of the territory of the republic takes place, the Soviet Union will help the Republic of Cyprus to defend her freedom and independence . . . and is prepared to begin negotiations on this matter immediately.[10]

However, by late August, Khruschev drew back from this partisan position. While upholding the territorial integrity and independence of Cyprus and urging Turkey to desist from further military operations, the Soviet government, in an oral message, reassured Turkey of Soviet neutrality,[11] and shied away from support of Makarios's aim of majority rule at the expense of the Turkish minority. Moscow was not going to alienate Turkey, after having sought a reconciliation for more than a decade.

An important Soviet concession to the Turkish position was the inclusion in the joint communiqué of November 6, 1964, issued at the end of Foreign Minister Erkin's visit, of the phrase "respect for the ... legal rights of the two national communities." The term "two national communities" effectively foreclosed enosis as an option. It was repeated in an interview with Izvestiia on January 21, 1965, when Gromyko called for a settlement respecting the rights of the "two national communities" that might "choose a federal form" of government.[12] The suggestion of a federated solution was the highwater mark of Moscow's move toward the Turkish position. In time the angry reaction of the Greek and Cypriot governments led to its adoption of a more equivocal stand, upholding the independence and territorial integrity of Cyprus without advocating any particular solution.

The prospect of Soviet backing on the Cyprus issue—even the minimal assurance that Moscow would not side with the Greeks or Makarios—accelerated the policy review in Ankara and contributed to the normalization process. The Soviet Union understood that Ankara wanted to utilize Podgorny's visit in January 1965 "only for strengthening its position on the Cyprus question," but Soviet analysts pointed out that the Turks were making a special effort to be accommodating, witness their courtesy in permitting Podgorny, over the opposition of a vocal minority, to address the parliament, and their decision announced during the visit not to participate in the U.S.-proposed multilateral nuclear force, a diplomatic action "regarded by the foreign press as a concession by Turkey to the Soviet Union."[13]

In May, Gromyko did not repeat his proposal of federation as a possible solution, but called for a settlement that would safeguard the rights of Greek and Turkish Cypriot communities and also denied that the Soviet Union had shipped arms to Cyprus.[14] This stand did not satisfy the Greek government, which then cancelled the scheduled visit of its prime minister to Moscow. By the time of Kosygin's visit in December 1966, the Soviet position had been fairly well developed in various statements, so the joint communiqué merely "confirmed the Soviet Union's attitude to the Cyprus question, as outlined in Soviet statements and also in the previously adopted joint Soviet-Turkish communiqué [of August 20, 1965]." Kosygin did express "regret" at the Czech sale of arms to Cyprus, and a second shipment was apparently not delivered, because of Moscow's orders.[15]

For the next eight years the international dimensions of the Cyprus situation remained unchanged, and UNFICYP kept the peace; but domestic developments in Greece, Cyprus, and Turkey fueled a new explosion. In April 1967 a military coup in Athens brought to power a group of incompetent zealots, who considered Makarios a "Red Monk" and worked to depose him; when they succeeded in July 1974, the consequences were unanticipated: an inadvertent crushing blow to enosis and their own downfall. From the late 1960s on, Makarios intensified pressure on the Turkish community and tried to retract the provisions of the Constitution that safeguarded minority rights. Ankara's fractured political alignments made any compromise on the Cyprus issue more difficult and the government intransigent on the matter of exercising Turkey's rights, as a guarantor power, on Cyprus.

At times, Moscow's desire to placate all the parties created problems. For example, at the end of Archbishop Makarios's visit to the Soviet Union in June 1971, the joint communiqué called for the "Cypriot people" to settle their problems and for the withdrawal of foreign troops from the island.[16] This immediately disturbed the Turks, since "Cypriot people" had replaced the term "two national communities" that the Soviets used since November 1964, and "withdrawal of foreign troops" seemed to include the small Turkish (and Greek) contingents permitted on Cyprus under a 1960 agreement and thus represented a change from previous Soviet opposition only to "foreign [British] bases." Soviet assurances that there had been no change in policy mollified Ankara, and the joint communiqué of April 17, 1972, issued at the end of Podgorny's visit, stated:

> The Soviet Union and Turkey reaffirmed their positions on the Cypriot question. They come out for a peace settlement of the Cypriot problem, against *enosis* in any form, and for the preservation of the independence, sovereignty and territorial integrity of the Republic of Cyprus, with the observance of the legitimate rights and interests of both communities in Cyprus—the Greek and the Turkish—which ensure their peaceful life in an atmosphere of complete security. The two sides went on record for the continuation of inter-communal talks, which should be held on an equal footing, and expressed the hope that these talks would have a successful outcome.

The issue of foreign troops and foreign bases was not addressed, presumably because of serious disagreement that both sides preferred not to air, fearing it would mar the friendly atmosphere they were nurturing.[17]

The 1974 Cyprus crisis had far-reaching consequences that served

Soviet interests and furthered the Soviet-Turkish accommodation. On July 14 Makarios was overthrown by a military group that was linked to the junta in Athens, which hoped an imposed enosis would bring it popular support and a new lease on power. The next day the Soviet government denounced the putsch by "Fascist extremists" who were out to make Cyprus "a NATO arsenal," and throughout the crisis it portrayed NATO as the arch culprit.

After failing to enlist Britain's cooperation to restore the status quo ante coup, Turkey, on July 20, landed forces and occupied almost 40 percent of the island. It justified its unilateral action as consistent with the responsibility of a guarantor power under the 1960 treaty, once Britain (and of course Greece) had refused to reestablish the original regime. Whatever the legal merits underlying Turkey's action—and they tend to be slighted—it was clear from the start that the Turks were intent on more than merely a restoration of the pre-coup situation; they wanted stronger safeguards for the minority ethnic Turks.

The action caught all the powers by surprise. An initial Soviet statement the next day extended implicit support. Pleased with the disarray in NATO, it did not condemn Turkey's unilateral use of force. When, at the end of July, the junta in Athens collapsed and a civilian government took over amidst a tide of anti-American sentiment, Moscow withheld criticism of the Greeks whose alienation from the United States and NATO (like that of the Turks) held out the prospect of considerable Soviet political advantage. Indeed, on August 1, the Soviet stand was praised by Prime Minister Ecevit, who said it was "from the very outset of the events in Cyprus ... characterized by great understanding and constructiveness." On August 14 Moscow applauded the decision of the provisional Greek government to remove its troops from NATO's military command—a decision prompted by its desire to blunt the appeal of the leftist Andreas Papandreou, who favored a total withdrawal from NATO and a nonaligned foreign policy. All of this suited Moscow, though a permanent Turkish occupation and de facto partition of Cyprus would be an undesirable outcome from its perspective. Therefore in repeated statements the Soviet government insisted on the return of Makarios and the preservation of the territorial integrity and independence of the Republic of Cyprus.

On August 22, although unable directly to affect the tortuous course of events, Moscow, in a major statement, accused NATO of "behind-the-scenes diplomatic maneuvers" intended to dismember Cyprus and create a "NATO stronghold in the eastern Mediterranean." It called for "an international conference within the framework of the United Nations" to ensure the "sovereignty, independence and territorial integrity of the

Republic of Cyprus"; and to ensure the "withdrawal of all foreign armed forces." None of the Western capitals, except Athens, thought internationalizing the problem would help; and Ankara was firm:

> The Turkish Government is not aware of any NATO move designed . . . to end the existence of the Cyprus Republic as an independent and sovereign state and to convert [it] into a NATO stronghold . . . . Turkey has fully respected the policy of nonalignment by Cyprus. The probability of Cyprus joining the joint NATO security system would have arisen if a part of Cyprus or the whole of it were annexed by a member of the alliance. But as in the past, Turkey is determined to prevent such an annexation . . . .[18]

The Turks opposed the involvement of outside powers, especially since in the recent past "some permanent members of the Security Council" have not demonstrated impartiality and objectivity in the solution of international problems. In mid-September Moscow dispatched a deputy foreign minister to Greece, Turkey, and Cyprus, but failed to obtain their support for a compromise proposal. By the end of the year, though, with the return of Archbishop Makarios to Cyprus, the Soviet fear of NATO's encroachment on Cyprus waned.

By early 1975 the Cyprus question was a cul-de-sac.[19] The Soviet Union could do nothing to arrange a settlement, and had little reason to try, for a new deterioration in U.S.-Turkish relations was grist for its diplomatic mill. Indeed, in February 1975 the U.S. Congress terminated military aid to Turkey, in an attempt to pressure Ankara to withdraw its troops from Cyprus; and Turkey shut down U.S. military installations. Lacking any real leverage in the Cypriote dispute—either in terms of inducements or pressures—the Soviet Union took the lofty road, advocating general principles that offered something to each. Thus, in all high-level meetings of Soviet and Turkish officials, beginning with Kosygin's visit to Ankara in December 1975, the following formulation (or some slight modification) was used:

> The sides believe that the Cyprus question should be settled peacefully . . . on the basis of respect for the sovereignty, independence, territorial integrity and policy of nonalignment of Cyprus . . . observing the legitimate rights and interests of the Turkish Cypriots and Greek Cypriots and ensuring their peaceful life in conditions of complete security.

This satisfied essential Turkish requirements and meant that Moscow saw Cyprus as no bar to closer ties. The USSR favored a broad-based international conference within the framework of the United Nations and, in early February 1975, dropped the distinction between "foreign troops" and "foreign bases" and called for the island's permanent demilitarization.[20]

Moscow's opposition to both enosis and *taksim* (partition), and championing of the independence and territorial integrity of Cyprus, gives it an opportunity to pose as an advocate of the rights of a small state threatened by encroachment of larger states. An independent Cyprus is a perennial bone in NATO's craw and helps Moscow's courtship of Turkey and Greece and their disaffection from the United States.

Since its rapprochement with Turkey involves prime strategic objectives, that is, access through the Straits, an end to U.S. bases in Turkey, and Turkey's decoupling from NATO, the USSR finds the status quo vis-a-vis Cyprus quite acceptable. For the moment, the dislodgement of Britain from its bases at Akrotiri (near Limassol) and Dhekelia (near Larnaca) and the United States from its radar installations and radio communications facilities on the island is not of prime importance. When Greece rejoined NATO's military command in October 1980 (having withdrawn after the junta was deposed in July 1974), a move made possible by General Kenan Evren (who had seized power in Ankara the previous month and dropped Turkey's opposition to Athens' return), one implication was a tacit Turkish-Greek understanding to continue to disagree over Cyprus, but to avoid recourse to war. The situation is troublesome but stable. Because of its overriding interest in assured access through the Straits, the USSR does not want a Turkish-Greek war, but it gets a lot of mileage out of existing frictions. Overall, the simmering Cyprus issue, a marginal matter for the Soviets but a significant one for the Turks, has helped Moscow's courtship of Ankara.

POLITICAL ACCOMMODATION

Since the late 1960s, Turkey's changed perception of the Soviet threat and the USSR's skillful response to regional opportunities have complemented their search for détente with each other. This was a period of Turkish disenchantment with the United States and interest in new foreign policy options, so that even though the USSR's military capability had grown enormously, Turkey regarded its activities in the eastern Mediterranean, including its permanent forward naval deployments and quest for military bases in the Arab world, with surprising equanimity.

Several considerations entered into Ankara's assessment.[21] First was the sharply diminished sense of Soviet threat. Soviet policy in the region is seen as a natural concomitant of the USSR's emergence as a superpower and its objectives as essentially political. Drawn by the region's instability in its quest for clients and advantage, Moscow exploits circumstances it did not create and seeks maximum gain at minimum cost. The Turks have by no means shed their historic wariness of Russia and its ambitions to control the Straits, but they see little immediate cause for alarm, because toward them Moscow has been almost benign. The 370-mile frontier has generally been quiet. Protocols were signed in 1967, 1972, 1973, and 1979 to adjust the border and arrange territorial compensation for losses incurred due to shifts in the river and the building of a series of dams—all in all requiring more than 1,000 individual protocols and dozens of sectional maps; and in 1978 there was an amicable demarcation of the continental shelf and territorial waters between the two countries in the Black Sea. There have been few threatening military buildups, and no rocket-rattling or serious incidents. In August 1979 Turkey's defense minister wrote that there was no "immediate threat from the Warsaw Pact" and no evidence of Soviet aggressive intentions.[22] A Soviet buildup in the Caucasus in late spring and summer of 1980 was probably linked to events in Iran at the time (see Chapter 5).

This Turkish perception is a function not only of Soviet moderation but of U.S. inconstancy. The Turks bitterly resented U.S. policy during the Cyprus crisis. They found the thesis of Charles de Gaulle—that the United States could not be expected to risk a nuclear exchange with the Soviet Union if Soviet conventional forces attacked a NATO member—validated by the alacrity with which the U.S. Congress weakened a NATO ally and disrupted the alliance because of the pro-Greek lobbying and partisan domestic interests of some of its members. They watched Washington's search for détente with Moscow since 1972 with a combination of expectancy and dismay, and were not impressed by its handling of the Iranian and Afghan crises. The result is that many in Ankara believe Turkey's security may be jeopardized more by allies than adversaries.

A second consideration that explains Turkey's receptivity to Soviet overtures is the leadership's feeling of having been neglected. Many officials are convinced that NATO headquarters, in its preoccupation with the ominous Soviet buildup in central and northern Europe, regards the eastern Mediterranean as an ancillary theater of operations. Since the U.S. arms embargo was lifted in late summer of 1978, the resources allocated to modernizing Turkey's armed forces have been, in Ankara's view, inadequate; "paltry" is a word often heard. They tell the story (hopefully apocryphal) of an official at NATO headquarters, who, when asked what could be done to strengthen NATO's southern flank, airily replied, "Lop it off."

The conviction that Brussels-NATO accords low priority to the eastern Mediterranean can be understood in light of the decisions taken on the allocation of AWACS (airborne warning and control system) aircraft.

Although the exact figures remain classified, NATO is supposed orginally to have sought the purchase of some 24 to 32 AWACS in order to cover its entire defensive arc from Norway to Turkey to safeguard against surprise attack.[23]

Owing to budgetary constraints, the number was steadily pared down, until approval for the purchase of 18 AWACS was reached by the NATO defense ministers at their semiannual meeting in December 1978. The reduced number means that some sectors of NATO's defensive perimeter will have to be shortchanged, and the eastern Mediterranean is lowest on the priority list. Among other developments reinforcing Turkey's perception of NATO's "benign neglect" may be included a 1978 study by the Office of Program Analysis and Evaluation of the Department of Defense suggesting "that the outbreak of a war on either of NATO flanks is either unlikely or impossible to successfully defend against"; and a statement of Secretary of Defense Harold Brown to a congressional committee: "*If* control of the Mediterranean were adjudged an appropriate planning objective . . . " (italics added).[24] Ever since the end of the World War II, control of the Mediterranean has been regarded as a prime objective of U.S. foreign policy. To have raised doubts concerning the validity of that strategy in such an offhanded fashion did little to reassure the Turks about either the intensity of the U.S. commitment or the coherence and perspicacity of Washington's Mediterranean-Middle East strategy.

The third consideration is Turkey's parlous domestic situation. The 1970s were very difficult. The economy was subjected to mounting annual inflation that reached 85 percent by the end of the decade; the balance-of-payments deficit rose from $86.1 million in 1970 to $3.5 billion in 1978; unemployment topped the 25 percent level; chronic mismanagement of state enterprises, the sharply reduced remittances from Turkish workers abroad, and soaring energy costs all served as the economic backdrop against which the level of political violence "built to nightmare proportions."[25] The strain of burgeoning urbanization, the return from Western Europe of hundreds of thousands of emigrant workers with new ideas, and the breakdown of traditional loyalties and patterns created a pressure-cooker society. The explosive situation brought warnings from the military: End the "anarchy, terrorism and separatism" (an allusion to the Kurdish movement in eastern Turkey) or face the consequences.[26] In late July 1980 the main political parties reluctantly agreed to steps to strengthen the authority of the army and the courts.[27] The Generals were unimpressed, however, and on September 12, 1980, they seized power under the leadership of General Kenan Evren. What all of this makes abundantly clear is Turkey's desperate need for time, and help, to put its house in order. Friendly relations with the Soviet Union would permit attention to internal problems to be the leadership's priority.

Finally, Turkey needs trade, investment credits, and economic assistance. Moscow's blend of checkbook and olive branch has conveyed an overall reasonableness, easing the way for an accommodation that is both symbolic and substantive. The USSR has tried to obtain political concessions, especially since 1979, but knowing Turkey it has acted with circumspection, as the unfolding of the political dimension of its policy shows.

Ever since they began their diplomatic courtship, the Soviets have wanted a nonaggression pact. In an interview with the publisher of the Turkish weekly news magazine *Akis*, on the eve of Prime Minister Urgüplu's visit in August 1965, Kosygin suggested that a topic for discussion might be a nonaggression pact similar to the 1925 treaty abrogated by Stalin in 1945, not because, said he, the Soviet Union felt threatened by Turkey or Turkey by the Soviet Union, but because "we are concerned over the possibility of a third country which has aggressive intentions against us, using Turkey as a vehicle."[28] Urgüplu did not take the bait, seeing it as an attempt to attenuate Turkey's ties to NATO. Progress on the political front was slow, as Kosygin acknowledged at the end of his visit in late December 1966: "We realize that we differ in our positions on some international questions; but this does not shut out the prospects of further developing Soviet-Turkish relations and we are convinced that the existing obstacles can be overcome."[29]

Each side recognized that closer cooperation was desirable and feasible and that it could be managed without sacrificing vital national interests. For Turkey this meant steering clear of issues between the Soviet Union and the United States that did not jeopardize Turkish security or commitments to NATO: Thus, during the October War Turkish leaders refused refueling facilities to the United States for its airlift to Israel, on the ground that the issue lay outside of NATO's sphere of competence. For its part, the Soviet Union showed "understanding" for the Turkish position during the Cyprus crisis and extended a sizable credit in June 1975, at a time when Turkey, embittered by the U.S. aid cutoff, badly needed a morale-booster, as well an infusion of machinery and materials.

Such was the improvement in relations that at the end of Kosygin's visit in late December 1975 the joint communiqué announced "agreement on the preparation of a political document on friendly relations and cooperation between Turkey and the USSR to be signed in the near future." Drafted under Demirel's Justice Party, the political document was finally signed by Ecevit's RPP in June 1978—an indication of the prevailing consensus for improving relations with the USSR, signalling Turkish annoyance to Washington, and exploring all political options.[30]

In an interview with the Istanbul newspaper *Hurriyet* a week later,

Demirel emphasized the need to diversify the country's foreign policy: "Our country's interests demand it should establish good relations with communist countries, despite differences in systems . . . Why should Turkey stand aside while the United States, Britain and France are in full cooperation with the Soviets?"[31] On February 25, 1976, at the Twenty-fifth Congress of the Communist Party of the Soviet Union (CPSU), Brezhnev observed that cooperation with Turkey "is gradually spreading from the sphere of chiefly economic to political questions," implying that the balance sheet was promising for the future. However, 1976 passed without any movement on the political front, with Prime Minister Demirel repeatedly postponing a projected trip to Moscow, largely in hopes that the U.S. Congress would ratify the Defense Cooperation Agreement of March 23, 1976, and end its embargo.

Before Foreign Minister Ihsan Sabri Caglayangil's visit in March 1977, Ankara informed Moscow that no political document would be signed. The talks centered on economic cooperation, especially in the energy field; and a protocol was signed on preventing the hijacking of civil aircraft. Of particular importance to the Turks was the section on Cyprus in the joint communiqué, which excluded any mention of the Soviet proposal for an international conference and called for a solution based on the interests of two national communities.[32]

After the shock of the U.S. arms embargo, the military began to evaluate "Turkey's domestic potential for meeting her national defense needs."[33] Apart from making Turkey's defense industries more self-reliant in essential types of weaponry, Ecevit floated a "new concept" (two years later he called it the National Security Concept), which included diversification of Turkey's source of arms supply, most notably by buying from the Soviet Union.[34] Moscow, unquestionably "motivated by a desire to demonstrate the high quality and potential availability of Soviet arms for Turkish use," invited Turkish military observers to attend manuevers in the Caucasus between January 25 and February 6, 1976, in keeping with the spirit of the Final Act signed on July 31, 1975, in Helsinki, at the Conference on Security and Cooperation in Europe (CSCE).[35] In May 1976 Deputy Chief of the General Staff Kenan Evren met with top Soviet military leaders and toured Soviet installations. After Caglayangil's visit the following March, the Turkish Service of Radio Moscow noted with satisfaction:

> . . . even though Turkey is a NATO member and the Soviet Union is a member of the Warsaw Pact, the two countries find it possible to promote their contacts in the military domain . . . .The Soviet initiatives, which involve implementation of a number of measures in the armament field, suit the interests of . . . the Turkish people.[36]

In January 1978 the RPP returned to office, a result of the revolving-door syndrome that reflected the failure of either major party to arrest the mounting inflation, unemployment, and trade deficits or the violence from extremist groups at both ends of the political spectrum. Against this background and strong anti–Americanism, Ecevit determined to alter the focus, if not the substance, of Turkish foreign policy and implement ideas that had been discussed in Turkish circles for several years.[37] He stressed the need for strengthening relations with the Soviet Union and the neighbors in the Balkans (Romania and Bulgaria); and for firmer ties to nonaligned countries, and especially the Arab world. Wasting no time, he announced arrangements for a visit to Moscow in June to negotiate a "political document"; and on March 23 he told the Turkish Senate that Turkey had contributed more to NATO than NATO had to Turkey, adding: "Turkey can no longer leave its national security only to its cooperation with the U.S. and NATO."[38] On May 15, at the prestigious International Institute for Strategic Studies in London, Ecevit outlined the reasons for a new defense orientation: the changes in the international system and in the sources of threat; the excessive dependence for arms supplies on the United States, which lacks credibility as an ally because "there is too great an interaction, an inter-relationship between her internal and her external politics"; the need for economic assistance to help Turkey through a very dangerous period; and the prominence of regional tension over Cyprus.[39] An admirer of Romania's Nicolae Ceausescu, Ecevit wanted an independent role for Turkey within NATO comparable to the one he thought Ceausescu had within the Warsaw Pact.

Adding to the uncertainty of how far Ecevit intended to take Turkey in a new foreign policy direction was the visit from April 24 to 29, 1978 of Marshal N. V. Ogarkov, the Soviet chief of staff and first deputy minister of defense. Ostensibly a return for the 1976 visit of General Kenan Evren, Ogarkov's visit was at a slightly higher military level (a nuance some thought politically important) and came at a time (just before Ecevit's trip to Moscow) that gave it added significance. Ogarkov apparently offered military assistance, though the specifics remain uncertain, and some Turkish officials insist no offer was ever made. The comment of Defense Minister Hasan Esat Isik at a press conference held on the day of Ogarkov's departure is perhaps the most revealing official statement we have: "During his visit here the Soviet Chief of the General Staff . . . said that should the Turkish Armed Forces need it, the USSR would extend it [arms aid] within its means. But he said nothing further than that."[40]

Despite the Turks' decision not to explore the matter, the Greek Cypriots were sufficiently disturbed for the Soviet ambassador to tell President Spyros Kyprianou (who had suceeded to the office on Makarios's death in 1977) that what Marshal Ogarkov had in mind was only "ordinary contacts in the military field, such as the exchange of visits by warships and military athletic teams."[41] Militarily, Ogarkov's visit was without results, but politically it conveyed Moscow's readiness to provide a military option, should the Turks be so inclined.

The Political Document on the Principles of Good-Neighborly and Friendly Cooperation Between the USSR and Turkey, signed during Prime Minister Ecevit's visit (June 21 to 25, 1978), was the best the Soviet-Turkish political accommodation could achieve.[42] The original draft, presented to Ankara in April 1976, had not been acted on until six weeks before Ecevit's arrival.[43] Far less than the nonaggression treaty and return to the 1925 level of political closeness that Moscow coveted, the political document was a compromise that added little to the 1972 Declaration of the Principles of Good-Neighborly Relations, though symbolically it reinforced various strands of the existing rapprochement. The core of the document was the principles contained in the Final Act adopted at Helsinki.

The political document was not quite the accomplishment Moscow had hoped for. Taken together with Ecevit's statements that the Soviet Union was not a threat, it did aid Soviet diplomacy elsewhere in the region. (The communist coup in Afghanistan in April 1978 and the emerging unrest in Iran were as yet too localized to affect regional or international politics.) Moscow did not object to Turkey's membership in NATO, though it later used the document as a basis for contending that Turkey's participation contravened the provision renouncing "the utilization of their territory for aggression or subversive activities against other countries." Moscow could take some satisfaction from the glowing reception it received in the Turkish press and from the call by some Turkish intellectuals for the legalization of the Communist Party. However, a year later, when Moscow tried to use the document to urge the institutionalization of political consultation (a term favored by the Soviets in dealing with Third World clients), it was rebuffed by Ankara, which agreed to political discussions but not political consultations, and only on an irregular, not institutionalized, basis.

For the Turks it was the joint communiqué of June 25 that was a bonanza. Henceforth, commercial agreements would be concluded for three years—the first time Turkey had entered into a long-term trade pact with any nation—thereby facilitating economic planning; the volume of trade for the 1979-81 period was more than doubled, helping Turkish exports; and the USSR agreed to supply 3 million tons of petroleum annually (about 25 percent of Turkey's import needs), repayable in Turkish goods and not in precious hard currency, during this period. Further assistance for industrial and energy-related projects was placed on the agenda of the October meeting of the Joint Economic Cooperation

Committee. The two governments agreed to demarcate the continental shelf of the Black Sea. Though of little practical value at present, "since Turkey is not engaged in seabed exploration in what could be disputed areas . . . it gives Turkey the chance to show Greece that their continental shelf dispute can be solved through 'direct negotiations' which Athens so far has been reluctant to accept."[44] On the all-important issue of Cyprus, the Soviet Union adhered to the formulation, satisfactory to Ankara, used in previous communiqués. There were assorted agreements on flight information and supervision in the Black Sea region and cultural and scientific exchanges. At Turkish insistence, the political document included a provision calling on both sides to respect each other's "public order." All in all it was an ample harvest.

For a number of reasons the Ecevit visit was the last top-level political exchange before the military took power in September 1980. First, Turkey's snowballing domestic difficulties demanded so much attention that neither Ecevit nor Demirel had the inclination or the support to proceed further: The preoccupation with internal affairs mandated caution in foreign policy. Under the military there has been no interest in flirting with a quasi-Soviet option.

Second, the USSR recognized that a pause was in order. It had achieved as much as it could for the moment, and would have to await new developments before proffering additional inducement. The ongoing economic programs were solid building blocks for the future. After the U.S. lifted the arms embargo in mid-1978, Moscow watched the United States and Turkey edge back toward a functioning but not particularly cordial working relationship. Soviet analysts shrewdly exploited the uneasiness over U.S. confusion vis-a-vis Iran, the Horn of Africa, OPEC, and Western Europe; and they played on the feelings of the Turks that they were neglected and taken for granted:

> . . . at present Turkey feels ill at ease in the company of NATO states which condescendingly slight their semi-Asian ally and, moreover, ward it away from its neighbors.
>
> Let us not exaggerate Turkish-American differences. It is, of course, a question not of a break but of a new equilibrium which, in Ankara's view, must not exclude either American dollars or American weapons or even American bases on Turkish territory, albeit on different terms— these are being drawn up. But the differences must not be belittled either. For, after all, they turn on different concepts of Turkey's place in the modern world. Washington strategists have a strictly functional view of Turkey: Until the recent demise of CENTO it was a connecting link between two military blocs, and it is still NATO's southeastern flank and an element in the encirclement of the Soviet Union. But, of course, the Turkish people do not want to be just a function, and a risky one too, or a

"connecting link" which does not link them very well with a peaceful future. As a counterbalance to Atlantic nations, Turkish statesmen, having shaken off cold-war delusions, emphasize that Turkey's very location at the crossroads of East and West, north and south, enables it to help the cause of bringing peoples and states closer together in the name of peace and good-neighborliness. This is a sensible approach, and it extends to relations with the Soviet Union. Turkey does not want—and demonstratively emphasizes this—elements in its relations with the United States which could harm Turkish-Soviet relations.[45]

When Ecevit's government fell in October 1979, some criticized him for having acceded to U.S. pressure and reopening U.S. bases, resuming arms acquisitions from the United States, and strengthening ties to NATO.[46] The RPP had proven something of a disappointment to Moscow.

A third development adversely affecting the political course of Soviet-Turkish relations was the USSR's invasion of Afghanistan in December 1979. The Turks were not nearly as upset about the upheaval in Iran, having resented the Shah's niggardliness toward them during Iran's affluent period in the 1970s, and always contemptuously regarded the Iranians as somewhat effete. The invasion of Afghanistan, however, showed the USSR was not as benign as improved relations had led many to believe and had a chilling effect on new exchanges. It was also a fresh reminder of the ominous potential of the Soviet buildup and capability in Europe. The effect was to push Turkey's search for security with a NATO framework.

Finally, U.S.-Turkish relations took a turn for the better after the end of the arms embargo and the signing in April 1980 of a new Defense Cooperation Agreement; and also when a Western consortium put together a hefty aid package to prevent a collapse of the Turkish economy.

THE STRAITS

Historically, control of the Straits was the crux of the tension in Russo-Turkish relations. Since the death of Stalin, after which Moscow dropped all claims for co-management of the Straits and elected to operate within the framework of the 1936 Montreux Convention, Turkey's interpretation of the key provisions accorded with Soviet interests. Nowhere have the far-reaching advantages accruing to Moscow from the Soviet–Turkish accommodation been more evident than in the ease with which Soviet ships are permitted to transit the Straits.

From time to time Moscow criticizes Turkey's stewardship, but this is minor when weighed against the strategic access the USSR enjoys. For example, in December 1968, the Soviet government protested the entry into the Black Sea of the U.S. destroyers *Dyess* and *Turner*, alleging violations on two grounds: first, that the *Dyess* carried antisubmarine rocket launcher missiles, which exceeded the eight-inch or 203-mm caliber permitted warships of non-Black Sea powers; second, that the convention forbade a belligerent power that is not a Black Sea power from sending its ships into the Black Sea, "and the United States is waging war—a war of aggression—against the Vietnamese people."[47] Ankara rejected both contentions:

> New arms have been developed since the Montreux Convention. These weapons were not listed in the Convention because they did not exist at the time of its signature. The Turkish Government takes the view that carrying such weapons is not conflicting with the Convention if they are not of an aggressive nature.[48]

It did not consider U.S. involvement in Vietnam belligerency in the international legal meaning of the term; and it dismissed as goundless Soviet charges that the brief visits by U.S. naval vessels in the Black Sea since 1965 were provocations.

These minor setbacks aside, Moscow has good reason to be satisfied with Turkey's flexible interpretation of the Montreux Convention. Since the mid-1960s, when the USSR began to maintain a permanent squadron on station in the Mediterranean, Turkey has permitted transit of the Straits with minimum formality. After the 1967 June War, to avoid the clause that requires "at least eight days' notification of the intention to pass" through the Straits, Moscow flooded "the Turkish Foreign Ministry with stand-by applications for transit . . . to obtain permissions whether they are effectively made use of or not."[49] The Turks did not object to this ploy. During the October War, despite Washington's objections, they permitted the Soviet government to conduct a major sea and air resupply of its Arab clients, very likely to avoid angering the Arabs, to whom they look for oil, loans, and markets.

However, lest Moscow see this as acquiescence for a corridor over Turkey to the Gulf and Horn of Africa, in December 1977-January 1978, at the height of the Soviet airlift to Ethiopia, Turkish authorities protested that the sharp increase of flights southward over their territory surpassed the "occasional flights" of "civil aircraft" permitted under Article 23 of the Montreux Convention. Whereas Turkey had been allowing 10 to 12 notified flights a month, in December the number exceeded 30.[50] After Turkey's admonition, the traffic returned to normal, and Moscow used a more roundabout route to Aden and the Horn.

Soviet marine transits of the Straits—military and commercial—are so numerous that the Turks as a concession and convenience have dropped virtually all pretense at restricting either numbers or types of Soviet ships, subject to the easily manipulated formality of prior notification.[51] Indeed, it is reported that Soviet submarines start their transit from the Black Sea through the narrow Bosporus shortly before first light, although Article 12 of the convention states they "must travel by day": By allowing the passage time to be pushed back to an hour of darkness the Turks enable the Soviets to minimize observation from the shore.[52] Furthermore, although the convention limits submarines to those permanently based in the Black Sea, the rotation of Soviet submarines in the Mediterranean from 8 to 16 (during the October War) suggests that some of those making the eastbound passage from the Aegean Sea through the Dardenelles, the Sea of Marmara, and the Bosporus to the Black Sea were neither built in Soviet Black Sea ports nor permanently stationed there. Admittedly, this traffic has been most uneven; no Soviet submarines transited the Straits in the period from December 1972 to December 1975, meaning that they entered the Mediterranean through the Strait of Gibraltar.

Perhaps the most dramatic instance of Turkey's adaptation to the USSR's growing naval capacity was the transit on July 18, 1976, of the *Kiev*, the Soviet Union's first genuine aircraft carrier. Whereas the transits of the helicopter ships, *Moskva* and *Leningrad*, starting in 1968, raised questions about violations of the Montreux Convention, which seemed implicitly to prohibit aircraft carriers from passing through the Straits, that of the *Kiev* was regarded by most Western analysts as a definite violation because, unlike the *Moskva* and *Leningrad*, it "mounts a large angled flight deck and carries not only helicopters but also 30 Yak-36 vertical/short take-off and landing (V/STOL) jet aircraft."[53] However, the Turks, having studied the problem for two years prior to the *Kiev*'s transit, accepted the Soviet description of the *Kiev* as an "antisubmarine cruiser." Turkey is the sole arbiter of the Montreux Convention and of what can transit the Straits only when its vital interests are involved; otherwise it must take the changing international environment and interests of the various parties into consideration. NATO, contended the Turks, knew six months prior to the transit that the *Kiev* was preparing for sea trials; it "discussed the issue but declined to take action."[54] Since neither NATO nor any country protested, they felt confirmed in the wisdom of their decision.

Eager to reinforce Turkey's de facto revision of the Montreux Convention, the Soviets followed up quickly with their own assessment. A high-ranking naval officer, Captain V. Serkov, argued that "as a constituent part of the Soviet Fleet, the Black Sea fleet needs to be in constant connection with our fleets, which are deployed in other maritime areas," the implication being that unfettered access through the Straits was vital "by virtue of objective geographic conditions." He dismissed the bankruptcy of the [Western] claims that certain new Soviet ships do not fall into the category of ships that ... have the right of transit through the Straits. As has been shown in the detailed analyses of the Montreux Convention, from a juridical point of view it can be considered that transit through the Straits of *any* ships of states on the Black Sea does not contradict the letter and spirit of the Convention (italics added).[55]

The Straits no longer represent a threat to Soviet security: No armada is going to attack the USSR from the Black Sea. Turkey's policy is testament to the growth of Soviet military power and to Turkey's recognition of the new international environment and the constraints to which it must adapt. At odds with the United States, seeing no immediate danger of war and convinced its security requires cooperation with the USSR, Turkey permits access through the Straits under a pragmatic application of the Montreux Convention. This satisfies the Soviets and enables them to pursue their "foward policy" in the Arab East and Africa with minimum inconvenience. Short of physical control of the Straits—indubitably the ultimate Soviet objective—Moscow gives Ankara every reason to continue, and to expand, its accommodation in the 1980s. On only one issue, namely, the existence of the U.S. bases on Turkish territory, is the USSR still really dissatisfied.

U.S. MILITARY BASES: MILITARY-POLITICAL CONSIDERATIONS

Since Turkey joined NATO in 1952 its most serious source of tension with the Soviet Union has been the presence on Turkish territory of a network of U.S. and NATO-related military installations. Designed to strengthen NATO's deterrent and intelligence-gathering capability, the bases are perceived as threats by Soviet leaders, who fear the use of these "provocative" bridgeheads for preemptive nuclear strikes and electronic espionage and accord priority attention to their removal.[56] Moscow has repeatedly criticized their presence as "unfriendly" acts that jeopardize Soviet-Turkish relations. After the removal of IRBMs from Turkey after the Cuban missile crisis, the USSR focused increasingly on the elimination of the U.S. bases and intelligence-gathering capabilities in Turkey.

After the 1974 Cyprus crisis, when the U.S. Congress voted an embargo on arms to Turkey, *Pravda* reported the comment of the Turkish foreign minister: "U.S. bases in Turkey represent an additional risk to us. We were prepared to accept this given further arms supplies. But now that arms supplies have been cut off, all that is left is the additional risk."[57]

In July 1975, as a reprisal, Turkey suspended operations at all 26 U.S. military installations, assuming direct control over them, and operating them solely for NATO purposes. The effect was a severe curtailment to all U.S. electronic monitoring of Soviet missile testing and troop movements in the southern region of the USSR. In addition to closing ammunition storage facilities, early warning radar stations, and supply depots, the move halted U.S. activities at the Incirlik air base (which provided military runways close to the Middle East), Kargaburun (a LORAN station on the Sea of Marmara that assisted U.S. Navy aircraft in fixing their positions in the Mediterranean), Sinop (a station on the Black Sea monitoring Soviet missile testing at the Baikonur Cosmodrome at Leninsk and the launching center at Kapustin Yar), Pirinclik (a long-range and communications complex located 15 miles from Diyarbakir in eastern Turkey and used for tracking Soviet missiles and listening in on radio transmissions between Soviet aircraft and their bases), and Belbasi (a major seismographic detection base located near Ankara and important for monitoring underground Soviet nuclear testing).[58] The suspension did considerable harm, as Secretary of Defense Harold Brown noted three years later in urging Congress to end the embargo:

> . . . it has resulted in the loss of some intelligence information not available from other sources. Data, some of which are not available from other sources [that is, satellite photography], have been lost on Soviet space, missile, and military systems development, operations, and training, thereby reducing our level of confidence in our knowledge of these subjects. Continued loss of information which can be collected only from sites in Turkey will hamper our ability to develop countermeasures to Soviet weapons systems under development.[59]

The deterioration in U.S.-Turkish relations that followed the arms embargo was paralleled by improved Soviet-Turkish economic and political relations. As one Turk observed, "the Kremlin couldn't have done it without help from the U.S. Congress."[60] Soviet commentaries stressed the anger in Turkish circles determined not to accede to U.S. pressure. A. Vasilyev, *Pravda's* correspondent, noted that officials "are hoping for some possibility of compromise with Washington [but] the general opinion is, however, that there can be no return to the former arrangement."[61]

The prospect of an end to U.S. military activities in Turkey seemed to put this preeminent Soviet objective within reach. During the next three years, the period of the embargo and the shutdown of the bases, Soviet commentators hammered at four basic themes, citing Turkish sources to support their arguments. First, Turkey should follow an independent and active foreign policy and not be captive to U.S. "imperialist" ambitions.

Turkey's efforts to improve relations with the Balkan countries and to forge closer ties with nonaligned countries were more consonant with Turkey's interests.

Second, Turkey should withdraw from NATO, since membership had brought nothing but economic trouble—inflation, unemployment, wasteful military expenditures—and made Turkey, NATO's poorest member, spend proportionately more of its national income on defense than any other NATO country. Leaving NATO and CENTO would ease the military burden and encourage economic development. Moreover, the "Atlanticist" focus of the Western countries had "always been determined by ulterior motives," which regarded Turkey important only as a "military strategic bridgehead in southern Europe and the Middle East in close proximity to the U.S.S.R. and the oil-rich Arab states."[62]

Third, the United States had shown itself an unreliable, capricious ally, insensitive and unsympathetic to Turkey's interests. Witness the imposition of the arms embargo to pressure Turkey on Cyprus and the efforts to gain a privileged position for "U.S. monopolies" as a sine qua non of economic assistance. (In a country where a statist mentality was deeply ingrained in the bureaucracy and the military, this Soviet criticism of U.S. efforts to promote "free enterprise" hit a responsive note.) As if to underscore U.S. neglect in the post-1973 period of economic difficulty, in December 1976 Moscow signed a ten-year agreement on economic cooperation, with emphasis on energy-related industries and activities.

Finally, a return of U.S. bases would threaten the Soviet–Turkish détente. Soviet commentaries maintained that "Turkey was not threatened by the USSR either before or after it had joined NATO," and that the United States was using "certain forces" to spread in Turkey "a myth about Soviet menace."[63] Quite prudently, during the period between the closure of the U.S. bases in 1975 and their reopening in October 1978, the Soviet government had never officially pressured Turkey on the issue, or, according to Turkish diplomats, even broached the matter. Moscow had learned that it could be more effective with a smile than a snarl.

Moscow hoped the end of the arms embargo would not lead to reactivation of U.S. military installations. At first it insisted that reports to this effect "are far removed from the truth."[64] Having less than two months earlier hosted Prime Minister Ecevit, signed the political document, and committed itself to massive additional economic assistance, it understandably had great expectations. TASS reminded Ecevit that the political document contained assurances that neither country would permit its territory to be used for aggressive purposes against the other and warned against upsetting the military balance in the region. Soviet broadcasts beamed to Turkey said the resumption of U.S. espionage against "Turkey's neighbors" was contrary to détente and Turkey's own security, the United

States had lifted the embargo only to promote U.S. strategic interests, and "no harm" had come to Turkey as a result of their closure. Nevertheless, in October Ecevit permitted the United States to resume operations at key bases.

Thus, despite a decade of generous developmental assistance, military quiescence, and political conciliatoriness, the Soviet Union could not prevent the Turkish government, even one more receptive to closer ties than any since Ataturk, from reversing a policy that Moscow strongly favored. The remembrance-of-things-past-with-Moscow overshadowed its current amicability.

Though disappointed, the Soviet leadership kept its perspective on what had been accomplished in the previous decade or two and showed itself possessed of historical understanding and political wisdom.

A few months later three aspects concerning the issue of military bases unleashed a flurry of Soviet commentary: Washington's effort to relocate in Turkey the monitoring stations ousted from Iran; its attempt to persuade Turkey to allow U-2 flights over Turkish territory in the vicinity of the Soviet border in order to monitor the prospective SALT II agreement; and its quest for a new agreement on U.S. bases in Turkey. The first two fell through, but not the third.

When, after the fall of the Shah in January 1979, Iran closed U.S. monitoring stations, Moscow orchestrated a campaign to forestall their relocation in Turkey. The Soviet media denounced the U.S. Central Intelligence Agency (CIA) for trying to install the secret eavesdropping equipment in Turkey, for spying on the Soviet Union: "Turkish public opinion will understand the consequences of this step by the United States. As a result of this step, Turkey may in the future be dragged against its will into a dangerous conflict—as has happened repeatedly in the past."[65] It accused Washington of deepening Turkey's involvement in America's imperialist ventures to ensure that Turkey remained the West's outpost in the area; and of using Turkish bases "to sabotage cooperation" between the USSR and Turkey. In a few months the Turks refused to grant the United States permission to relocate the equipment from Iran to Turkey, and Washington had to accept the consequent diminution in its capability to monitor Soviet missile testing.

To compensate for this loss of data formerly obtained from the listening posts in Iran, Washington made a concerted effort to obtain permission for its U-2 reconnaissance planes to fly in Turkish air space close to the Soviet border in order to monitor Soviet compliance with the SALT II agreement (that President Carter signed with Brezhnev in Vienna in June 1979 but never forwarded to the Senate for ratification). Mindful of Moscow's position that the request was a pretext to "spy" on the Soviet Union, on May 8, 1979, Prime Minister Ecevit turned

Washington down, agreeing to the surveillance flights only if Moscow assented. He viewed the SALT II treaty as between the United States and the USSR, and not between Turkey and the United States, and said the question of U-2 flights was one the superpowers should answer in the context of the overall verification procedures they establish. Ecevit was supported by the opposition leader, Suleiman Demirel, who said: "These flights are against Turkish interests."[66] On June 24 the Turkish chief of staff, returning from a visit to the United States and being informed that the U.S. House of Representatives had voted down a $50 million grant in military aid, declared: "Aid should not be linked with the issue of U-2 flights ....Even if they gave 150 million dollars,we can make no concessions. Under these circumstances we cannot allow U-2 flights over Turkey."[67]

In September the U.S. government dropped the matter. Moscow had carried the day, though, ironically, in so doing it weakened Carter's case for the treaty, whose ratification was a major objective of Soviet foreign policy.

Where Moscow stood virtually no chance of influencing Turkish policy was on the all-important issue of U.S. basing privileges. The Kremlin apparently confused the pervasive anti-Americanism in Turkey with opposition to the agreement's renewal, witness Soviet sources asserting that "broad circles of the Turkish public are resolutely opposed to the American military presence [which] not only infringes the country's national independence and sovereignty but also poses a threat to the very existence of Turkey's 44 million people."[68] It was disappointed when Washington and Ankara finally agreed on new terms in February 1980. *Pravda* was not only critical but threatening. Writing that Washington had "succeeded in imposing" its will on Ankara, A. Filippov said

> the military deal [caused] rejoicing in the camp of the right wing forces oriented toward the United States and the West, [and warned that] the permission to allow the Pentagon to use bases on Turkish territory for its own purposes ... could cause complications in relations with the countries of the region.
>
> The question is, either Turkey will live under conditions of peace with its neighbors and the peoples of the Near and Middle East or, surrendering its territory to U.S. bases, it will spoil relations with its neighbors and in the event of a conflict become a nuclear cemetery. Therefore ... it is not worth the risk for the sake of the interests of those who live across the ocean.[69]

Filippov's article made front-page news in Turkey: the Soviet ambassador was called in by the foreign minister for an explanation, and editorial opinion was very critical of Moscow.[70]

Under the five-year Defense Cooperation Agreement signed between the United States and Turkey in Ankara on March 30, 1980, the United States retained the use of 12 bases, including the major airbase at Incirlik and key intelligence-gathering facilities at Sinop, Pirinclik, Karagaburun, and Belbashi. Of the lesser stations, 13 reverted to exclusive Turkish use.

Moscow's inability to block the agreement was hardly surprising, given Turkey's membership in NATO and urgent need for massive assistance. However, nothing indicates that Moscow will change its approach: It need only recall the fate of the Shah and his agreements with the United States to sustain its present efforts.

THE LIMITS OF RAPPROCHEMENT

The transformation of the Soviet-Turkish relationship from the bristling suspicion that impelled Turkey's alliance with the West to an accommodation that restrains Turkey from actions that would unduly antagonize Moscow is an undoubted Soviet achievement. It has altered the strategic environment in the region.

Turkey is still a member of NATO, not from expectation of imminent Soviet attack but from lack of an attractive option. It no longer fears a Soviet thrust for Kars and Ardahan or the Straits and believes its interpretation of the Montreux Convention satisfies Soviet needs. If war were to come, Turkish leaders are convinced the main Soviet attack would be against NATO's central front, with Turkey a minor theater of operations. They see no promising alternative to NATO—the nonaligned movement is too fragmented to offer any security and too anti-Turkish on the Cyprus issue (even the Palestine Liberation Organization, to which Ecevit extended full diplomatic recognition in 1979, has sided with Greek Cypriots).

What is remarkable about the past decade or so of Soviet-Turkish relations is that it has been so unremarkable: no crises, no periods of high tension; no issues on the agenda that demand attention. The nearest thing to serious agitation was *Pravda's* crude criticisms of the U.S.-Turkish base-renewal agreement, and this was short-lived. Even Turkey's membership in NATO is seen by Moscow as a temporary phenomenon, because it senses an underlying incompatibility between Christian Western Europe and Islamic Turkey.

The record suggests that on the issues that concern it the most, that is, control of the Straits, Turkey's membership in NATO, and U.S. bases, Moscow has had little direct influence. Still the Soviet Union continues to provide Turkey with substantial economic assistance. The reasons may be applicable to donors in general: A donor may derive more benefit from the broad consequences of a donee's policy than from the actual returns from its specific inputs.[71] It may well be enough for Moscow that Soviet policy has helped to transform the strategic environment within which Soviet-Turkish relations and Turkish foreign policy are carried on; and that the Soviet Union can pursue its goals in the Eastern Mediterranean and Middle East without hindrance from Turkey. Thus, though unable to impose its preferences on Turkey's domestic or foreign policy behavior, the USSR may nonetheless be quite satisfied with the relationship because of the regional advantages that stem from Ankara's sensitivity to its policy needs and desires. In a word, the transformation of the strategic context within which a superpower pursues its foreign policy may be the ultimate power-political grail driving it on.

The specific hypotheses postulated at the beginning of this study tend largely to be unprovable or refuted. First, there was no correlation between inputs and influence. Soviet goods and services did not produce any changes in Turkish policies. Their utility lay in making Turkey receptive to Soviet overtures for better relations. What is clear is that economic inputs may be useful for improving the general milieu within which government-to-government relations are conducted but that they do not convert into dividends on specific political issues. Perhaps it was the absence of a military relationship that diminished the political returns the Soviets hoped to obtain from their economic programs.

Second, an increased Soviet presence did not lead to greater influence. Soviet technicians came with the economic assistance, but they were restricted to the projects on which they were working and had no privileged access to the Turkish elites, thus rendering Moscow incapable of penetrating any key bureaucracies. There were no Soviet military advisers, no student exchanges, and few cultural ones. Though the Soviet presence in Turkey increased after 1965, it did not have any effect on the political sector.

Third, there was no correlation between the number of missions and influence. It may well be that a supplicant goes to a benefactor more often than vice versa, but that does not mean the benefactor, that is, the recipient of the greater number of missions, wields influence. What may be true at the individual or small group level is not true at the nation-state level. However, specific missions are important for illuminating a political relationship, especially when analyzed in conjunction with evaluation and comparison of joint communiqués. The hypotheses concerning the media as an index of influence and the possible correlation between sophistication of weaponry delivered and influence could not be tested because of the paucity and absence of data, respectively.

The constraints on closer Soviet-Turkish ties and on Soviet influnce are profound. The military is anticommunist and suspicious of the USSR. Moscow's support of illegal communist activities and terrorism is a continuing reminder of its unregenerate ambitions. Periodic Soviet calls for legalization of the Turkish Communist Party keep vivid this perception of threat.[72] The ultimate constraint is a deep-rooted historical consciousness. Centuries of suspicion cannot be expunged in a decade or two when reinforced by the inevitable uneasiness of a small power lying in the shadow of an expansion-minded imperial power and membership in politically hostile alliance systems.

NOTES

1. Richard D. Robinson, *The First Turkish Republic: A Case Study in National Development* (Cambridge, Mass.: Harvard University Press, 1963), 181-82.

2. As quoted by Süleyman Tekiner, "Soviet-Turkish Relations and Kosygin's Trip to Turkey," *Bulletin of the Institute for the Study of the USSR* 14, no. 3 (March 1967):8.

3. *The Guardian*, September 30, 1975.

4. *Financial Times*, June 6, 1979. Foreign Broadcast Information Service (hereafter referred to as FBIS)/USSR, June 27, 1979, G4.

5. FBIS/USSR, February 4, 1980, G4.

6. FBIS/USSR, August 22, 1979, G5-G6. See *Pravda*, August 4, 1980, for an account blaming Turkey's economic difficulties on its membership in NATO.

7. In March 1976, *Pravda*, for example, assigned a full-time journalist, Aleksandr Filippov, to Ankara. Lidiya Suyetina broadcasts regularly (in Turkish) from Moscow.

8. T. W. Adams and Alvin J. Cottrell, "Communism in Cyprus," *Problems of Communism* 15, no. 3 (May-June 1966):24-27.

9. New York *Times*, February 8, 1964.

10. *The Observer*, August 16, 1964.

11. New York *Times*, August 30, 1964.

12. *Izvestiia*, January 22, 1965.

13. B. M. Potskhveriia, *Vneshniaia politika Turtsii posle vtoroi mirovoi voiny* [The foreign policy of Turkey after the second world war] (Moscow: Nauka, 1976), 31-32.

14. New York *Times*, May 23, 1965.

15. New York *Times*, December 22, 1066.

16. *Cyprus Bulletin* 8, no. 22 (June 13, 1971).

17. *Soviet News*, April 25, 1972, 135.

18. FBIS/The Middle East and North Africa, August 28, 1974, Q4-Q5.

19. Potskhveriia, 263. See also Aleksandr Bovin, *Izvestiia*, January 29, 1976, for an analysis of the intractability of the three parties.

20. See B. Vladimirov in *Krasnia zvezda*, February 1, 1975; and *Izvestiia*, February 20, 1975.

21. This analysis is developed in Alvin Z. Rubinstein, "The Soviet Union and the Eastern Mediterranean: 1968-1978," *Orbis* 23, no. 2 (Summer 1979):299-315.

22. Neset Akmandor, "Turkish and European Security—The Role of Eurogroup," *NATO Review* 27, no. 4 (August 1979):7.

23. AWACS have great flexibility, combining routine aircraft detection and tracking with command, control, and communications capabilities. They can detect and track low-flying planes at ranges of up to 200 nautical miles, and can simulataneously detect and track

high-altitude targets at ranges of up to 360 nautical miles, thus greatly reducing the need for highly vulnerable ground-radar stations. By looking several hundred miles into Soviet-bloc territory, they can detect enemy troops and tank concentrations and provide an additional 15 minutes' warning of enemy air attack.

24. New York *Times*, April 9, 1978.

25. A particularly cogent analysis is Justin Galen (pseudonym), "Turkey As a Self-Inflicted Wound: The Narrowing Options for U.S. Defense Policy." *Armed Forces Journal International*, June 1980, 62-63. See also Lincoln P. Bloomfield, Jr., "Anarchy in Turkey: The Growing Pains of a Young Democracy," *Conflict: An International Journal* 2, no. 1 (1980):31-56; Aryeh Shmuelevitz and Esther Lidzbarski-Tal, "Turkey," in Colin Legum, ed., *Middle East Contemporary Record*, Vol. I:1976-77 (New York: Holmes and Meier, 1978), 622-46; Dankwart A. Rustow, "Turkey's Travail," *Foreign Affairs* 58, no. 1 (Fall 1979):82-102; and Andrew Mango, "The Multiple Crisis in Turkey," *Asian Affairs* 10 (June 1979):125-31.

26. New York *Times*, January 3, 1980.

27. New York *Times*, July 26, 1980.

28. New York *Times*, June 26, 1965.

29. *Soviet News*, no. 5350 (December 28, 1966), 131.

30. Judging by the tone of its commentaries and reportage, Moscow preferred the RPP, which was less staunchly pro-NATO, more interested in a quasi-nonaligned foreign policy, and a bit softer on domestic communists, who are still not able to function in the open politically. For example, on the occasion of the RPP's electoral victory in June 1977, *Izvestiia*, June 8, 1977, observed: "The defeat of the rightists attests to the electorate's wish for democratic changes and also the voters' rejection of the anticommunist hysteria which the reactionary groupings chose as their weapon for the election campaign." As quoted in FBIS/USSR, June 13, 1977, G1.

31. FBIS/USSR, January 15, 1976, G1.

32. See the joint communiqué of March 18, 1977. FBIS/USSR, March 21, 1977, G1-G3.

33. Michael M. Boll, "Turkey's New National Security Concept: What It Means for NATO," *Orbis* 23, no. 3 (Fall 1979):614.

34. *The Pulse: A Daily Review of the Turkish Press* (Ankara) (hereafter referred to as *The Pulse*), Supplement No. 131 (April 20, 1976), 2.

35. Boll, 617. The Final Act, though only a political statement of intent and not a treaty or a legally binding document, in effect recognized the territorial status quo in Europe and Soviet hegemony over Eastern Europe; and it called for confidence-building measures and disarmament, economic and technical cooperation, and the freer flow of people, ideas, and information. It represented the high point of the East-West détente in the 1970s.

36. *The Pulse*, no. 3428 (March 9, 1977), 1.

37. For example, Hamit Batu, "New Developments in Turkish Foreign Policy," *Dis Politika/Foreign Policy* 5, no 4 (1976):5-7 (the author was director-general of research and policy planning in the Turkish Ministry of Foreign Affairs); and An Observer, "A Multi-Faceted Foreign Policy As a New Approach," *Dis Politika/Foreign Policy* 6, nos. 3-4 (1977):7-17.

38. Sami Kohen, *Christian Science Monitor*, March 28, 1978.

39. Bulent Ecevit, "Turkey's Security Policies," *Survival* 20, no. 5 (September-October 1978):203-08. See also the interview given to Bernard Gwertzman, while attending a NATO summit meeting in Washington, D.C. New York *Times*, May 30, 1978.

40. *The Pulse*, no. 3711 (May 2, 1978), 1. Author's interviews.

41. *Financial Times*, May 6, 1978.

42. The text is available in *Soviet News*, no. 5935 (June 27, 1978), 227.

43. *The Pulse*, no. 3724 (May 22, 1978), 7.

44. *Christian Science Monitor*, June 28, 1978.

45. See S. Kondrashov, *Izvestiia*, June 30, 1979, as cited in FBIS/USSR, July 6, 1979, G1-G2.

46. Aleksandr Filippov, *Pravda*, October 18, 1979.

47. *Soviet News*, December 10, 1968, 100.

48. As cited in Ferenc A. Váli, *The Turkish Straits and NATO* (Stanford, Calif.: Hoover Institution Press, 1972), 103.

49. Ibid.

50. *The Pulse*, no. 3647 (January 27, 1978), 3.

51. By 1978, more than 7,000 Soviet ships transited the Straits each year. FBIS/USSR, August 8, 1979, G 10.

52. New York *Times*, February 8, 1969.

53. Barry Buzan, "The Status and Future of the Montreux Convention," *Survival* 18, no. 6 (November/December 1976): 243.

54. Ihsan Gürkan, *NATO, Turkey, and the Southern Flank: A Mideastern Perspective* (New York: National Strategy Information Center, 1980), 50. *The Pulse*, no. 3270 (July 23, 1976).

55. V. Serkov, "Pravovoi rezhim chernomorskikh prolivov" [The legal regime of the Black Sea Straits], *Morskoi sbornik*, Summer 1976, 86.

56. For example, see Alvin J. Cottrell, "Soviet Views of U.S. Overseas Bases," *Orbis* 7, no. 1 (Spring 1963):77-95. Representative Soviet articles are: P. Katin, "Na yuzhnom flange NATO" [On the southern flank of NATO], *Mirovaia ekonomika i mezhdunarodnye otnosheniia* (hereafter known as MEMO) no. 5 (May 1972), 77-80; and Ia. Bronin, "Imperialisticheskaia strategiia v vostochnom sredizemnomore" [Imperialist strategy in the Eastern Mediterranean], *MEMO*, no. 1 (January 1973), 31-40.

57. *Pravda*, February 28, 1975.

58. U.S. Senate, Committee on Foreign Relations, "Turkey, Greece, and NATO. The Strained Alliance," (Washington, D.C.: U.S. Government Printing Office, March 1980), 8-9.

59. U.S. Senate, Committee on Armed Forces, "The Military Aspects of Banning Arms Aid to Turkey," *Hearings*, 95th Cong., 2d sess. June 28, 1978, 8. For further information on the value of the bases at Karagburun and Sinop, see "Turkey: Intel Base Characteristics," *Defense & Foreign Affairs Daily* 7, no. 191 (October 6, 1978).

60. Interview at the Turkish Embassy in Moscow, April 1979.

61. *Pravda*, July 30, 1975.

62. V. Shmarov, "Turkey: Control Over Bases," *New Times*, no. 32 (August 1975), 12.

63. FBIS/USSR, April 11, 1978, G2.

64. *Pravda*, August 7, 1978.

65. FBIS/USSR, February 1, 1979, G2.

66. New York *Times*, May 24, 1979.

67. New York *Times*, June 25, 1979.

68. P. Mezentsev, "Leasing Both Earth and Sky," *New Times*, no. 5 (February 1, 1980), 12-14.

69. *Pravda*, February 27, 1980.

70. The Legation of Israel (Ankara), *A Weekly Review of the Press*, March 7, 1980, 2.

71. This was true of Soviet-Egyptian relations during the 1967–76 period. See Alvin Z. Rubinstein, *Red Star on the Nile: The Soviet-Egyptian Influence Relationship Since the June War* (Princeton, N.J.: Princeton University Press, 1977), Ch. 10.

72. A. Filippov, in three successive articles, called for an end to the ban on the TCP. *Pravda*, September 26, October 23, and November 17, 1978.

3

RUSSIA AND IRAN:
THE ROOTS OF ENMITY

Apart from occasional travelers, the first contact between Russia and Iran[1] came in the middle of the sixteenth century as a consequence of Czar Ivan the Terrible's abortive attempt to seize Persian territory in the Muslim-dominated mountain areas of the Caucasus. In the seventeenth century, Russia's expansion concentrated on the Far East and on Europe, where it absorbed the Ukraine in 1654. Peter the Great resumed the pressure against Persia, but no permanent acquisitions were made until the early years of the nineteenth century.

Like Ottoman Turkey, Iran was afflicted by dynastic debilitation, economic backwardness, and military weakness, and was forced to relinquish land to Russia. In 1801 Russia annexed Georgia and part of Azerbaijan and turned the Caspian Sea into a Russian lake. Despite warring in Europe against Napoleon, it continued to expand in the south. In 1813, under the Treaty of Gulistan, Russia's preeminence in the Caucasus was acknowledged by Iran, and Moscow acquired economic privileges, which enabled it to meddle in Iran's internal affairs. Fifteen years later the Czarist advance resumed, as Russia took additional chunks of Armenia and Azerbaijan. After an ill-conceived war against Russia, Iran was forced by the Treaty of Torkamanchay (1828) to yield additional territory and economic concessions, which made it a virtual vassal state of Russia's. The treaty established what is basically the present border between the two countries.

Russia's broad advance in Central Asia, which set the stage for the Anglo-Russian rivalry later in the nineteenth century, was impelled mainly by the military for whom "a nationalist-imperialist ideology of the Panslavist type" meant everything: "quick promotion, decoration, fabulous loot, unlimited opportunities for enrichment through dishonest management of army funds, excitement and adventure."[2] By the 1880s all of Central Asia up to the northern frontiers of Iran and Afghanistan were under Russian control. Influential segments of the Russian military-political elite, writes an eminent scholar on the period, regarded domination of Iran as part of Russia's manifest destiny:

> The Tsar, his ministers, and his generals firmly believed that sooner or later Russia was destined to incorporate Iran in its empire. Count S. Iu. Witte, who as minister of finance was deeply involved in Russia's foreign relations, believed that "the entire northern part of Persia was intended, as if by nature, to turn, in the future, if not into a part of the great Russian Empire, then, in any case, into a country under our complete protectorate."[3]

This view was shared even by a moderate like V. N. Lamsdorff, for a time minister of foreign affairs under Nicholas II at the turn of the century:

> The principal aim pursued by us ... through various ways and means during long years of our relations with Persia can be defined in the following manner: to preserve the integrity and inviolability of the possessions of the Shah; without seeking for ourselves territorial acquisitions, without permitting the hegemony of a third power, gradually to subject Persia to our dominant influence, without violating, however, the external symbols of her independence or her internal regime. In other words, our task is to make Persia politically an obedient and useful, i.e. a sufficiently powerful instrument in our hands.[4]

In the late nineteenth-early twentieth centuries, Iran survived as a nominally independent country because Russia and Britain preferred to preserve the plum whole. The British navy kept Russia at bay in the south, but in the north Russian influence was paramount. Shahs reigned at the sufferance of the Czars. In 1879, at Tehran's request, Russia organized and officered a Persian Cossack Brigade, which, though Persian in composition, was more loyal to its Russian officers than to the Shah. Trade followed the flag and helped keep it flying,[5] but it was strategic advantage and not commerce that impelled Russia's policy. Moscow used a variety of means, including the Brigade and social unrest, to bend the government to its will.

For Moscow, the year 1900 seemed an opportune moment to establish a military presence in the Persian Gulf: Britain was mired in a war in South Africa against the Boers, and northern Iran was more than ever an undisputed Russian sphere of influence, and the Shah was pro-Russian. British warnings to the Shah against granting bases in the Gulf to any foreign power caused Russia to pause, however. By 1905 Russia's situation had changed. Defeated by Japan, worried by Germany's growing power in Europe, and beset by unrest at home, the Czar sought a rapprochement with Britain and an end to the Anglo-Russian rivalry in Central Asia. Moreover, a revolution in Iran temporarily undermined the Russian position: In December 1905, encouraged by the British, a coalition of Tehrani bazaris (small merchants) and mullahs (religious leaders) brought the populace into the streets and forced the Shah to grant a Constitution (a situation similar to the constellation of social forces that would topple another Shah in January 1979). In January 1907, a week after granting the Constitution, the Shah died and was succeeded by his son, who was pro-Russian and anti-Majlis (parliament).

The Anglo-Russian Convention of August 31, 1907, gave lip service to the "integrity and independence of Persia" but divided the country into three spheres: the northern part of the country was allocated to the Russian sphere, the southern to the British, with a neutral zone in between. The Majlis tried, unsuccessfully, to shed Russian influence, but Iranian nationalist anger was particularly directed against the British, from whom they felt safe from retribution. By 1010 Moscow felt confident enough to resume inroads into Iran, notwithstanding the 1907 convention. It forced Tehran to fire an American expert, W. Morgan Shuster, who had been invited to reform the country's chaotic financial structure, and sent troops to occupy parts of Iranian Azerbaijan, where they remained until 1920. Thus, on the eve of World War I, Iran had again become a virtual Russian protectorate.

> In 1912 Russian troops entered Mashad and shelled the tomb of Imam Reza, the holiest shrine in Persia. The civil administration of the northern provinces was openly taken over by Russian consuls. They, as well as Russian army officers and hundreds of other subjects of the tsar, bought vast tracts of land, in violation of Persian laws but with the firm support of the Russian government. By the summer of 1914 the Persian government virtually ceased to exist.[6]

BETWEEN TWO WARS: 1917 TO 1941

Involvement in World War I in pursuit of imperialist objectives in the Balkans and the Middle East eroded the last pillars of Czarist rule. In 1917 the collapse of the Romanov dynasty and the emergence of the Bolsheviks ended one type of Russian imperial expansion and gave birth to another. For a short while, the combination of defeat in war and revolution at home loosened Russia's grip on Persia. After almost a century of vassalage, the country was on the threshold of regaining its independence.

Lenin and Stalin, though occupied with survival in European Russia, nonetheless sensed the significance of the East. Two months after seizing power they made their famous appeal "To All the Toiling Moslems of Russia and the East," exhorting them to resist the imperialists. Repudiating the Czarist treaties, they declared: " ... the treaty for the partition of Persia has been torn up and destroyed. As soon as hostilities cease, the troops will be evacuated from Persia and the Persians will be ensured the right freely to determine their destiny."[7]

A year later, World War I having ended, the Bolsheviks' concern in this area was to keep Britain from entrenching itself in Iran and threatening their rear in the Caucasus and Transcaspia regions by giving aid to the White armies bent on overthrowing the Bolshevik regime. Britain's attempt, through the proposed Anglo–Persian Treaty of August 9, 1919, to place Iran under its tutelage failed. The Majlis refused to ratify the treaty, realizing Britain's position was weakening when its forces in northern Iran retreated in the face of a Soviet-supported rebellion that in May 1920 spawned a "Soviet Republic of Gilan" (the northernmost region contiguous to Soviet Azerbaijan). Though some Bolsheviks urged a revolutionary tack, Lenin opted for pragmatism: He normalized relations with Tehran and encouraged it to resist British encroachments. As in Turkey, nationalism and national independence, not communism or the Communist Party, presented the fledgling Soviet regime with the best prospect for thwarting the British threat and enhancing its security.

On February 21, 1921, a military coup mounted by Reza Khan, the head of the Cossack Brigade (about 6,000 men), strengthened Lenin's conviction that nationalism was the antidote to imperialism. Reza Khan, concerned about the ineptness and corruption of the Qajar dynasty and about the inroads of communism in Gilan, and encouraged by the British (who by this time realized they were too thinly stretched globally to take over Iran), imposed himself on the weak Ahmad Shah, the nominal ruler since 1910. On February 26, in order to remove any pretext for a British presence, Moscow signed a treaty of friendship with Iran and withdrew its support from the puppet Soviet Republic of Gilan. By late 1921 Reza Khan's troops reasserted Tehran's authority over all of Iranian territory in the north.

The treaty, formally ratified by the Majlis in December 1921, reaffirmed the cancellation of "the whole body of treaties and conventions concluded by the former Russian Government with third parties in respect of Persia"; settled the issue of the frontiers between the two countries; and prohibited interference by each in the internal affairs of the other. Articles V and VI merit extensive quotation, because they were to be important for defining Soviet-Iranian relations in 1941 and in the post-World War II period.

Under Article V, the two parties undertake:

1. To prohibit the formation or presence within their respective territories of any organizations or groups of persons . . . whose object is to engage in acts of hostility against Persia or Russia, or against the allies of Russia.

They will likewise prohibit the formation of troops or armies within their respective territories with the aforementioned object.

2. Not to allow a third party or any organization, whatever it is called, which is hostile to the other Contracting Party, to import or to convey in transit across their countries material which can be used against the other Party.

3. To prevent by all means in their power the presence within their territories or within the territories of their allies of all armies or forces of a third party in cases in which the presence of such forces would be regarded as a menace to the frontiers, interests or safety of the other Contracting Party.

Article VI stipulated:

If a third party should attempt to carry out a policy of usurpation by means of armed intervention in Persia, or if such power should desire to use Persian territory as a base of operations against Russia, or if a foreign Power should threaten the frontiers of Federal Russia or those of its allies, and if the Persian Government should not be able to put a stop to such menace after having been once called upon to do so by Russia, Russia shall have the right to advance her troops into the Persian interior for the purpose of carrying out the military operations necessary for its defence, Russia undertakes, however, to withdraw her troops from Persian territory as soon as the danger has been removed.[8]

Although a subsequent "exchange of letters between the two governments made it clear that this clause" referred only to anti-Bolshevik Russian forces, "the remnants of broken armies which had fought the Bolsheviks in the Civil War," in 1941 the USSR invoked the treaty to justify its occupation of northern Iran and, in the mid-1950s, to condemn Iran's membership in pro-Western alliance systems.[9]

In 1925 Reza Shah abolished the Qajar dynasty, which was of Turkish origin, and had the Majlis proclaim him Reza Shah Pahlavi, adopting a name that unmistakably derived from Iran's language and history. A ruthless autocrat, he embarked on a program of modernization and secularization that sought to emulate Ataturk's pioneering effort in Turkey. He normalized relations with the USSR and in October 1927 signed a treaty of guarantee and neutrality, reaffirming the 1921 accord. He expanded trade and intensified the pace of economic development, of which the most notable achievement was the construction of Iran's first railroad, a 900–mile link between the Caspian Sea and the Persian Gulf. However, Reza Shah's fear of communism and Russian intriguing prompted him to look to Germany for advisers and assistance, especially after Hitler came to power in 1933. The result was a chilling of Soviet-Iranian relations.

The outbreak of World War II found Stalin neutral and a prime beneficiary. His territorial appetite whetted by the Nazi–Soviet pact of August 1939—which gave the USSR half of Poland, the Baltic states, and parts of Finland and Romania—he was ready for further deals. On November 26, 1940, Molotov informed the German ambassador in Moscow that the Soviet Union was prepared to enter into a pact with Germany, Italy, and Japan, delineating spheres of influence, provided that among other things "the area south of Batum and Baku in the general direction of the Persian Gulf is recognized as the center of the aspirations of the Soviet Union."[10] This much was agreeable to Berlin, but Stalin wanted too much in the Balkans, so Hitler attacked the USSR on June 22, 1941. (The ensuing alliance between Moscow and London was reminiscent of the one that had existed during World War I.)

Despite the Shah's proclamation of neutrality after the start of World War II, his known pro-German sympathies and toleration of Nazi activities in Iran prompted a joint Anglo-Soviet occupation on August 25, 1941, as much to forestall Iran's drift to the German camp as to protect the Persian Gulf oilfields and assure a safe transit route for shipments of war material to the Soviet Union. The country was divided into two zones of occupation: The Soviets occupied the provinces of Azerbaijan, Gilan, Mazanderan, Gorgan, and Khorasan; the British, the southern part of the country. Tehran was treated as a neutral enclave. In justifying its intervention, the Soviet government referred to Article VI of the 1921 Soviet-Iranian treaty. By the tripartite treaty of alliance signed on January 29, 1942, Britain and the USSR agreed that allied forces would be withdrawn from Iranian territory "not later than six months after all hostilities between the Allied powers and Germany and her associates have been suspended by the conclusion of an armistice or armistices, or on the conclusion of peace between them, whichever date is the earlier." Reza Shah was forced to abdicate in favor of his son, Mohammed Reza Shah, and was sent into exile. He died in South Africa in 1944.

STALIN'S IMPERIAL POLICY

During the war Soviet officials ruled their areas like conquerors. No Iranian troops were permitted into the northern provinces. Separatist movements were encouraged among the non–Farsi-speaking Kurds,

Azerbaijanis, and Azaris. Tehran's authority was continually weakened. Propaganda was aimed to instill pro–Soviet attitudes, and pro-Soviet groups were established, including in 1943 the Iranian-Soviet Society for Cultural Relations. The Tudeh (Communist) Party, which was established in October 1941, operated freely, as Moscow prepared the ground for restoration of the former Russian position in northern Iran.

In September 1944 Deputy Foreign Minister Sergei I. Kavtaradze was sent to Tehran with a demand for oil concessions in the northern provinces, ostensibly to match British privileges in the south. Despite Soviet-inspired demonstrations and labor unrest in the capital, Prime Minister Muhammad Saed refused. In a show of determination, the Majlis, prompted by Dr. Mohammad Mossadeq, passed a law on December 2 prohibiting any official from granting oil concessions to foreigners without its express approval. Only the Tudeh Party deputies opposed the measure. A week later Kavtaradze returned empty-handed to Moscow. Control in Tehran, not oil, had been Stalin's goal. Whereas he was to succeed at the Yalta Conference in February 1945 in regaining Russia's pre–1905 position in the Far East, he was not able in Iran to restore the status quo ante 1907.

Once the war was over, Stalin strengthened Soviet forces in the occupied provinces, frustrated the Iranian government's efforts to regain its authority there, and set off separatist revolts. Moscow had no intention of withdrawing in accordance with the 1942 tripartite agreement. On December 12, 1945, the Tudeh established the "Autonomous Republic of Azerbaijan," under Jafar Pishevari, an old line communist; and on January 22, 1946, Qazi Muhammad, the head of the Democratic Party of Kurdistan, proclaimed Kurdish autonomy in Mahabad. Although nominally still part of Iran, the Azerbaijani and Kurdish provinces were to be autonomous under "Soviet protection."

At an allied foreign ministers conference in Moscow in December 1945, the Soviets refused to grant permission to any outside commission to investigate Iran's complaints. Dismayed by the lack of Western support and unintimidated by Soviet threats, Tehran brought its case to the UN Security Council on January 19, 1946; it argued that Soviet interference in Iranian internal affairs was contrary to the tripartite treaty of January 29, 1942, the Tehran Declaration of 1943, and the UN Charter. When the Security Council counseled Iran and the USSR to negotiate their differences, Qavam as-Saltaneh, a wily old diplomat who had been appointed prime minister a few days earlier, convinced that the West would not fight to uphold Iran's independence, decided to try to placate Stalin.

On February 19 Qavam went to Moscow, where he negotiated under great pressure. On March 2, the date that all foreign troops were to have left Iran (the British and American troops left on schedule), Stalin informed him that Soviet forces would leave some areas but remain in others, in accordance with the provisions of the 1921 treaty. For the next few weeks the situation was tense, but on April 4 Moscow agreed to a full withdrawal, even though reinforcements had poured into the provinces under its control in the previous month.[11]

In return for Stalin's assurances that Soviet troops would be withdrawn within one to two months, Qavam—in apparent accommodation—agreed to establish a joint Soviet-Iranian oil company before the end of the year, subject to the approval of the Majlis, and to satisfy peacefully in some unspecified fashion the demands of the Azerbaijanian and Kurdish separatist movements in a way that was consistent with Iranian laws and sovereignty.

When Soviet troops withdrew on May 9, most Western officials publicly asserted that Stalin's retreat was prompted by pressure from the UN Security Council and criticism, especially from various pro-Soviet bourgeois intellectual groups in the West. But they really feared that Qavam had acquiesced to Iran's becoming a Soviet puppet; and indeed, in late spring and summer, Qavam's policy seemed to bear out this gloomy assessment. He expressed warm friendship for the Soviet Union, encouraged anti-American newspaper articles, granted the Azerbaijanian rebel government considerable autonomy, supported a labor strike against the Anglo-Iranian Oil Company (AIOC) in the south, and brought three Tudeh members into his cabinet.[12]

Qavam established his own party to contest in the fall elections for Majlis, all the while assuring the Soviets that given the support of deputies from the Soviet-controlled provinces of Azerbaijan and Kurdistan he would be able to obtain the Majlis' approval for the oil concessions to the USSR. In the summer there was an uprising by the Bakhtiaris and Qashqais in the south. Although the British may have been involved, for Qavam the significant factor was the tribes' hostility to the Tudeh. Emboldened, he dismissed the Tudeh ministers, set elections for early 1947, and sent troops into Azerbaijan to evict the rebel regime, which collapsed on December 13, 1946. Moscow faced a dilemma:

> She could send her troops back into Iran to prevent the Iranian army from occupying Azerbaijan. Such an action in a rapidly deteriorating climate of world opinion [and a worsening of U.S.-Soviet relations] could lead to dangerous consequences. It would most certainly prevent the election of the fifteenth Majles, since under Iranian law no election could be held while foreign troops were on Iranian soil. Without the Majles the oil concession promised by Qavam would vanish into thin air. Or she could abandon Pishevari's separatist regime in the hope that the subsequently elected Majles would ratify the oil agreement.[13]

A week later the Kurdish Republic also collapsed, as the Shah's troops marched in without any reaction from the Soviet Union and mopped up the sporadic resistance.

The denouement of Qavam's artfully managed policy of procrastination came in 1947. The elections were held in January but the Majlis was not convened until August. On October 22 a coalition of Qavam's party and the National Front, headed by Dr. Mohammad Mossadeq, by an overwhelming majority rejected the oil agreement with the Soviet Union and the award of privileged treatment to any foreign country. Moscow was furious, but in the year since its prospects in Iran had seemed so bright, much had changed in the international environment: The polarizing Cold War in Europe and America's growing support for countries threatened by the Soviet Union (the Truman Doctrine had been proclaimed in March and the Marshall Plan in June) had raised the costs of armed intervention. Stalin accepted defeat and turned to more serious developments, in Eastern Europe and China. For the first time since the end of the war, a targeted victim had escaped the Soviet net.

For the remainder of Stalin's era, Soviet-Iranian relations were poor, trade was negligible, and the Tudeh was outlawed after an attempt on the life of the Shah in February 1949. Moreover, as a result of Soviet hostility and Mossadeq's effort to gain control of the army (he had been elevated to the post of prime minister in April 1951 after forcing through a bill nationalizing the Anglo-Iranian Oil Company), the Shah turned increasingly to the United States for support. Like Turkey, Iran was looking to Washington for security in order to offset a perceived threat from its communist neighbor to the north.

THE DRIFT TOWARD NORMALIZATION, 1953-63

Soon after Stalin's death in March 1953, a struggle developed between the Shah and Prime Minister Mossadeq. The Shah relied on the army, the police, and the Americans; Mossadeq, on the ultraconservative clergy and the extreme left, dominated by the Tudeh Party, which, though outlawed, had honeycombed the military with agents. Washington's belief that Mossadeq was leaning toward a pro–Soviet orientation was buttressed by certain conciliatory phrases in Soviet Premier G. Malenkov's speech on August 8 reviewing the world situation: "The experience of thirty-five years has shown that the Soviet Union and Persia are interested in mutual friendship and collaboration . . . . At present, on the initiative of the Soviet Union, talks are being held concerning the settlement of a number of frontier problems and mutual financial claims."

A week later the Shah tried to oust Mossadeq, but he failed and fled the country. *Pravda* echoed the Tudeh in denouncing the Shah's conspiracy and calling for an end to the U.S. presence. A revolution seemed imminent; but the Tudeh leadership hesitated, "uncertain whether it could defeat the army and the non–Communist forces; at a decisive moment, it was felt, Soviet help would be needed."[14] Moscow, however, was not prepared to intervene; and "at a meeting of the Tudeh's Central Committee in the basement of a house behind the [Soviet agency] VOKS a fight was going on between the extremists and the moderates," a struggle that ended with the decision not to mount an armed revolt.[15] With assistance from the CIA, the Shah was returned to power, after which he came increasingly to rely on U.S. economic and military aid. In 1954 the Tudeh's cadres were ruthlessly purged from the officer corps, and for the remainder of the Shah's rule the communists were an insignificant factor in Iran's internal affairs.

Notwithstanding the decimation of the communists in Iran, the post-Stalin Soviet leadership sought to normalize government–to-government relations with Tehran, as part of its stress on peaceful coexistence with all the nations along its southern tier. Thus, in late June 1954, it offered to negotiate unsettled boundary problems and all financial claims arising out of World War II. Relevant protocols were signed in Tehran on December 2, 1954, and entered into force on May 20, 1955, with the final treaty concerning the Soviet-Iranian border being signed in Moscow on May 14, 1957.[16] Satisfactory settlement of the border issue removed an old source of tension and led to a Soviet-Iranian agreement on joint sharing "of all water and power resources of the frontier parts of the rivers Aras and Atrek for irrigation, power generation and domestic use."[17] In late June-early July 1956 the Shah visited Moscow and impressed Soviet leaders with his desire for improved relations. During the next few years trade slowly increased, and Moscow extended numerous offers of economic assistance, of which only one (for the construction of dams on the Aras and Atrek Rivers) was accepted prior to the mid-1960s, because of the Shah's fear that Soviet economic aid and experts would somehow be used as a wedge for subverting his rule. Moscow's conciliatory gestures could not dispel deeply imbedded suspicions from the past.

Though normalization was clearly a priority objective, Moscow was critical of Iran's membership in U.S.-sponsored military pacts. As early as July 1954 it had protested the Shah's tilt toward participation in what became the Baghdad Pact in February 1955 (an alliance initially composed of Iraq, Turkey, and Great Britain). For more than a year the Soviet leadership cautioned Iran against neglecting its obligations under Article 3 of the 1927 Soviet-Iranian treaty, which stipulated that neither party would take part, "*de facto or de jure*, in political alliances or agreements directed against" the security or territory of the other, and warned of the harm that would result to their relations. The Shah, seeking security against a possible future Soviet repetition of 1945-46, persisted, and on October 11, 1955, Iran announced that it would join the pact.

In a note on November 26, 1955, Moscow denounced Iran's decision, declaring that "no one has threatened or threatens Iran" and that the pact serves

> the purposes of certain powers which are seeking to turn the countries of the Near and Middle East, Iran included, into their military *place d'armes*, and to ensure thereby the presence of foreign armed forces and the organization of their military bases on the territories of those countries . . . . The situation that is being created by Iran's accession to the aggressive Baghdad bloc is fraught with danger to the frontiers of the Soviet Union. Therefore the Soviet government cannot remain indifferent to Iran's accession to the Baghdad pact.[18]

It feared that the United States and Great Britain intended to establish bases on Iranian soil from which to deploy long–range bombers and intermediate-range missiles capable of striking targets in the southern regions of the USSR. Moscow believed the introduction of U.S. forces into Iran would come as a logical outgrowth of the globalization of the containment policy pursued by the Eisenhower-Dulles administration, of which the Baghdad pact was the military instrument in the Middle East.

The Iranian government repeatedly reassured Moscow on the defensive character of its military relationship with the West and insisted that no nuclear bases would be established in Iran. This must have mollified the Kremlin, because, as Khrushchev later noted, during the Shah's visit in June 1956 "we had sensed on his part considerable interest in improving relations."[19] Moscow offered economic assistance on favorable terms, and a number of agreements were reached in 1957 (though not ratified until late 1962), but for the moment Tehran was leery and kept its distance.

On July 14, 1958, the pro-Western Hashemite monarchy in Iraq was toppled. This coup, coupled with the growing Soviet presence in Syria and Egypt, heightened the Shah's fear of encirclement, prompting him to draw even closer to the United States, while at the same time seeking a way to mollify the Soviet Union. A Soviet aide-memoire in December 1958 warned Tehran against a U.S.–Iranian military pact and suggested that a nonaggression treaty be negotiated. Tehran agreed, in principle, but specified that no new treaty could contain clauses like those in the 1921 and 1927 treaties that permitted a Soviet intervention. Deputy Foreign Minister Vladimir Semenov arrived in late January 1959 to discuss the matter. He asked that Iran quit the Baghdad Pact and refrain from signing a military alliance with the United States, but he was apparently prepared to settle for assurances that Iran would not conclude with any third party agreements directed against the Soviet Union or permit foreign military bases on its territory. For its part Iran insisted, first, on Soviet renunciation of the provisions of the 1921 treaty sanctioning, under certain conditions, unilateral Soviet interventions in Iranian affairs; and second, on a definition of "military bases" that would not preclude Iran from entering into defense treaties with other nations. The view of one scholar is that by so doing the Shah thought "alliance with the West and coexistence with the Soviet Union would be possible"; the Shah was probably trying "to test the potential and the limits of the Soviet policy of peaceful coexistence."[20] Other interpretations are: a more Machiavellian approach, arguing that the Shah was using the negotiations with Moscow to obtain a speedy and satisfactory pact with Washington;[21] and a hybrid argument that "the very nature of the [brief Iranian-Soviet] talks rings somewhat false . . . the more immediate Iranian concern was to maintain an effective and viable security position while dealing with pressing and long overdue internal economic and social problems"; and the Shah succeeded in extracting a stronger U.S. commitment without ceding military bases that would have really disturbed Moscow "more out of genuine weakness and indecision than of calculated shrewdness and skill."[22] Whichever explanation is closest to the truth, the upshot was a three-year deterioration in Soviet-Iranian relations.

On February 12, 1959, when Moscow was convinced that the Shah intended to sign a military pact with the United States, the Soviet press agency TASS issued a statement charging the Shah with "pursuing a two-faced insincere policy toward the Soviet Union which cannot but lead to grave consequences, first of all to Iran."[23] The condemnation crescendoed after March 3, when the Iranian government formally declared Articles V and VI of the 1921 treaty "obsolete" and no longer applicable, and March 5, when Iran signed a defense treaty with the United States. *Pravda* rejected the Iranian renunciation, asserting that the 1921 treaty remained fully in effect.[24] Soviet Ambassador Nikolai M. Pegov was called home (and did not return until mid-September) and for the next three years the Soviet media carried bitter attacks against the Shah and his policy. A communist clandestine radio station, calling itself the National Voice of Iran, started broadcasting from the Soviet Caucasus, calling for a revolution against the Pahlavi dynasty.

The watershed in the Shah's relations with the Soviet Union was September 15, 1962. Using an opening that Moscow had provided three years earlier during Semenov's visit, the Shah instructed the Iranian Foreign Ministry to inform the Soviet government that "the Shah-in-Shah government of Iran will never permit Iran to become an instrument of aggression against the territory of the Soviet Union"; and it, specifically, "will not grant any foreign nation the right of possessing any kind of rocket bases on Iranian soil."[25] This decision allayed the key Soviet security concern and eliminated a major stumbling block to diplomatic normalization. For the next 16 years of the Shah's reign, Soviet–Iranian relations were characterized by good political ties and extensive, expanding economic cooperation.

The Shah—in 1962 not yet the ambitious, overconfident ruler he was to become a decade later—proceeded to improve his ties to Moscow with a number of considerations in mind. First, the United States would not object, since it was moving to upgrade its IRBM capability already inplanted in Turkey to an ICBM and SLBM (submarine-launched ballistic missile) deterrent. Second, since the United States (as well as Western Europe) was exploring an improved relationship with the USSR (a process that continued after the dangerous but fleeting interruption of the Cuban missile crisis in October 1962), the Shah saw no reason for Iran not to do likewise, especially since he was unimpressed with U.S. forcefulness in the Middle East, and he did not want Iran to be at a permanent disadvantage, alienated from the Soviet Union and unrewarded by the United States. Finally, he was embarking on a "White Revolution," designed to reform and modernize Iran's archaic economic and social system, and he wanted to minimize the threat of a "Red Revolution" by giving the USSR a stake in his regime.[26] An accommodation on security matters might lead Moscow to curb support for the outlawed Tudeh and give him time to cope with the clergy and landowners opposed to his vision of a secular state.

For its part, Moscow was pleased with the Shah's commitment to prohibit all missile sites and foreign military bases on Iranian territory and so did not insist on his scrapping the network of U.S. intelligence-gathering stations. Having neutralized Iran as a source of direct military threat, it hoped through economic and diplomatic means, over time, to attenuate Iran's ties to the West. In addition, rapprochement with Iran enhanced the image of moderation being cultivated by Moscow as it carried on its courtship of new nations in the Middle East, Southern Asia, and Africa.

During the next few years prominent exchanges of missions lent substance to the budding accommodation: In November 1963 then President Leonid Brezhnev (that is, chairman of the Presidium of the Supreme Soviet) visited Iran. Shortly thereafter the Soviet attitude toward the Shah's domestic programs underwent an abrupt change from sharp denunciation to guarded approval, and the media adopted a more balanced coverage of Iranian internal developments. In June 1964 Princess Ashraf, the Shah's twin sister, and a strong economic delegation went to Moscow; one year later the Shah made his second trip to Moscow.

The resulting agreements greatly influenced the pattern of expanding economic cooperation and realistic political interactions. Over the next decade or so, the Soviet-Iranian relationship became a showpiece of Moscow's policy of peaceful coexistence.[27]

NOTES

1. Iranians have always called the name of their country Iran. However, Europeans used the term Persia until 1925, when Reza Shah's government formally requested that all governments use the name Iran.

2. Firuz Kazemzadeh, "Russia and the Middle East," in Ivo J. Lederer ed., *Russian Foreign Policy: Essays in Historical Perspective* (New Haven, Conn.: Yale University Press, 1962), 497.

3. ibid., 508

4. ibid., 509

5. For an exhaustive and authoritative study of Russia's economic penetration and policy, see Firuz Kazemzadeh, *Russia and Britain in Persia, 1864–1914: A Study in Imperialism* (New Haven, Conn.: Yale University Press, 1968).

6. Kazemzadeh, "Russia and the Middle East," 519–20.

7. *Lenin-Stalin, 1917: Selected Writings and Speeches* (Moscow: Foreign Languages Publishing House, 1938), 666.

8. J. C. Hurewitz, ed., *The Middle East and North Africa in World Politics: A Documentary Record*, 2d ed., revised and enlarged, vol. 2, *British-French Supremacy, 1914-1945* (New Haven, Conn.: Yale University Press, 1979), 241-42.

9. Kazemzadeh, "Russia and the Middle East," 523.

10. Raymond J. Sontag and James S. Beddie, eds., *Nazi-Soviet Relations 1939-1941: Documents from the Archives of the German Foreign Office* (Washington, D.C.: Department of State, 1948), 258-59.

11. For a detailed examination of the diplomatic maneuvering and international consequences at the time, see the following: Bruce R. Kuniholm, *The Origins of the Cold War in the Near East* (Princeton, N.J.: Princeton University Press, 1980), Chapter V; George Lenczowski, *Russia and the West in Iran, 1918-1948* (Ithaca, N.Y.: Cornell University Press, 1949), pp. 220–315; William Eagleton, Jr., *The Kurdish Republic of 1946* (New York: Oxford University Press, 1963), which relates the developments in Kurdistan; and Rouhollah K. Ramazani, "The Autonomous Republic of Azerbaijan and the Kurdish People's Republic: Their Rise and Fall," in Thomas T. Hammond ed., *The Anatomy of Communist Takeovers* (New Haven, Conn.: Yale University Press, 1975), 448-74.

12. Kuniholm, 346-48.

13. Firuz Kazamzadeh, "Soviet-Iranian Relations: A Quarter–Century of Freeze and Thaw," in Ivo J. Lederer and Wayne S. Vucinich, eds., *The Soviet Union and the Middle East: The Post World War II Era* (Stanford, Calif.: Hoover Institution Press, 1974), 63-74.

14. David J. Dallin, *Soviet Foreign Policy after Stalin* (Philadelphia: Lippincott, 1961), 213.

15. Ibid. See also Sepehr Zabih, *The Communist Movement in Iran* (Berkeley: University of California Press, 1966), 202-07

16. Robert M. Slusser and Jan F. Triska, *A Calendar of Soviet Treaties 1917-1957* (Stanford, Calif.: Stanford University Press, 1959), 320, 382.

17. As quoted in Rouhollah K. Ramazani, *Iran's Foreign Policy 1941-1973* (Charlottesville: University Press of Virginia, 1975), 307.

18. Royal Institute of International Affairs, *Documents on International Affairs, 1955* (London: Oxford University Press, 1958), 309-13.

19. *Khrushchev Remembers* (New York: Bantam Books, 1971), 185.

20. Ramazani, 299.

21. For a thoughtful, sophisticated interpretation of these important negotiations, see Ramazani, 294-304.

22. Shahram Chubin and Sepehr Zabih, *The Foreign Relations of Iran* (Berkeley: University of California Press, 1974), 60-61.

23. New York *Times*, February 13, 1959

24. New York *Times*, March 16, 1959.

25. Ramazani, 316

26. "None of the goals of our White Revolution could have been achieved if we had not been able to maintain peace with our neighbors in a strategic region of the world of which Iran is the focal point." Mohammad Reza Pahlavi, The Shah of Iran, *Answer to History* (Briarcliff Manor, N.Y.: Stein and Day, 1980), 131.

27. "Recent Soviet Writing on Persia," *Mizan Newsletter* 6, no. 7 (July-August 1964):11–15. By the 1970s Soviet scholars, though steering clear of controversial subjects, were nonetheless writing solid works on Iranian history, linguistics, culture, and economics. Jacob Landau, "More Soviet Works on Iran," *Middle Eastern Studies* 15, no. 3 (October 1979):408–11. See also E. A. Orlov, *Vneshniaia politika Irana posle vtoroi mirovoi voiny* (Moscow: Nauka, 1975).

4

THE KREMLIN AND THE SHAH:
1968-78

The decade of 1968 through 1978 witnessed the most intensive and fruitful pattern of interaction between Moscow and Tehran in their long and troubled history. Political and especially economic missions were regularly exchanged (see Appendix 2) and resulted in tangible achievements. Trade expanded, and more than 100 Soviet-assisted industrial projects began to dot the Iranian landscape, including a major steel complex, an engineering works, and a natural gas pipeline. Cooperation with the Soviet Union was important for the economic development of Iran and the hopes of the Shah for his White Revolution.

Political relations were of two kinds: accommodating and antagonistic. The former, focusing on their mutual interest in a peaceful, stable situation along the 1,200 miles of border, was epitomized by such reciprocities as the prompt return of defectors in accordance with the August 7, 1973, agreement to prevent the hijacking of civil aircraft; and the deployment of only modest military forces on either side of the frontier. The latter included the USSR's arming of Iraq and heavy engagement in Afghanistan, and Iran's military buildup and policy in the Persian Gulf and its agreement to permit five U.S. intelligence-monitoring facilities on Iranian soil. Neither party had any illusions about the other: Moscow viewed the Shah's alignment with the United States as inherently anti-Soviet, and the Shah suspected the USSR's ambitions and subversive activities, which emanated from East Germany, source of the anti-Shah National Radio Iran and training ground for Tudeh cadres. Both sides had a sure sense of their priorities and the parameters and possibilities of their détente. For most of the decade they carried on their relationship in a calculated, businesslike manner that ended only with the internal upheaval in Iran.

GEOSTRATEGIC OVERVIEW

The environment in which Soviet-Iranian diplomacy strove for accommodation was one of systemic change. First, there was the Shah's increasing skepticism of the credibility of the United States as a protector of Iranian national interests. Having departed in the 1950s from a policy of unalignment to one of alignment with the West, he had joined the Baghdad Pact in 1955 and concluded a bilateral defense agreement with the United States in 1959. Soon thereafter, however, the realization that Washington was interested in détente with Moscow, the reluctance of the United States to provide the economic and military assistance that he considered essential for Iran's development and security, and the concern over Moscow's growing presence in neighboring Iraq and Afghanistan all contributed to the formulation of an "independent national policy." This policy was characterized by normalization of relations with the Soviet Union, determination to rely less directly on the American connection for political guidance, and awareness that Iran's security vis-a-vis Iraq and the Persian Gulf would require greater national assertiveness.[1] What probably steeled the Shah's determination was the failure of the United States to help its ally, Pakistan, in the Indo-Pakistani war of September 1965, because a few months later he observed to an American journalist: "Now we know that the United States would not come to aid us if we were attacked. It is no longer 1946. Things have changed!"[2]

After the 1970-71 Indo-Pakistani war, he dismissed the value of CENTO (the successor to the Baghdad Pact), saying it "has never been really serious."[3] He no longer thought much of the U.S.-Iranian defense pact, which, though it guarantees "Iran against a communist threat, grants the United States the privilege of interpreting what 'Communist' meant, no matter what we called it. Moreover, it was not an automatic defense pledge";[4] and he resolved to strengthen Iran's military capacity so that it would not have to depend on any power in the event of nonnuclear attack.

London's announcement in January 1968 that the British military presence in the Persian Gulf would be terminated in late 1971, coming as it did on the heels of the relinquishment of the Aden protectorate (now known as the People's Democratic Republic of Yemen [PDRY]) some months earlier, heralded a second profound change in the region. It heightened

> the Shah's fears of a political-military vacuum in the Perisan Gulf [arising out of] the multitude of territorial disputes and claims among the littoral states of the Gulf, and the certainty that these claims would be strongly reasserted once the restraining force, which the British had traditionally wielded in the region, would be retracted . . . [5]

and encouraged his rapid military buildup.

The Shah acted firmly to safeguard Iran's security. In a show of statesmanship, he relinquished Iran's claim to the oil-rich Arab island Sheikhdom of Bahrain, thereby reassuring the other ministates on the Arab side of the Persian Gulf of Iran's peaceful intentions; but proceeded, on November 30, 1971, "one day before the expiration of the British treaties which had given Britain control of the external relations of the Gulf Sheikhdoms," to occupy the two Tumb Islands and Abu Musa, barren, virtually unpopulated specks of land, "which are located so strategically close to the narrow—twenty-six mile—entrance to the Straits of Hormuz."[6] With this, the Shah signalled Iran's intention to play the role of keeper of the peace in the Gulf region. Iran patrolled the Strait of Hormuz and between 1972 and 1975 helped Oman suppress the Dhofari rebels who operated with Soviet supplies from sanctuary in the PDRY. Iran settled an old dispute with Afghanistan over the Helmand River in 1973; helped Pakistan through the difficult period following its defeat by India and the secession of Bangladesh; and courted India, offering concessionary prices on purchases of oil, as well as investment credits for an oil refinery. During a visit to Australia in September 1974, the Shah proposed some kind of collective security arrangement among the countries bordering on the Indian Ocean that would persuade the United States and the Soviet Union to withdraw their naval forces from the area and accept the Indian Ocean as "a zone of peace and collaboration."[7] The Shah's ambition to police the Persian Gulf was reasonable and not inappropriate, given the political environment of the decade.

A third systemic change in the region was the emergence of Iraq as a radical, antimonarchical, anti-Western state, armed and primed with Soviet weaponry. Though not the only cause for Iran's military buildup, the militarization of Iraq under a leadership that manipulated the appeal of Arab unity in order to advance its own ambitions heightened tensions in the region and inevitably attracted superpower involvement. (After Ayatollah Rouhollah Khomeini came to power in February 1979, tensions between Iran and Iraq over conflicting territorial and strategic aims were aggravated by historic cultural-religious animosities and antithetical revolutionary outlooks.)

Finally, for most of the decade, the Shah had a free hand to carry out his new foreign policy, because of a convergence of U.S. and Iranian aims, and the inability of the Soviet Union to interfere directly in the region. His policy of national assertiveness accorded with the Nixon Doctrine of August 1969, which said the United States would not intervene directly on behalf of friendly states but would provide them with the wherewithal to defend their own (and presumably U.S.) national interests. Mired as it was in Vietnam, the United States had little power to deploy in the Persian Gulf and was only too willing to see the Shah assume responsibility for safeguarding the region. For its part, the Soviet Union lacked both the presence and the power required to play a leading role in the Gulf. Besides, détente with the United States still held sway in the Kremlin, which preferred low-risk, indirect challenges only, as in Angola in 1975 and the Horn of Africa in 1977-78. Though the Soviet-Iraqi relationship placed limits on the Soviet-Iranian rapprochement, none of these systemic changes seriously interfered with the promotion of improved bilateral relations between Moscow and Tehran.

ECONOMIC DETENTE

The flowering of economic ties that followed the thaw in the political field was insulated throughout the decade from episodic political tensions. On October 6, 1965, and January 13, 1966, in the aftermath of the Shah's visit the previous June, far-reaching economic agreements were signed, under which the USSR advanced a $300 million credit and agreed to construct a steel mill near Isfahan, a machine tool plant, a hydroelectric power station, and a natural gas pipeline. Moscow's terms were generous: Iran was to pay only 2.5 percent interest and to repay the loan in natural gas from the pipeline after it was completed. The Shah was particularly pleased with the Soviet offer to build the steel complex, because Washington had rejected the project on the economic grounds that Iran's coal and iron resources were too limited and distant from one another and had discouraged the Soviet alternative, arguing that Iran's security might be compromised by

> having any larger Russian representation in Iran than geography makes necessary.
> One thing is certain [he remarked], the Russians will build our steel mill! That your [U.S.] people want to build now, having opposed it before, I find amusing!
> Your people have warned me that if we are friendly to the U.S.S.R. and let them in, they will subvert Iranians. To this I reply that the last attempt on my life was organized in Manchester, England, and I suspect that the "forty-year-old students" in the United States would do it too.[8]

In 1967, the year the United States phased out the economic aid program it had operated since 1954, Iran signed an agreement with the USSR to expand trade and economic cooperation, increase the quantity of natural gas to be delivered, and added oil to the list of commodities to be sold. (Iran also entered into its first arms agreement with the USSR, a decision that, paradoxically, was to benefit mainly the revolutionary regime that overthrew the Shah, enabling it to resist the Iraqi invasion of September 1980.) All of this suited the Shah's plans for rapid industrialization, the increase in Soviet assistance compensating greatly for the termination of U.S. aid. Between 1965 and 1968, Moscow extended about $700 million in credits to Iran, approximately 20 percent of total Soviet aid commitments to Afro-Asian countries for that period. By the end of the 1960s, total credits extended to Iran by the Soviet block exceeded $1 billion.

The intensive economic interactions of the early 1970s were the most tangible payoff from the political rapprochement of the 1960s. Total trade quadrupled, expanding from more than $250 million in 1970 to in excess of $1 billion by 1978. In 1976 Moscow undertook a threefold expansion of the Isfahan steel complex (to 6 million tons annually) and development of additional sources of iron ore and coal. Soviet participation in Iran's development program accounted for 90 percent of Iran's coal, iron ore, and cast iron production, and for 70 percent of its steel capacity. By early 1978, 78 of the 134 projects in which Soviet assistance was involved had been completed. In addition to being the largest Third World purchaser of Soviet machinery and equipment, Iran negotiated contracts worth several billion dollars, including "(a) a second trans-Iranian gas pipeline, with a total cost of $3 billion; (b) a new seaport on the Caspian coast; (c) two new hydro-power projects; (d) uranium development; (e) a $500 million aluminum plant; and (f) expansion of highway, railroad, and port facilities."[9] To this impressive array of economic interactions must also be added the growing links between Iran and the East European countries. Overall, then, the picture was one of activity and growth.

THE NATURAL GAS INCIDENT

The lone exception to the gratifying Soviet-Iranian economic relationship during the Shah's final decade of rule, the natural gas affair of 1974-75, demonstrates the influence that can be excercised over a superpower by a Third World leadership if it is in a fortunate bargaining position and in a situation that is devoid of strategic significance or vital national concerns. Business is business, and despite the degree of his indebtedness, the possessor of a valued commodity is in a position to bargain stiffly.

One result of the Shah's visit to the USSR in June 1965 was the construction of the Iranian Gas Trunkline (IGAT-1) from Khuzistan in southwestern Iran to the Soviet border at Astara. Of the 630-mile-long pipeline, the Soviets laid and tested 340 miles of 40-inch pipe from Kuh Namak to Astara, plus a feeder line between Kuh Namak and Tehran, a distance of about 80 miles. They also installed a gas-measuring complex at Astara. The southern portion of the line was built by British, French, and

German companies. A Soviet credit of $50 million covering part of the costs marked the beginning of the USSR's purchase of Persian Gulf energy and its financial involvement in Iran's modernization.[10] Prior to this, most of Iran's natural gas burnt off and was wasted.

Soviet interest in the project was threefold. First, Moscow wanted to sell its own gas to Western Europe for the hard currency needed to help finance its importation of advanced technology and equipment. The USSR has vast reserves of natural gas, but the fields are located in remote areas where the climate makes exploitation of the resources very expensive. It was therefore cheaper to invest in and purchase Iranian natural gas than to develop its own reserves. Second, the purchase of Iranian gas freed Soviet supplies for sale in energy-poor Eastern Europe, thus contributing to Moscow's policy of promoting bloc cohesion. Finally, Moscow saw the project as a major step linking Iran and the USSR more closely economically, creating an atmosphere of goodwill, and furthering political accommodation.

IGAT-1 was completed in 1970, less than five years from the first feasibility studies, a notable achievement for a project of this size and complexity. On October 28, 1970, the Shah and Soviet President Nikolai Podgorny inaugurated the pipeline at a ceremony in Astara, on the Iranian side of the border. Iran quickly became the Soviet Union's "number one foreign supplier of natural gas with Afghanistan far behind as its only other foreign supplier. In the period 1970-75 Iran provided the USSR with 41.15 billion cubic meters [bcm] of gas while Afghanistan supplied 16.39 bcm."[11] Agreement for a second line was reached, but construction was stopped shortly after Khomeini assumed power.[12]

When IGAT-1 started operating in 1970, the price of natural gas exports was set at 18.7 cents per 1,000 cubic feet. In early 1973, since the USSR was selling its own gas to Europe for four times this amount, the Iranian government asked Moscow to accept a price hike. On July 18, apparently without much resistance, Moscow agreed to an increase of 35 percent.[13]

One year later the situation was considerably different. Before the terms were finally settled in August 1974, Moscow and Tehran had experienced their first serious economic strains since the Stalin period and, as in July 1972 when Egyptian President Anwar Sadat abruptly expelled Soviet military personnel, Moscow had to suffer the slings of a resolute Third World autocrat.

The first indication of Iran's desire for new negotiations was the visit in January 1974 of a delegation of Iranian experts from the Ministry of Finance and the Central Bank of Iran to meet with Soviet officials "to discuss and exchange views . . . on matters related to payments between the two countries in light of recent world monetary developments," an allusion to the quadrupled oil prices levied by the Organization of

Petroleum Exporting Countries (OPEC) in the wake of the Arab-Israeli War of October 1973.[14] An alert that all was not well was sounded in a commentary on Moscow Radio, March 14, when I. Savchenko criticized an article in *Tehran Journal* (the English-language daily published by *Ettelaat*) for anti-Soviet falsifications in alleging that the Soviet Union made a profit in reselling Iranian natural gas to Western Europe at a higher price than it had paid to Iran.[15] He slyly circumvented the truth in maintaining that the USSR did not sell a single drop of Iranian gas, since he knew the use of Iran's gas to service the needs of the Soviet republics in the Caucasus and Central Asia made available for sale to the West the gas produced in the European part of the USSR. Three weeks later, another Soviet commentator declared that "rumors that Iranian gas was being exploited were nonsensical."[16] (While this set of talks was in progress, tripartite negotiations on the export of gas from Iran to the Federal Republic of Germany [FRG] via the USSR were simultaneously being carried on.)

On May 26 *Ettelaat* reported that Iran had officially demanded an additional 60 cents per 1,000 cubic feet and that "negotiations regarding Iran's demand have been agreed upon, but Moscow has not yet designated its delegation nor set a date for the negotiations," and it added that "any delay in the negotiations directly and immediately affects Iran's income."[17]

In the beginning of June, *Kayhan International*, a leading Tehran newspaper, discussed the matter fully, observing that

> the escalation clause provided for the automatic adjustment of one-third of the gas price for any movement in fuel prices of under thirty per cent, and for negotiations between the two parties to set new prices for gas whenever the price of fuel at Bander Mahshahr fell or rose by more than thirty per cent.[18]

According to the article, this clause had been added at the request of Moscow, in its expectation that the price of crude oil would drop. However, the price having risen from $2.99 to $11.65 per barrel between October and December 1973, Iran was asking for another increase.

Under the provisions of the 1966 agreement, this quadrupling in the price of crude petroleum meant negotiations for a new price of natural gas were in order. Noting that the Soviet Union was paying 30 cents per 1,000 cubic feet, the article said that an increase to $1.24 would be justified, yet Iran was asking for only half, that is, 62 cents, to reflect higher prices on world markets:

> The Soviet Union has often cited the prices paid to the producing states by the international oil cartel for crude as an instance of their exploitive

policies towards developing countries. How, Iranians are bound to ask, do the Russians justify the under-valued price they pay for Iranian gas?[19]

Positions hardened, and both sides began to give a political slant to the issue: Radio Moscow labelled a reporter for *Tehran Journal* who wrote on Soviet profits from Iranian gas a "paid agent of Western interests," and *Pravda's* criticisms of Iran's demands assumed a hostile tone.[20] Tehran Radio ran general commentaries on the justice of Iran's request for price revisions, perhaps to prepare the public for some untoward development in relations with the Soviet Union.

On June 24, negotiations resumed in Moscow, with the managing director of the National Iranian Gas Company, Taqi Mossaddeqqi, leading the Iranian delegation. The Soviets rejected Iran's proposed increase to 62 cents, and after only two days the talks were broken off abruptly. A week later, Iran announced it would unilaterally double its price for gas.[21] (It also requested indefinite postponement of the tripartite talks, scheduled to reopen in Essen on July 1, a signal of Tehran's determination to see the matter through to the end.) The Iranian press called the proposed increase a "friendly gesture" to the USSR and, in effect, a discount demonstrating Iran's goodwill and desire for cooperation.[22] Responding to reports that the USSR might double the price of the capital goods already sent to the Isfahan steel mill, it emphasized the point that the escalation clause in the gas agreement had been included at Moscow's specific request, while the Isfahan project had provided for a fixed price. One acerbic editorial suggested that the USSR's failure to live up the agreement was

> inviting the Iranian people, and the developing countries as a whole, to take another hard look at the self-professed "friend" of Third World countries.
>
> [The Russians] can hardly expect Iranians to applaud a great power that secures Iranian gas cheaply and sells it at a handsome profit in Europe. This smacks of what the Russians like to describe as capitalistic exploitation ... It is not only a question of money. Relations nurtured carefully over a decade could be affected.[23]

Another detailed the instances in which Iran had to pay the Soviet Union the prevailing international price for goods that it imported; for example, "until a few months ago, Russia charged Iran $50 for a cubic-metre wood block for which Iran now pays $230."[24] Such commentaries by the tightly controlled Iranian press conveyed Iran's dissatisfaction with the character and pace of the negotiations and, what is more, its intention to air the disagreement.

With negotiations broken off and each side adhering, not only in private but in public as well, to its official position, an impasse had been reached. In this frozen environment on July 11, Tehran radio reported that shipments of natural gas to the Soviet Union had stopped the previous morning "due to a fire" along the pipeline and that "the fire on this pipeline was of such a magnitude that it will not be possible to dispatch gas to the USSR for the next two weeks."[25] Accident or design, operations were resumed on July 16; but the disruption certainly brought home to Moscow the vulnerability of its position. The 800 million cubic feet of gas piped monthly to the southern part of the Soviet Union was more necessary to Soviet economic planning and activity than was the income it yielded Iran, whose export earnings had soared with OPEC's successful escalation of oil prices in late 1973. Tehran may very well have been signalling Moscow: Pay what we consider a just and reasonable price or be prepared for the consequences, which will inconvenience you more than us. Never before, in relations with a Third World country, had Moscow been put over a barrel, so to speak, in commercial dealings in which all trumps were held by the small power.

On August 3, a Soviet mission arrived in Tehran, and another round of negotiations began on August 6. Tehran Radio reflected the Iranians' confidence: "Informed quarters foresee that the USSR will have no answer but to agree to Iran's demand."[26] On August 17 Tehran announced an agreement raising the price by approximately 85 percent, to 57 cents per 1,000 cubic feet, retroactive to January 1, 1974. This was 5 cents less than the price it had requested and represented an increase of 10 cents over the Soviet offer made in Moscow in June.

Kayhan International called the agreement a "quiet but immensely important victory" for Iran, which "normalized relations between the two neighboring countries."[27] The Iranians had not viewed the dispute as an isolated incident but as integral to overall economic cooperation. Moscow put on a good face, a Soviet broadcast in Persian calling the agreement "yet another proof of Soviet-Iranian trade and economic cooperation" and citing an Iranian commentary that said the negotiations took place in "an atmosphere of complete understanding."[28]

What can be adduced about the nature of the Soviet-Iranian influence relationship from the natural gas controversy and its resolution? Iran's behavior is easy to understand. Its request was entirely appropriate, since the 1966 agreement permitted an increase in the price of natural gas whenever that of crude oil fluctuated by 30 percent or more.

Tehran considered its asking price reasonable, being well below the world market price Moscow was receiving for its gas in Western Europe. It had a strong case and did not feel constrained by the heavy Soviet involvement in Iran's industrialization program. Soviet assistance was

evidently not considered to mean dependency. In suspending the tripartite talks and shutting down the pipeline, ostensibly because of fire,
Tehran may even have been engaging in a bit of low-key high-pressure
tactics. By requesting an increase that was still far below world market
levels, however, Iran signified its desire to avoid jeopardizing the significant economic relationship that both countries had developed since the
mid-1960s.

Soviet acquiescence entailed far more complex and varied considerations. First, Moscow accepted the adjusted terms because Iran had
strong grounds for its request. The Soviets, who are zealous legalists in
their foreign commerical transactions, recognized this. Their delay may
have stemmed from a natural reluctance on the part of the affected
bureaucracies to concede more than they felt they absolutely had to; their
tardy recognition that the disruption in Iranian gas shipments would cost
them more than Iran; and their belief that by prolonging the negotiations
they might obtain greater concessions from the Iranians, who did in fact
somewhat reduce their price. Second, Iran's willingness to raise the
threshold of disputation surprised Moscow. Once convinced that Tehran
was resolute, Moscow quickly settled. Third, when the Iranians went
public, Moscow was increasingly embarrassed by the implication, em-
bellished by the Chinese, that it was exploiting a less developed country. A
basic theme in its diplomacy in the Third World was that, unlike the
capitalist countries, the Soviet Union did not take economic advantage of
the new nations. To seek to perpetuate a clearly low price level that had
been rendered blatantly anachronistic by the advent of the energy crisis
placed the Soviet Union in an unattractive light. Fourth, Moscow did not
want to disrupt the impetus toward political as well as economic détente in
Soviet-Iranian relations. Given the expansive character of these relations
and the USSR's deepening involvement in Iran's development planning,
the case for settling the matter was strong. Finally, accommodation in Iran
lent credence to détente in Europe, then the centerpiece of Soviet foreign
policy. Moscow espoused the convening of a Conference on Security and
Cooperation in Europe not only to obtain Western recognition for the
territorial and political status quo in Europe but also to entice Western
bankers to underwrite Soviet purchases of advanced technology and
equipment. The Soviet concessions paved the way for the 20-year
tripartite agreement of November 30, 1975, concerning the sale of natural
gas among Iran, the FRG,and the USSR.

In this instance Iran was unmistakably able to be the influencer,
because it had a strong hand, kept the bargaining confined to the
immediate issue, optimized rather than maximized an initial advantage,

and exploited a favorable milieu in which the USSR had more important stakes to push.

THE IRAQI DIMENSION

Iran's perception of threat from the Soviet Union was heightened by Moscow's military buildup of Iraq. After Colonel Abd al-Karim Qasim toppled the pro-Western monarchy in July 1958, Iraq pursued an anti-Western policy that received, over the years, varying degrees of Soviet support. By the late 1960s the Soviet-Iraqi arms relationship that started in 1959 when Iraq quit the Baghdad Pact began to make the Shah uneasy about the security of his border, especially along the disputed Shatt-al-Arab estuary across from Iraq, where the oil refineries of Abadan and the oil-loading installations at Kharq Island were within easy striking distance of Iraqi troops.

Whatever his faults as an autocrat torn between a desire to modernize and a belief in benevolent despotism, the Shah was an astute student of international politics. He understood that under conditions of loose bipolarity between the superpowers, small states have greater manueverability in the regional game of power politics and can avoid domination by the stronger powers, if they play their diplomatic hand skillfully.

In January 1967, to the surprise of many in the West, Iran signed its first arms agreement with the Soviet Union. Worth about 110 million dollars, the agreement called for relatively unsophisticated weapons—armored personnel carriers, antiaircraft guns, trucks, and some types of artillery. But coming so soon after the 1966 economic accords for constructing the Isfahan steel mill and IGAT, it created a stir. The government stressed its loyalty to CENTO and the 1959 treaty with the United States, but the Shah was annoyed with Washington for restricting the sale of advanced weapons to Iran and for downgrading CENTO in Western strategy, and foreign diplomats felt he was cautioning Washington not to take Iran for granted. Also he wanted to induce Moscow to accord Iran greater importance and, by holding out the prospect of extending Soviet-Iranian ties to the military field, to dissuade Moscow from becoming too heavily committed to Iraq. In a sense, he hoped the agreement would loosen the arms tap in Washington and tighten it in Moscow as far as Iraq was concerned. The initiative was a calculated demonstration of his determination to pursue an "independent national policy."

The arrival in Tehran in January 1968 of a Soviet parliamentary delegation presaged a year of high-level exchanges. In April, Alexei Kosygin became the first Soviet premier to visit Iran. The joint communiqué issued on April 7 called particular attention to "the Middle East situation"—an allusion to Britian's announced intention of withdrawing militarily from the Gulf by the end of 1971:

> The two sides declared themselves against foreign interference in the internal affairs of other states, and against the use or threat of the use of force to solve disputed relations between states. Touching on the dangerous rise in tension in the Middle East, the two sides stressed particularly that it was necessary for all the states in the area to have an opportunity for free and independent development, without any pressure or interference from alien forces which wanted to preserve colonial order and their influences in the area.

The Shah interpreted this to mean that Moscow would neither support Iraq's irredentist claims against Kuwait nor oppose Iran's policy of preserving stability in the Gulf. Satisfied with the results of the Kosygin visit, he ignored the Soviet invasion of Czechoslovakia on August 22 and subsequent Western criticism, and proceeded in late September with his previously scheduled trip to Moscow, his third since 1956. As one Iranian paper observed: "Closer ties with the Soviet Union should not be interpreted narrow-mindedly as opposition to our Western friends. What encourages and urges this friendship is having thousands of kilometers of common border with the Soviet Union."[29] The joint communiqué of October 5 made no specific mention of the Gulf, but like the one in April it advocated a hands-off policy by extraregional powers. So far Moscow's relations with Iraq were still fairly uneven, and its détente with Iran was promising enough for it to cultivate closer ties to Tehran. However, "the Soviet leadership, still doubting the British intention to relinquish their hegemony in the Gulf at the end of 1971," and apprehensive lest Iran and the United States enter into an alliance with the Arab nations of the Gulf and thereby allow U.S. influence to replace that of the British, sought also to deepen its ties to Iraq.[30]

The Soviet courtship of Iraq assumed new intensity after a coup in July 1968 brought the Baath (Arabic for Renaissance) Party back to power. The Baath (which had originally seized power in February 1963, but had been ousted eight months later) faced insurrection at home from the Kurdish minority seeking greater autonomy, tensions with Syria and Egypt over rivalry in the Arab world, and difficulty with Iran over the Shatt-al-Arab, which Baghdad unwisely chose to reaffirm as an integral part of Iraq's territory. This led Tehran on April 19, 1969, to declare the 1937 treaty, which had been foisted on Iran by a British–controlled Iraq, null and void "because of Iraq's alleged nonadherence to the treaty [its failure to conclude a convention for maintaining the navigability of the estuary] for thirty-two years and because of 'change of circumstances.' "[31] Iran's assertiveness, coupled with the Baath's own ambitions to play a leading role in the Gulf, motivated Baghdad to seek closer ties with Moscow. For its part, the Soviet Union wanted to encourage the Baath's anti-Western policy and establish a firm presence in the area, without alienating Iran, if at all possible.

On April 9, 1972, the Soviet Union and Iraq signed a 15-year treaty of friendship and cooperation that included provisions for immediate consultations "in the event of a situation developing which endangers the peace of either of them" (Article 8) and "cooperation in the strengthening of the defense capabilities of each" (Article 9). (Both of these seemed timely because Iraq-Iranian tensions had mounted dangerously since Iraq's expulsion of some 50,000 Iranians the previous fall.) Two days after the treaty was signed a Soviet naval squadron paid a goodwill visit to the Iraqi port of Umm Qasr. The USSR's alignment with Iraq further exacerbated tensions between Iraq and Iran. Despite Moscow's reassurances, the Shah feared it was a Soviet stepping-stone to the Gulf and determined to strengthen Iran militarily.

Iraqi-Iranian frictions became a factor in Soviet-Iranian relations, especially because of the Shah's covert assistance to the Kurdish insurrection. An unassimilated, fiercely nationalistic, non-Arab minority, constituting about one-quarter of Iraq's population and inhabiting the northeastern part of the country, the Kurds had mounted uprisings in 1944 and again in 1961, the latter dragging on inconclusively for almost nine years. A provisional agreement in March 1970 between the Baath and the Kurds collapsed, and sporadic fighting erupted in late 1971. The Baath knew the Kurds' ability to engage in a protracted war depended on military assistance from Iran, whose relations with the Soviet Union were improving, so it calculated that a commitment of Soviet support on its behalf would keep Iran on the sidelines.[32] The treaty with Moscow was thus motivated in part by Baghdad's desire to use the Soviet connection to settle its Kurdish question.

After the Arab-Israeli War of October 1973, Iraq resumed diplomatic relations with Iran, which then cut back its assistance to the Kurds. This normalization was a prelude to the Baath's concentrating on ending the Kurdish challenge by force if necessary and on terms less lenient than those set forth in the agreement of March 11, 1970, between the Baath and the Kurdish Democratic Party of General Mustafa Barzani. On the fourth anniversary of the agreement, the Iraqi government announced a watered-down plan for Kurdish self-rule, which, as it expected, Barzani termed inadequate. Thereafter heavy fighting began anew. To add to the complexities of the situation, a few weeks earlier there had been border clashes between Iraqi and Iranian troops that reversed the short-lived improvement in their relations and threatened to complicate the Kurdish campaign, as well as to trigger hostilities between the two long-term regional rivals.

Though long a partisan of the Kurds, Moscow could not remain indifferent to the government's needs without risking its evolving special relationship with the Iraqi Baathists, and so complied with their requests for military assistance. It knew that a Kurdish revolt threatened the stability of a regime whose predecessors had fallen because of this intractable issue and might undermine all that the Iraqi connection had brought: namely, close ties with an important Arab country in the Persian Gulf area; access to Umm Qasr, whose significance for Moscow was political rather than military (not only is the port poorly equipped to repair modern vessels, but its location at closed end of the gulf limits its value in times of crisis); participation of the Iraqi Communist Party (ICP) in the government; expanded economic ties and a major role in the exploitation of Iraq's rich oil fields; and an opportunity to improve relations with both Iraq and Iran, thereby creating a more favorable strategic environment for the advancement of Soviet objectives in the region as a whole.

Baghdad exploited Moscow's dilemma, knowing the Kremlin preferred a political solution but would in the interests of better standing with the Baath reluctantly go along with a military solution rather than allow the Kurds and their "imperialist" supporters (Iran and covert U.S. and Israeli assistance) to threaten the Soviet position in the country.[33]

Moscow wanted to prevent a war between Iraq and Iran. It expected that Baghdad's need to draw on its support would help increase Soviet influence on the Baathists and, at the same time, impress the Kurds with the futility of fighting and the need for compromise, and deter Iran from deepening its involvement. Moscow's arms shipments to Iraq, heavy throughout 1972 and 1973, increased in 1974. In late May 1974 Soviet ships unloaded surface-to-air missiles in Umm Qasr, possibly to protect Iraqi troops against Iranian air strikes.[34] Moreover, as the Iraqi army prepared a major offensive, Soviet air power played an important part. Soviet pilots, flying MIG-fighters and Tupolev supersonic bombers with Iraqi markings, the handling of which was known to be beyond the capability of the Iraqis, bombed Kurdish villages and flew reconnaissance missions. The Russians presumably calculated the willingness to use their personnel in support of the Iraqi offensive would be taken as a commitment to the Iraqi regime and would give the Shah cause to reassess direct Iranian involvement on behalf of the Kurds. The risks to Moscow were minimal, given the very limited number of pilots and planes and their minor role in the fighting, but their symbolic value was enormous.

The critical phase of the problem as a factor in Soviet–Iranian relations began in late summer 1974 and lasted for about six months. At about that time the Iraqi offensive against the Kurds had advanced farther than any had before, squeezing the Kurds into a narrowing strip along the Iranian border. However, the Iraqis could not achieve a knockout blow because Iranian protective artillery barrages and supplies of antitank missiles and ammunition stiffened Kurdish resistance. With the onset of fall and winter and the Iranians apparently willing to escalate their involvement, the Iraqis feared another indecisive campaign and pressed Moscow for additional assistance. In late September, in closely spaced visits, Iraq's foreign minister and its chief of staff each went to Moscow to discuss ways of "strengthening cooperation and friendship." A month later First Secretary of the ICP Aziz Muhammad, a Kurd elected to his post in 1964 and strongly identified with Moscow and ICP participation in the Baath's National Progressive Front, met with Politburo alternate member Boris N. Ponomarev. According to *Pravda* Aziz Muhammad emphasized the importance of the ICP-Baath cooperation and the Front's progressive line in pressing socioeconomic reforms and a solution to the Kurdish problem,[35] and presumably backed Baghdad's request for additional weapons.

Two events proved crucial: The Shah's visit to Moscow from November 18 to 20; and Soviet Army Chief of Staff and Deputy Minister of Defense Viktor Kulikov's visit to Baghdad a week later. During the Shah's visit Soviet President Podgorny declared: "We must say outright that the tension existing in relations between Iran and Iraq is not in the interests of peace," and it is up to the parties themselves to reach a settlement. To this the Shah had replied, "I would only observe that if in its relations with us Iraq will adopt the same position which you, our great neighbor, observe in your relations with us, and will refrain from following with such addiction the legacy of British imperialism, there will be no problem between us in this matter."[36]

Disagreement between the two governments was evident in the joint communiqué issued at the end of the visit. Compared with the communiqués published on October 21, 1972, March 17, 1973, and August 12, 1973, during visits by the Shah to Moscow, Kosygin to Tehran, and Prime Minister Hoveyda to Moscow, respectively, the one of November 20, 1974, was noteworthy in a number of ways. First, it was the briefest of all, an immediate indication of trouble and the pressing primacy of Soviet-Iranian relations, since visits by heads of states or prime ministers usually conclude with lengthy statements of accomplishment and global concerns. Second, whereas in 1972 and 1973 the discussions were described as having taken place "in a friendly and frank atmosphere on the basis of mutual understanding," in 1974 the talks were described as having taken place "in a businesslike and frank atmosphere," the previously used phase "mutual understanding" having been omitted. Third, in the former communiqués, when referring to the Persian Gulf, the two sides "expressed their strong belief that Persian Gulf affairs should be settled by the states in the area on the basis of the UN Charter and without any interference by foreigners"; in 1974 the phase about foreigners not interfering was left out, an omission signifying that Moscow intended to take a more direct part in the politics of the region and would not accept exclusion. Elsewhere the exchange of options on "other questions relating to the situation in the Middle and the Near East" (the former referring to the Gulf, the latter to the Arab-Israeli sector) was described as having been "reciprocally outlined" . . . in a "spirit of frankness" (the term "frank" indicating that differences were aired but unresolved). Finally, the Shah did not invite Podgorny to visit Iran. In all previous communiqués an invitation had been extended to the host to visit the other nation. When the Shah left, he did so with the realization that although no direct Soviet threat was implied, Moscow intended to back the Iraqis in any showdown.

If there were any doubts about Moscow's intentions, General Kulikov's visit to Baghdad on November 27 to evaluate the situation first hand confirmed Tehran's fears and anticipated Arab reports that Iraq and the Soviet Union had concluded their largest arms agreement.[37] What set Moscow's course is not known: whether the breakdown in December of secret Iraqi-Iranian talks in Istanbul, the downing of two Soviet aircraft by Iranian missiles supplied by the United States,[38] the growing strain on the capability of the Baath, who had been forced to call up reserve officers in their mid-thirties to continue the campaign, or the indication that covert U.S. and Israeli support was sustaining the Kurdish revolt. However, on January 13, 1975, a few days before the arms agreement was reportedly signed, *Pravda* accused the CIA, in cooperation with Israel, of having stirred up the Kurds, strongly implying that Moscow was disturbed by Washington's effort to undermine a Soviet client through regional proxies. The buildup of Iraq's armed forces proceeded quickly. Soviet shipments noticeably increased in late spring and, combined with the sorties by Soviet-piloted MIG-23 aircraft, played a key role in the settlement reached between Iraq and Iran on March 5, 1975.

The Iraqi-Iranian settlement, which took place at a meeting of OPEC in Algiers, doomed the Kurdish rebellion. Although the Kurds were not specifically mentioned in the communiqué issued by the Shah and Vice President Saddam Hussein, the reference to the restoration of "security and mutual confidence along their joint borders" and the maintenance by both sides of "strict and effective control over their joint borders in order to put a final end to all subversive infiltration from either side" meant that the Kurds could no longer obtain Iranian arms or sanctuary. The agreement also reestablished the border along the Thalweg line in the middle of the deepest shipping channel in the Shatt-al-Arab estuary, where it had been prior to the 1937 treaty. (Dissatisfaction with this concession was one of reasons given by Iraq for its invasion of Iran on September 22, 1980.) The Shah made peace, abandoning the Kurds, because he obtained desired border adjustments and an end to anti-Iranian activity on Iraqi territory, and because he realized that Moscow was prepared to raise the arms ante on Iraq's behalf, the consequences of which would surely have weakened Iran and jeopardized the Soviet–Iranian detente.

Moscow also had reason to be satisfied. A month earlier it had noted with concern the seriousness of the border clashes and, reminding the Shah of Podgorny's comment the previous November, had urged a peaceful settlement.[39] The Baath had solidified its internal position as a result of timely Soviet support, and prospects for Soviet-Iraqi relations seemed bright. The elimination of territorial and political irritants from the Iraqi-Iranian relationship meant that Moscow, not having to take sides with one against the other in an armed conflict, could proceed with its policy of improving relations with both countries. In this situation, through indirection, it shaped an Iranian response that resulted in a preferred outcome. That the resolution was also satisfactory to Iran glossed over the role that Soviet power had played, but it, coincidentally, intensified the Shah's determination to continue his military buildup, project Iran's influence in the Gulf, and counter future Soviet imperial probes and provocations on the Arabian Peninsula.

IMPERIAL RIVALRY IN THE GULF

Soviet policy in the Persian Gulf-Arabian Peninsula region, though opposed to the Shah's, did not prevent improvement in bilateral Soviet-Iranian relations. It was viewed by Tehran as imperial, not national, in character, with the result that each party pursued its aims convinced that the differences were tolerable to the other. None of the issues was acute enough to upset their detente.

In the early 1970s Soviet leaders reiterated their position that the interests of the two countries were compatible and that the USSR did not pose a threat in the Persian Gulf, such as would justify Iran's projected high level of arms procurement. Soviet broadcasts combined professions of friendship with warnings of the dangers of arms races and "warmongering" policies. Similarly, when Kosygin visited Iran in March 1973 to dedicate the Isfahan steel mill, he declared the Soviet Union wanted "true security" based "on reduction of tension and strengthening of mutual confidence between the countries" and not an arms race, adding that a "warmongering policy by any country will necessarily lead to a crisis in an entire region and, more frequently, in the whole world and will force the neighbors of such countries to adopt this or that measure aimed at defending their national interests."[40]

In general, Soviet criticisms of Iran may be grouped under the following headings: Iran's arms buildup; its role as gendarme for the United States in the Gulf; the Shah's interest in organizing cooperation among the regional powers; and Sino–Iranian relations.

Iran's Arms Buildup

During President Nixon's visit to Tehran in May 1972, where he went directly after signing the SALT I agreement in Moscow, he opened the U.S. arms tap to the Shah. By early 1973 Tehran had placed multibillion-dollar orders for the most sophisticated weaponry in America's arsenal: F-14 fighter aircraft, a Hawk surface-to-air missile system, Spruance-class Destroyers, and helicopters (and Chieftain tanks from Britain).

Averring that the arms buildup was draining Iran's economy of resources it vitally needed for economic and cultural growth and that the Soviet Union had no intention of becoming a threat, Moscow counselled restraint. Kosygin told Prime Minister Amir Abbas Hoveyda, on his visit to the USSR in August 1973, that inflated military budgets and reliance on power politics did not make "states any stronger."[41] Time and again, Moscow reaffirmed "there is no justification for such a large-scale buildup of Iran's armaments—it cannot be explained by imaginary 'threats,' the need to create a 'self-defense perimeter' or the danger of 'falling behind' in the development of the "technical thinking of the age.'"[42] Iran's arms deals, it said, went far beyond the scope of legitimate defense needs and created a dangerous situation in the region. After all, wrote one Soviet commentator, it is known that "Soviet Union invariably pursues a consistent policy of good-neighborliness toward Iran and, on the admission of the Iranian leaders themselves, the Soviet-Iranian state border is a border of peace."[43]

The Role of Gendarme

Moscow perceived Iran as a surrogate protecting U.S. strategic and economic interests in the Persian Gulf:

> The USSR cannot remain indifferent to the attempts of the U.S. imperialist quarters, under the pretext of wishing to expand cooperation with Iran, to turn Iran into an agent of their policy, something that is fraught with danger for the cause of peace. The USSR does not wish Iran

to be turned into an instrument for exacerbating tensions in the Persian Gulf region, in the Middle East area....It is axiomatic that the USSR cannot remain indifferent to this state of affairs. Indeed, the USSR has often declared that it wishes Iran to be an independent, prosperous and strong country and to be the object of complete confidence and deep respect and not a tool for carrying out the adventurist policy of the aggressive forces of imperialism in the eyes of the peace-loving peoples.[44]

Throughout the 1973-75 period, Moscow denounced the use of "Iranian mercenary units" in suppressing the Dhofari uprising in Oman on behalf of Sultan Qabus.[45] Whatever reasons Tehran might give for its actions, it was doing Washington's bidding and advancing U.S. objectives. One Soviet journal put the matter thusly: one can "smell oil, the mercantile spirit of arms dealers, and the desire to make Iran, by dint of ruses, a shield for protecting the U.S. interests in the Persian Gulf and in the Arab lands south of it."[46]

Iran's Efforts to Promote Regional Cooperation

With growing naval power, the USSR sought a role for itself in the Persian Gulf quadrant of the Indian Ocean basin and increasingly resisted attempts at exclusion. At first, as a newcomer to the region, having diplomatic relations only with Iraq, Iran, Kuwait, and the geographically distant two Yemens, it aimed at "the weakening of the Gulf States' ties with Western countries and the encouragement of alternative governments or policies more congenial to Soviet interests."[47] Accordingly, it reacted strongly against the Shah's suggestion in April 1974 that the littoral states of the area established a common market, fearing that such a grouping would bar closer Soviet ties while strengthening pro-Western alignments. Soviet writers warned against the plans of "Western militarists" who, under the rubric of "stabilization" of the Gulf region, seek "to reanimate the CENTO bloc and pave the way to the creation of a new military-political line-up";[48] they charged that the U.S. arms sales were intended, on the one hand "to bring back the oil dollars into the safes of U.S. concerns, and on the other to tie the countries" of the region to the United States, thereby ensuring U.S. strategic control.

Concurrent with these criticisms were Moscow's attempts to sow discord between Iran and Arab countries by harping on Iran's working relationship with Israel, which included covert sales of oil; its close ties to Sadat, whose interest after the 1973 War in a settlement with Israel was a polarizing factor in intra-Arab politics; and its expansionist designs in the "Arabian Gulf," as the Persian Gulf was called in Soviet programs beamed to the Arab world. Soviet propaganda minced no words in denouncing

Iran and was in complete contrast to Moscow's efforts to improve diplomatic and economic relations at the government–to–government level.

Sino-Iranian Relations

Iran established diplomatic relations with the People's Republic of China in August 1971. It hoped thereby to make Moscow more accommodating and to frustrate Brezhnev's attempt, launched in June 1969, to create an Asian collective security system, whose purpose was to isolate China and expand the USSR's influence. Iran received tangible benefit from the new links with Peking when, in 1972, China cut its aid to the PDRY and the rebels in Oman. The Sino-Iranian relationship continued to improve, culminating in a visit in August 1978 by Hua Kuo-feng, then chairman of the Chinese Communist Party and Mao's apparent heir. Both the Shah and Hua publicly expressed alarm at the communist coup in Afghanistan in April, the situation in the PDRY, and the danger to the region from outside powers, that is, the USSR. The following joke that made the rounds in Tehran at the time of Hua's visit turned out to be prophetic, for five months later the Shah's domestic troubles came to a head. The Shah asks Chairman Hua, "In your country, how many people are against you?" Hua answers, "About 35 million." The Shah thinks a minute and says, "Its about the same here."[49]

THE FALL OF THE PAHLAVIS

The collapse of the Shah's regime may be considered to have begun with the outbreak of massive antigovernment riots in the holy city of Qum in January 1978. They were ignited by "an article attacking the exiled Ayatollah Khomeini and alleging that he was a homosexual and a British stooge," published "under the inspiration of the Minister of Information (responsible for the supervision of the news media)" on January 8, 1978, in the daily *Ettalaat*.[50] The agitation on this occasion, which was also the sixteenth anniversary of the Shah's land reforms that the mullahs had bitterly opposed, spread to other cities. Throughout the spring and summer, disturbances, strikes, and protests against the Shah broke out in the key cities of Isfahan, Ahvas, Kumas, Arak, Kermanshah, Tabriz, and Tehran. Religious opposition merged with growing discontent over the inflation, corruption, gross economic inequities, and appalling poverty and alienation of the peasant masses who had migrated to the cities, and become a mighty surge of political protest. Wildcat strikes, especially in the oil fields, began to take their toll and paralyze sectors of the economy.

On September 8 martial law was declared in Tehran and quickly extended to all of Iran's major cities.

Moscow watched the Shah's troubles swell to incipient revolution. Beginning in September, daily reports gave fairly straightforward accounts of the unrest and violence. As the situation worsened, the tenor of the reporting changed, and news gave way to criticisms of the country's economic and social weaknesses and the activities of the SAVAK (the Iranian secret police) and the CIA. A mood of impending disaster was communicated by the Soviet media, which depicted the United States as the main culprit, assisting the regime in suppressing "Islamic revolutionary activity." The Shah was not criticized directly, because well into November Moscow may still have expected he would somehow quell the unrest.

In the face of the internal troubles, the Shah cancelled a number of scheduled trips abroad. However, Soviet-Iranian bilateral relations proceeded along the lines established in the previous decade, but at a dwindling pace. Three Soviet missions—two economic groups to conclude an agreement for a new natural gas pipeline and one scientific delegation—came in February and April, but none thereafter. Iran sent only an insignificant trade union delegation to Azerbaijan in August. Amidst the evidence of the demise of the Pahlavi regime, a session of the joint Soviet-Iranian F. Firdowsi prize committee met in Moscow on October 18-19, an anachronism from an era that was almost over.

Time was running out on the Shah, and Moscow prepared to show its hand. The first official Soviet statement on the events in Iran was made on November 19. Leonid Brezhnev, responding to a question allegedly from a *Pravda* correspondent concerning reports of U.S. interference and even possible military intervention, issued an unequivocal warning to "certain powers" to stay out of Iran:

> The Soviet Union, which maintains traditional, neighborly relations with Iran, resolutely states that it is against foreign interference in Iran's internal affairs by anyone, in any form and under any pretext. The events taking place there constitute a purely internal affair, and the questions involved in them should be decided by the Iranians themselves. All States should abide in this matter by the principles in the UN Charter and a number of other basic international documents, and should respect the sovereignty and and independence of Iran and its people.
>
> It must be also clear that any interference, especially military, in the affairs of Iran—a state directly bordering on the Soviet Union—would be regarded by the USSR as a matter affecting its security interests.[51]

The question-and-answer format was very likely a prearranged exercise, whereby *Pravda* was the venue in which the Soviet government could take a public stand on the Iranian situation and possible U.S. intervention without incurring the obligations inherent in a prepared foreign policy speech. Given the turmoil in Iran during the months preceding the fall of the Shah and the mixture of confusion and concern emanating from the United States, there was good reason for maintaining a flexible position. Brezhnev's warning, which was repeated in *Izvestiia* on November 21 and again in *Pravda* on November 26, drew a disclaimer from the U.S. secretary of state, who announced two days later that "the United States has no intention of interfering in the internal affairs of any country." The effect was to put the Shah on notice that he was on his own—at the very moment when he desperately needed every bit of support he could muster. Encouraged, the Soviet media escalated its coverage and criticisms. According to one Western observer:

> At some point between the appointment of the military government in early November and the second week in December, when the chances of the Shah's survival began to be questioned in the Soviet media, Moscow had come to the conclusion that it must prepare itself for a possible change of regime in Iran. It had hitherto been reluctant to criticize the Shah, fearing the emergence of an even more unfriendly regime to the south. The Soviet press had largely relied on quoting Western sources on the course of events in Iran. Soviet accounts therefore remained descriptive. Criticism, often of a most aggressive and irresponsible kind, was reserved for the West, especially the United States. Some Western observers have suggested that the Soviet Union actively sought to bring about the fall of the Shah. Even if this is true, it is likely that Moscow only decided to do so when it was convinced that the monarchy could not be rescued.[52]

By the time the Shah was forced to leave the country, the Soviet media had become vituperative, abandoning all pretense of impartiality. On January 25, 1979, *Izvestiia* wrote: "On January 16, His Majesty Mohammad Reza Pahlavi, Shah of Shahs, of Iran, left the country accompanied by the curses of his people and the lamentations of his parasites."[53] On February 12, 1979, Ayatollah Rouhollah Khomeini, the exiled cleric who had been the catalyst of the revolution, returned to Iran and established a revolutionary Islamic republic. The story is told that when Khomeini was exiled in 1963 to Iraq, the Shah telephoned and warned him to be good or else the Shah would put on his father's shoes and boot the Ayatollah. Khomeini replied that Reza Khan's boots were too big for the son. Apocryphal, but the Ayatollah did prove mightier than the Shah, and it was he who was to transform Iran's political system and relations with the outside world, including the Soviet Union.

OBSERVATIONS

During the period treated here, the Soviet Union and Iran dealt with each other on the basis of mutual advantage. Despite different systems and antithetical ideologies, they developed valued economic relations, kept their border quiet, and handled their regional rivalry pragmatically and prudently. Each derived considerable benefit from the normalized relationship, and Moscow must have watched the fall of the Shah with mingled uneasiness and expectancy.

Moscow had hoped that the start of a period of "peaceful co-existence" between the Soviet Union and Iran would eventually lead to friendly ties and a loosening of Iran's links to the West. The Shah's "independent national policy" was an improvement over his previous subservience to the United States. Given the stability such a policy brought to the Soviet-Iranian border, the autocratic consolidation of the Shah's internal power was not seen as a negative development, even if it did result in suppression of the Tudeh Party.

The Shah used the accommodation with Moscow to strengthen his rule. Diminished tension with the USSR gave him increased freedom to pursue regional ambitions in the Gulf.

If one uses the 1968–78 period as a time frame for assessment, the hypothesis that the greater the interaction the greater will be the influence of the stronger power is disproved. Although political, economic, as well as cultural, scientific, and military interactions significantly increased during this period, there is nothing to buttress the case that the USSR's influence increased.

On none of the issues in Soviet-Iranian relations did the Shah succumb to Soviet wishes: It must be remembered that the settlement of the Iraq-Iranian conflict on terms favorable to Iran developed out of a demonstration of Soviet military power on behalf of Iraq, and not out of anything intrinsic to the Soviet-Iranian relationship. The corollary that the larger the number of A's missions to B, the greater will be B's influence is difficult to evaluate because of the relatively small number of missions in most years. Overall, however, there was an approximate symmetry of exchanges: In some years Soviet missions visited Iran more often, while in others, the opposite was the case. The clustering of missions had little to do with the outcomes of issue areas.

The proposition that the greater A's aid to B, the greater is A's influence was not true. Soviet assistance to Iran (credits not grants) was important for Iranian industrialization, but there is no evidence that it brought influence. The most obvious argument against this proposition was the Shah's victory in obtaining a renegotiation of the price Moscow paid for natural gas. Economic assistance did not translate into political influence, or, for that matter, any kind of influence. Paradoxically, Soviet aid may almost be said to have subtly increased the Shah's options and influence in his dealings with C, that is, the United States.

Finally, the proposition that the greater the presence of A in B, the more likely is A to exercise influence over B proved false. The presence of some 1,500 Soviet technicians in Iran did not affect the Shah's foreign or domestic policies. Soviet technicians were kept under tight surveillance and they did the specific job for which they were hired. The Soviet presence alone was not enough to ensure the exercise of influence.

Judging by the experience of the decade under consideration, the Soviet Union's influence was, at best, indirect, and not at all the consequence of specific inputs affecting directly related issue areas.

With the Shah's fall, uncertainty reappeared as a norm in Soviet-Iranian relations, and with it new tensions and a need for a restructured set of ties.

NOTES

1. Rouhollah K. Ramazani, *Iran's Foreign Policy 1941-1973* (Charlottesville: University Press of Virginia, 1975), see Chapter XIII.

2. E. A. Bayne, "Notes Toward a Study of Iranian Foreign Relations, Part II: The King as Policymaker," American Universities Field Staff (hereafter referred to as AUFS), Reports Source, Southwest Asia Series 14, no. 3 (Iran) (November 1965):12.

3. *Kayhan International*, January 22, 1972.

4. New York *Times*, April 22, 1973.

5. Alvin J. Cottrell, "The Foreign Policy of the Shah," *Strategic Review* 3, no. 4 (Fall 1975):36.

6. Ibid.

7. New York *Times*, September 29, 1974.

8. Bayne, 11-12.

9. CIA, National Foreign Assessment Center, *Communist Aid to Less Developed Countries of the Free World, 1977* (Washington, D.C., November 1978), 31.

10. William H. Cooper, "The Impact of the Iranian Revolution on the Soviet Union," in U.S. Congress, Joint Economic Committee, 96th Cong. 1st sess., November 19, 1979, *Economic Consequences of the Revolution in Iran* (Washington, D.C.: U.S. Government Printing Office, 1980), 164.

11. Ibid.

12. The agreement for IGAT-2 was signed in 1975 and involved Iran, the USSR, and the Federal Republic of Germany. Predicated on close, long-term Soviet-Iranian economic ties, it called for Iran to deliver 13.4 billion cubic meters of gas to the USSR annually until 2001, and for the USSR to provide the same quantity to the FRG. During a visit to Tehran on April 12, 1978, the chairman of the USSR State committee for Foreign Economic Relations, S.A. Skachkov, signed the agreement for the final section, the project being scheduled for completion in 1980.

13. FBIS/IRAN, July 26, 1973, K2.

14. FBIS/IRAN, January 25, 1974, K1.

15. *USSR and Third World* 4, no. 3 (March 4-April 21, 1974):152.

16. Ibid., 153.

17. FBIS/IRAN, June 5, 1974, R4.

18. *Kayhan International* 5, no. 318 (June 1, 1974):7.

19. Ibid.

20. *The Times* (London), July 1, 1974.

21. *The Times*, July 3, 1974.

22. *Kayhan International* 5, no. 323 (July 6, 1974):1.

23. Ibid.

24. *Kayhan International* 5, no. 325 (July 20, 1974):4.

25. FBIS/IRAN, July 12, 1974, R1.

26. *USSR and Third World* 4, no. 3 (July 29-September 8, 1974):360.

27. *Kayhan International* 5, no. 331 (August 31, 1974):6.

28. FBIS/USSR, August 22, 1974, F4.

29. As quoted in Daniel Dishon, ed., *Middle East Record, Vol. Four: 1968* (New York: John Wiley, 1973), 58.

30. A. Yodfat and M. Abir, *In the Direction of the Persian Gulf: The Soviet Union and the Persian Gulf* (London: Frank Cass, 1977), 67.

31. Ramazani, 417.

32. For details of the complex Iranian-Iraqi-Soviet diplomacy in this crisis, I have drawn on my essay, "Air Support in the Arab East," in Stephen S. Kaplan, ed. *Diplomacy of Power: Soviet Armed Forces As a Political Instrument* (Washington, D.C.: The Brookings Institution, 1981).

33. On September 29, 1980, Prime Minister Menachem Begin disclosed that Israel had armed and trained Kurdish rebels when they fought the Baath from 1965 to 1975. New York *Times*, September 30, 1980.

34. *Middle East Intelligence Survey* 2 (June 15, 1974):48.

35. *CDSP* 26, no. 44 (November 27, 1974):19.

36. Quoted in *USSR and Third World* 4, Nos. 7 and 8 (October 14-November 24 1974):466-67.

37. *Washington Post*, January 21, 1975.

38. *Arab Report and Record*, December 16-31, 1974, 576.

39. *Pravda*, February 2, 1975.

40. FBIS/USSR, March 16, 1973, B2-B3.

41. FBIS/USSR, August 7, 1973, B3.

42. FBIS/USSR, September 1, 1976, F1.

43. FBIS/USSR, September 10, 1976, F10.

44. FBIS/USSR, December 2, 1976, F7.

45. FBIS/USSR, November 5, 1975, F6.

46. P. Mezentsev, "Iran: Petrodollars and Politics," *New Times*, no. 5 (January 1978), 14.

47. Shahram Chubin, *Soviet Policy Towards Iran and the Gulf* (London: International Institute for Strategic Studies, Adelphi Paper 157, 1980), 14.

48. Dmitry Volsky, "Security or Confrontation?" *New Times*, no. 2 (January 1976), 8.

49. *Washington Post*, September 2, 1978.

50. George Lenczowski, "The Arc of Crisis: Its Central Sector," *Foreign Affairs* 57, no. 4 (Spring 1979):806.

51. *Pravda*, November 19, 1978.

52. Stelianos Scarlis, "Two Examples of Soviet Reporting: Coverage of the Shah of Iran and Idi Amin," Radio Free Europe-Radio Liberty, RK 251/79 (August 23, 1979), 6.

53. *Izvestiia*, January 25, 1979.

5

THE SOVIET-IRANIAN INFLUENCE
RELATIONSHIP UNDER KHOMEINI

Moscow watched the toppling of the Shah and the unfolding of the Iranian revolution with mingled anticipation and anxiety: No other internal upheaval and political turnabout in the Third World had brought such immediate gain and promising opportunity. But the end of stability in Iran had also created new problems for the USSR along its southern border and in its relations with the United States.

The boon for Moscow was a grave defeat for Washington. The new revolutionary government, deriving its authority from Ayatollah Rouhollah Khomeini, quickly reversed the political-strategic orientation of the former regime, and the process of de-Westernization began. First, the multinational corporations, especially the American firms, were expelled. Khomeini considered it essential to remove the underpinnings of the Shah's industrialization program in order to Islamicize Iran, a step that consequently proved to be a major cause of the country's economic decline. Second, the two American-manned electronic intelligence collection stations, one adjacent to the Soviet border near Bandar Shah on the shores of the Caspian Sea, and other in Kabkam, a desolate spot in the mountains 80 miles south of Meshed, were shut down. No longer could the United States use them to gather data on Soviet nuclear and missile testing in Soviet Central Asia. (Ironically, their loss was a blow to Soviet hopes of U.S. ratification of the SALT II treaty, because it strengthened the position of those in the U.S. Senate who opposed the treaty on the ground that effective verification of Soviet compliance had been seriously weakened.) Third, Iran immediately reduced arms purchases and withdrew from the role of policeman for the Persian Gulf, thus depriving the United States of a reliable ally who could safeguard Western interests in the region. Should the Soviet-backed People's Democratic Republic of Yemen attempt to foment another insurrection in the Dhofar province of Oman, Iran would not now send troops to defend the pro-Western Sultan as it had in 1973-75. Nor would it help any of the other Arab monarchs on the Arabian Peninsula, to whom in the long run Khomeini's religious fundamentalism is a far greater threat than the Shah's imperial ambitions ever were—though since the start of the Iraqi-Iranian war in September 1980 their fear that the Iranian revolution would spread has markedly subsided.

Fourth, Iran opted for a policy of nonalignment. It withdrew from CENTO, thereby removing a link from the U.S. chain of containment. Interestingly, however, the Iranian government has to date not explicitly abrogated its 1959 mutual security agreement with the United States, thus suggesting a cautious desire to retain a possible U.S. option. Though too much should not be made of what was an executive agreement and not a formal treaty ratified by the legislative bodies of both countries, Soviet propagandists often raise the matter in their broadcasts in Persian to Iran:

> ... it is natural that one of the most pressing points for Iranian foreign policy should be the earliest possible cancellation of Iran's unequal agreements with imperialist countries, particularly the 1959 agreement with the United States. Bearing in mind that the danger of imperialist attempts on the national sovereignty of Iran and other Persian Gulf countries has not only remained constant but, on the contrary, has increased, it is clear that the earliest possible shedding of the heavy burden from the past is of the utmost importance.[1]

Fifth, Khomeini embraced the anti-American grouping in the Arab world. He stopped selling oil to Israel and severed all connections with it by the end of February 1979; broke off diplomatic relations with Egypt on April 30, 1979; and recognized the Palestine Liberation Organization (PLO), turning over to it the Israeli embassy. Iran's alignment with the Arab states who opposed President Jimmy Carter's Camp David initiative and the settlement between Egypt and Israel was a stunning setback not only for Israel but for Egypt as well, as E. M. Primakov, director of the Institute of Oriental Studies of the USSR Academy of Sciences, indicated in an interview with a Lebanese journalist:

> The Iranian revolution greatly complicates the American game in the Middle East. Actually, Iran is not only fully out of this game after taking, under the Shah, a very active part in it, but has also become a force openly hostile to the anti-Arab machinations of the USA and Israel. Iran has given unreserved support for the PLO and the right of the Arab people of Palestine to establish their own state. It spoke out strongly against the capitulatory deal of As-Sadat, the American-Israeli model for a Middle Eastern settlement.[2]

Khomeini's triumph was a blow to U.S. credibility, and as such a boost to Soviet diplomacy. Perhaps more than any other defeat experienced by the United States in the 1970s, it signified abroad that for the defense of even its closest clients, the United States was no longer able, or willing, to ignore the cost. The Soviet media had only to quote from U.S. newspapers, lamenting the record of retreat and defeat from Vietnam to Angola and the inconstancy of Washington's policy toward South Korea and Japan, to buttress its contention that the United States was not a reliable patron.

Finally, the communist and pro-Moscow Tudeh Party was permitted to emerge into the open after a long period of illegal existence under the Shah. It quickly came out in support of Khomeini and aligned itself with the revolution, notwithstanding serious ideological differences between it and the Islamic Republican Party (IRP), the political instrument forged by the activist religious leaders around Khomeini to institutionalize theocratic power.

Thus, the Khomeini regime virtually eliminated all the persistent sources of tension between Moscow and the Shah: the operation of U.S. intelligence bases on Iranian territory, Iran's role as surrogate of the United States in the Persian Gulf, Iran's alliance with the West, and its suppression of the Communist Party. There were seemingly no bars to even better relations than had existed during the final decade of the Shah's rule—at least not from the Soviet side. During these early days of the revolution and the confusion attending the move from alignment to nonalignment, Moscow learned a great deal about some of the most advanced military hardware in the U.S. arsenal. It undoubtedly obtained manuals and photographs of the F-14 Tomcat fighter aircraft, as well as samples of the A1M-54A Phoenix air-to-air missile, the improved version of the Hawk antiaircraft missile, and other sophisticated weapons. Presidents Nixon, Ford, and Carter, in selling the Shah virtually all of the advanced weaponry that he wanted (but could not possibly use effectively), provided the Soviet military, through its KGB operatives in Iran, with a windfall of top-secret U.S. arms.

Though Soviet journals described the Iranian revolution as a gain for progressive forces, the terms "national-democratic revolution" and "victory for socialism" are not used unreservedly as they are for the Afghan revolution that brought to power the Communist Party, "the vanguard of progressive forces." Whereas the fashioning and consolidation of the Afghan revolution was considered to have been swift and decisive, the "crash of absolutism" in Iran was qualifiedly praised: "With the fall of the monarchy, with the victory of the anti-Shah revolution, real prerequisites are being formed for the successful solution of problems of democracy and social changes in the country."[3] But, the argument continues, since the revolution is not a completed communist revolution, the period ahead, to which the USSR is "not indifferent," can be expected to face hardship: "The changes in the country are monumental, but ahead lies a difficult time for the creation of the new [society]."[4]

Moscow regarded the Iranian situation as "complex" but promising, and sought early to develop friendly relations with the new government. It contrasted the USSR's offer of friendship with the dangers from U.S. plots to generate a CIA-backed counterrevolution.[5] On March 1, 1979, *Pravda* noted the worldwide support for the new regime, but warned of the danger from "imperialism," that is, the United States:

> Thus, a process of stabilization of the revolutionary regime in Iran— a strengthening and deepening of the positive changes that the Iranian people have won in a difficult and bloody struggle—has become apparent in both its domestic and international aspects. *However*, this outcome clearly does not suit imperialist strategists. There are repeated calls for the use of force in the Persian Gulf region to defend American interests. At the same time a mythical Soviet threat to Iran is being noised about. Everything possible is being done to incite protests and plots by Iranian reaction within the country.

As events unfolded with unforeseeable confusion, verging on quasi-anarchy, relations between the Soviet Union and Iran entered a troubled period. Moscow has watched the turmoil, disappointed by the chaotic environment, occasionally attempting an initiative, but for the most part circumspect and unhurried in its approach. It senses that out of the turbulence may emerge a rare opportunity for even further strategic and political advantage.

Soviet-Iranian relations in the Khomeini period are not easy to analyze, because of the absence in Tehran of a stable government or a coherent foreign policy. Thus the notion of influence, which presupposes an interactive process between essentially stable political leaderships who were able to formulate policy on specific issues in a fairly consistent and rational manner, is difficult to apply in any systematic way. The criteria, indeed even the kinds of data, that were salient in assessing the Soviet-Iranian relationship in the Shah's period are not always applicable (for example, there are no longer any joint communiqués) and must, for the moment, be used more tentatively.

The issues wax and wane in importance, largely as a consequence of the vagaries of Iranian domestic factional strife, but also because they are overshadowed by Iran's absorption with its relations with Iraq and the United States. Those issues that have loomed large in the Soviet-Iranian relationship since Khomeini came to power are the Soviet attempt to normalize relations, the communist takeover of Afghanistan, the Iraqi-Iranian war, the price of natural gas, and Soviet interference in Iran's domestic turmoil.

THE LIMITS OF NORMALIZATION

After the fall of the rump Regency Council established by the Shah on the eve of his flight from Iran, the Soviet Union promptly recognized the provisional government of Prime Minister Mehdi Barzagan, who took office in mid-February 1979 with the sanction of Ayatollah Khomeini, the father of the revolution. Khomeini was not without a sense of geopolitical realities, for his first meeting with a foreign envoy was with Soviet Ambassador Vladimir M. Vinogradov on February 25.[6]

On March 3 Brezhnev publicly hailed the triumph of the revolution and expressed the hope that "good neighborliness will fruitfully develop"; a month later he congratulated Khomeini on the occasion of the proclamation of the Islamic Republic of Iran.[7] Soviet officials repeatedly noted that "during the Iranian people's struggle against the monarchy the USSR resolutely sided with the Iranian revolution and did everything to prevent outside interference in Iran's affairs and to block plans for armed intervention against the revolution," an allusion to Brezhnev's warning of November 19, 1978, against outside interference.[8] Barzagan called for "strengthening understanding and cooperation" between Iran and the USSR and in May sent Dr. Mohammad Mokri to assume the post of ambassador in Moscow. The signs seemed promising for continuation of the good state-to-state relationship that had existed during the previous decade.

Nevertheless, dissonant voices were soon heard, and domestic considerations began to strain Soviet-Iranian relations. Many in Khomeini's entourage were suspicious of the Soviet Union for a variety of reasons: ingrained anticommunism, hostility to Soviet atheism, traditional Iranian fear of the covetous imperialist neighbor to the north, the communist coup in Afghanistan in April 1978, and Moscow's insistence on reaffirming the operativeness of Articles V and VI of the 1921 Soviet-Iranian treaty, under which Soviet forces could intervene in Iranian affairs in the interests of self-defense if a third country threatened to attack the USSR from Iranian territory or if Moscow considered its border threatened. The conciliatory attitude expressed by Ambassador Mokri in May and June 1979 was not the mood in Qum, the holy city where Khomeini made his headquarters.

The immediate cause of tension was Ayatollah Khomeini's charges of Soviet aggression in Afghanistan and involvement in Iraq's fueling of Arab discontent in the oil-producing province of Khuzistan in southern Iran.[9] An exchange of messages in July between Khomeini and Brezhnev did nothing to ease the growing acrimony. In early September Soviet commentators criticized the concept of an Islamic state and attacked Khomeini by name for the first time.[10] Moscow's response to the anticommunist and anti-Soviet expressions emanating from Khomeini, his crackdown on Kurdish separatists, and his hostility toward the secularist National Democratic Front, which was a major rival of the Islamic Republican Party, reflected its concern over what it viewed as the unfavorable course of the Iranian revolution. The juxtaposition of both critical and laudatory commentaries in the Soviet press suggested the existence of contradictory assessments in the Kremlin.

The Kremlin was its own worst enemy on the matter of normalization. Its insistence on the validity of the Soviet-Iranian treaty of February 26, 1921, notwithstanding repeated repudiations by Iranian authorities, both under the Shah and Khomeini, served as an ever-present reminder of Russian imperial ambitions. Moscow's reaffirmation of the treaty on February 27, 1979, two days after Khomeini's meeting with the Soviet ambassador, aroused Iranian uncertainty about Soviet intentions and may well have been Moscow's heavyhanded way of making Tehran sensitive to its wishes. The Soviet press's frequent citations of the treaty as evidence of the USSR's commitment to the independence of Iran were perceived by the Iranians as an implicit threat.[11] Tehran explicitly abrogated the offensive articles on November 5, 1979, but Moscow blandly ignored the move.[12]

THE AFGHAN CRISIS

Afghanistan has been a disquieting factor in Soviet-Iranian relations ever since the communist coup in Kabul in April 1978, though the Iranian government had little time to devote to the matter in the final chaotic months of the Shah's rule. However, almost from its first days in power, the Khomeini regime criticized Soviet intervention in the internal affairs of Afghanistan, and leading figures such as Ayatollah Shariatmadari openly espoused the cause of the Afghan freedom-fighters who were resisting the Soviet-backed Taraki government. The Afghan government responded with denunciations of interference, interspersed with reconciliatory offers of friendly relations.

The Soviet presence in Afghanistan became a prominent issue in Soviet-Iranian relations after June 12, 1979, when Khomeini warned Ambassador Vinogradov against interfering in Afghanistan or fomenting unrest in the Kurdish and Baluch areas of Iran. Vinogradov denied all Soviet involvement, though the Soviet press presented the agitation in Kurdistan in a sympathetic light.[13] The meeting put Moscow on notice of Khomeini's anger, which was vented two months later in a call for the Afghans to rise against the puppet communist regime. After Hafizullah Amin ousted Taraki in late September, Iran's deputy prime minister and government spokesman, Sadeq Tabataba'i, said this "quiet coup d'état" in

Kabul meant a hardening of policy toward the freedom-fighters and an indication that Moscow would not give up Afghanistan as a Soviet base, because it could in the future provide easy access to the Indian Ocean.[14] Regarding the reassurances that the Soviet ambassador had sent Ayatollah Khomeini concerning the USSR's noninterference in the internal affairs of Afghanistan, he noted that after reading the message Khomeini laughed and said, "Sometimes a liar does not realize that the person spoken to knows that he is lying, and sometimes the liar knows that he is lying and knows that the one spoken to has not believed him. What Soviet ambassador said was the second type of lying." Iranian leaders had no illusions about their northern neighbor.

A sudden and dangerous deterioration in U.S.-Iranian relations, already poor in the post-Shah climate of recrimination and condemnation of past U.S. policy, provided the Soviet Union with a rare opportunity to demonstrate its support for Iran's revolutionary regime and divert attention away from its involvement in Afghanistan. On November 4, 1979, Iranian militants seized the U.S. Embassy in Tehran, precipitating a 444-day crisis. Moscow moved to exploit the mounting tension and improve its standing with the Khomeini government. It upheld the essential justifiability of the incarceration of the 52 Americans, though not openly sanctioning the embassy takeover. Its attempted manipulation of the hostage crisis took on added intensity after the full-scale Soviet military invasion of Afghanistan in late December 1979. As matters turned out, however, the Soviet leadership was too clever by half: Its transparently pro-Iranian position on the hostage issue failed to ingratiate it with Tehran or to deflect Iranian criticism away from the Soviet intervention in Afghanistan. Moreover, it had itself to blame for the stepped-up deterioration of U.S.-Soviet relations and for the U.S. Senate's unwillingness to consider ratification of the SALT II treaty.

The Soviet official attitude was at first one of studied correctness. It endorsed the various UN Security Council resolutions calling for release of the Americans, but never came out openly and unequivocally for their release nor even explicitly condemned the seizure itself. On November 21, during a visit to Madrid, Soviet Foreign Minister Andrei Gromyko expressed the hope that "this problem is going to have a satisfactory solution."[15] Two days later, in Bonn, he said:

> We support the international convention requiring respect for diplomatic immunity for those who represent their governments abroad. This is the stand we have adopted, and when the matter was brought before the Security Council we made it known to the governments of the United States and Iran. I would like to express the hope that this affair will be resolved to the mutual satisfaction of both parties. But the parties, including the United States, must display restraint and clear-headedness so as not to allow emotions to spill across borders.[16]

This was the strongest Soviet statement made during the lengthy crisis. Whenever criticized by Washington for its unhelpful attitude, Moscow invariably referred back to Gromyko's Bonn statement.

It was quickly evident that Moscow was currying Iranian good will. Soon after returning from Bonn, Gromyko met with the Iran's ambassador, who said that the question of the hostages inside the U.S. Embassy in Tehran "was never once raised."[17] The Soviet media concentrated more on denouncing U.S. imperialism in Iran than on upholding the principle of diplomatic immunity. One Soviet official told an American journalist that the USSR favors "observance of the relevant international convention on respecting the diplomatic immunity" of the American hostages, but significantly added, "I think it would be a mistake for you to expect us to do more than that."[18]

On December 5, in an editorial in *Pravda*, signed with a pseudonym (Alexei Petrov), always an indication of an authoritative statement, the Kremlin made its first comment. It accused the United States of intensifying the crisis and turning it "into one of the serious conflicts of the postwar period." By the "flagrant military-political pressure" being brought to bear on Iran and by the extensive military preparations in the adjacent area, the United States

> is actually resorting to blackmail against another sovereign state.... it is claimed that this is happening in answer to the fact that members of the U.S. embassy staff in Tehran are being held as hostages, which is contrary to the standards of international law. The seizure of the American embassy is undoubtedly not in keeping with the international convention on respect for diplomatic privileges and immunity. This act, however, cannot be taken out of the overall context of American-Iranian relations.[19]

The article then denounced past U.S. interference in Iran on behalf of "the arbitrary and lawless rule of the Shah," deplored Washington's refusal to extradite the Shah or return his wealth, and declared that "the present attempts by the United States to blackmail Iran by massing armed forces on her frontiers and dictate a line of conduct to her by force are a gross violation of the standard of international law." It made no mention of UN Security Council resolutions calling for the hostages' release; nor did it criticize the Iranians in any way. Instead, the onus was placed squarely on the United States.

All pretense at objectivity disappeared after the Soviet invasion of Afghanistan later in the month. Inflammatory attacks on the United States and sensationalist reports of imminent U.S. military action against Iran intensified in the wake of the growing Soviet repression in Afghanistan. The Soviet press spawned dire warnings about the dangerous situation created by the United States and insinuated Iran's need to rely on the good-neighborliness and support of the Soviet Union. This was the message also of all broadcasts beamed to Iran in Persian and Arabic, the most scurrilous being that of the "National Voice of Iran," which operates out of Baku in Soviet Azerbaijan, not far from the Iranian border.

The Soviet Union's partisanship on the hostage crisis did not succeed in muting Tehran's criticisms of the military intervention in Afghanistan. On December 29, 1979, the Iranian foreign minister, Sadeq Ghotbzadeh, issued a strongly worded protest:

> The Islamic government of Iran cannot agree with military inter-
> vention by any country in another country, especially military inter-
> vention by a superpower in a small country . . . because Afghanistan is a
> Moslem country and a neighbor of Iran, the military intervention of the
> government of the Soviet Union . . . is considered a hostile measure not
> only against the people of the country but against all Moslems of the
> world.

Despite Moscow's assurance that it would "not tolerate any outside interference in Iran's internal affairs,"[20] and its veto on January 14 of a UN Security Council resolution calling for economic sanctions against Iran, Iranian officials, caught up in the election campaign for the first president of the Islamic republic, sharply denounced the USSR's military intervention: Ghotbzadeh alleged a Soviet buildup near the Iranian border; and Abolhassan Bani-Sadr, the finance minister, said Moscow wanted to partition Iran and drive on from Afghanistan to the Indian Ocean. Criticisms reached the point that Gromyko felt impelled, on January 27, 1980, to deny any troop movements or threat to Iran's territorial integrity.

On February 4, 1980, on the occasion of his inauguration as president, Bani-Sadr dismissed Moscow's claim that its intervention had been a response to American, Chinese, and Pakistani interference, and he insisted on its unconditional withdrawal. The next day, replying to a congratulatory message from Brezhnev on the occasion of the revolution's first anniversary, Khomeini rebuked the Soviets for their invasion of Afghanistan and ordered a boycott of the Moscow Olympic Games. To these and similar reprimands, Moscow reacted with relative mildness, avoiding any direct attack on Khomeini, while upholding Iran's case against the the United States, and reiterating the "complexity" of internal developments in Iran.

In early April 1980, TASS denounced President Carter's new economic pressures against Iran and the military buildup in the Persian Gulf region. The Soviet government, sensing a tightening of the economic noose, printed a full page ad in its English-language newspaper, *Moscow News*, offering Iran full use of transit privileges across the USSR.[21] Its frequent warnings that the United States would use force against Iran seemed vindicated by the U.S. rescue attempt of April 25 (albeit abortive). However, Ghotbzadeh pointed out that the Soviet Union had done nothing to contribute to the failure of the U.S. effort, and he persisted in his criticisms of Soviet Afghan policy, eliciting sharp rejoinders from the Soviet press.[22]

On June 30, 1980, an important Soviet diplomat was expelled from Iran—the first expulsion since the Shah's overthrow—allegedly for spying. Ghotbzadeh accused the Soviets of meddling and the Tudeh of operating as an agent of the Soviet Union. As a result, he closed the USSR's consulate in Rasht and reduced the number of its diplomats in Iran.

It was against this background that Iran's foreign minister sent an extraordinary diplomatic note to Soviet Foreign Minister Gromyko.[23] Much of Ghotbzadeh's florid style, contempt, and irony is apparently lost in translation,[24] but what emerges in English is sufficiently pungent and revealing of Iranian thinking. Professing "utmost respect" for Gromyko's "distinguished status" as "the most experienced foreign minister in the world" and a desire to discuss Soviet-Iranian relations "frankly and without any concealment," but "in such a way as not to cause offense . . . particularly when your next-door neighbor witnesses your government's great effort in establishing and strengthening its domination over certain parts of this world, the most recent of which is the military invasion of Afghanistan," Ghotbzadeh mentioned the struggle of "our young Islamic Republic" against the hegemonistic United States, but focused his contumely on the Soviet Union. Iran will not forget the USSR's attack on Iran in 1941 "under the pretext of the presence and activities of the Nazis in Iran in accordance with the imposed Articles V and VI of the 1921 friendship treaty"; or the emergence of "a party which from its inception up to the present has been and continues to be your government's fifth column on the soil of our dear country"; or the absence of any anti-Shah demonstrations by Iranians residing in the USSR in the 25 years after the coup d'état of August 19, 1953; or the USSR's participation in "the shameful festivities marking the imperial regime's 2,500th anniversary," such that "our nation could not see much difference between your socialism and U.S. capitalism." Coming to the present period, he accused the USSR of being as "satanic" (a favorite phrase of Khomeini's) as the United States; of shipping arms to rebels in Kurdistan; of failing to call the Iranian Islamic revolution by its correct title; of refusing to acknowledge Iran's abrogation of Articles V and VI of the 1921 treaty, thus compounding Iran's fear of the treaty's serving "as a pretext to launch aggression and attacks against our country;" of using the difficulty between Iran and the United States, suddenly, "under an imaginary pretext," to send troops into "our neighboring and coreligionist country,

Afghanistan," and crush its people. "Your utterances," charged Ghotbzadeh, "are socialistic while your deeds are imperialistic." How can we rely on your assurances "that our Baluchistan, on the borders of Afghanistan, will not be attacked by your troops?" He asked for a Soviet withdrawal from Afghanistan and an end to espionage activities by the Soviet embassy in Tehran. His concluding call for "true neighborly relations" in effect emphasized the severity of the censure.

If Ghotbzadeh's intent was to provoke an angry Soviet response that could be used internally to discredit Moscow and to strengthen the Iranian factions who wanted to keep *all* foreign policy options open, including even a deal with the United States on the hostages and on other outstanding problems, then it clearly failed. Gromyko's reply was cool and low-key and was not delivered until late August, when Moscow knew that Ghotbzadeh was to be removed from the post of foreign minister and from the cabinet. Soviet broadcasts labeled the contents of Ghotbzadeh's note "a collection of illusions and discredited imperialist items and propaganda and distortion of facts."[25] But if the substance of his arguments reflects the views of a broad spectrum of the Iranian political scene, then it is likely that no prospective leadership group on the horizon is apt to have any illusions about ultimate Soviet intentions toward Iran.

The Soviet occupation of Afghanistan is a major impediment to improved relations between Moscow and Tehran, certainly as long as Khomeini lives. Not even the eruption on September 22, 1980, of the Iraqi-Iranian war, with Iran's obvious desire that the USSR be a disinterested observer instead of a partisan patron of Iraq as could be expected from the Soviet-Iraqi friendship treaty of April 1972, diminished Tehran's hostility on the Afghan issue. In the late fall of 1980, as the hostage crisis drew toward an end, Iran did downgrade the Afghan problem, but that was because of preoccupation with the United States and not the result of a policy shift. On December 27, thousands of Afghans demonstrated violently in front of the Soviet embassy in Tehran, as they had a year earlier, and Moscow issued a stern warning: "No one should have any doubt that the Soviet Union will have to protect the legitimate rights and interests of the Soviet state and its citizens if the Iranian government does not want or is not in a position to do its duty regarding the insurance of the safety of Soviet institutions and their personnel in Iran." Iranian authorities, not eager for trouble, kept the demonstrators in check and concentrated on bringing the hostage issue to an end. The settlement on January 20, 1981, was, judging by the cynical and incendiary commentaries of the Soviet media, a keen disappointment to Moscow, which had expected the 444-day crisis and the accompanying anti-Americanism to perpetuate U.S.-Iranian hostility and divert attention away from the war it was waging in Afghanistan.[26]

THE IRAQI-IRANIAN WAR

Since Iraq invaded Iran on September 22, 1980, the Soviet Union has adopted a position of official neutrality and tried to avoid actions that would irreparably alienate either side. It eschewed labelling Iraq the aggressor, which Iraq obviously was, in order not to foreclose any option. In Moscow, on September 23, the Iranian ambassador said he had been "formally assured" that the Soviet government "intended to remain neutral" in the conflict.[27] That day, too, *Izvestiia* laid out the essential Soviet line: that the conflict was a vestige of the two countries' colonial past; that the United States sought to exploit the war in order to gain control over the region's oil; that the United States hoped the conflict would lessen Iran's ability "to resist the imperialist pressure that is being brought on it" (in the context of the hostage crisis); and that Washington saw Iraq's involvement in a war against Iran as a chance to reorient Iraq's foreign policy toward the United States.[28]

As in 1974-75, the Iraqi-Iranian conflict created dilemmas for Soviet leaders. Whereas previously the tilt had been toward Baghdad, with whom they had a friendship treaty, in 1980 the subtleties of their policy suggested more a desire to court Iran than to reinforce Iraq. The potential for further strategic gains was greater in Iran, where the phobia about the United States, the internal unrest and disruption, and the rational case for friendship with the USSR appeared tailored to closer Soviet-Iranian relations. Morover, Moscow was disenchanted with Iraq, which had condemned Soviet policy in Afghanistan, threatened the pro-Soviet regime in Syria, effected a rapprochement with monarchical, pro-Western Saudi Arabia, made its major purchases of industrial equipment from Western suppliers, and suppressed the Iraqi Communist Party. A hint of how far Moscow was prepared to go in order to cement Soviet-Iranian ties was revealed by Iranian Prime Minister Mohammad Ali Rajai, according to whom Soviet Ambassador Vinogradov had on October 4 made Iran an offer of Soviet arms. The offer was rejected, and Rajai condemned Soviet interference in the internal affairs of Iran and Afghanistan and cast doubt on Moscow's asseverations of neutrality in the Gulf conflict.[29]

Iran's occasional accusations that the Soviet Union was helping Iraq with arms shipments[30] and supplying military advisers for Iraqi troop operations[31] were promptly denied by Soviet sources. In early February 1981, an Iraqi official declared that the USSR was no longer "implementing prewar contracts with Iraq,"[32] but precise information on Soviet arms deliveries to Iraq or Iran is difficult to obtain. However, given Moscow's continuing objective of maintaining close ties with both Baghdad and Tehran and forestalling a decided shift by either toward the United States, the reality may be that Moscow sends modest amounts to

Iraq, using East European countries as conduits, and holds open the offer of similar sales to Tehran, which reportedly has received some shipments of Soviet arms from Syria, Libya, and North Korea.

Throughout the early stage of the war, when it overlapped with the hostage crisis, Moscow seemed especially patient with Iranian criticisms of Soviet policy, believing that this would allay Iran's concern and induce a turn to the Soviet Union, the only power willing to help Tehran. Conversely, Moscow treated Iraq with a coolness that belied their treaty relationship. Indeed, at the Twenty-sixth Congress of the CPSU in Moscow in late February 1981, the leader of the Iraqi Communist Party, presumably with the Kremlin's approval, denounced Iraq's Baathist leadership for waging war against Iran and called for a withdrawal from Iranian territory occupied since the conflict began. Moreover, the Baath, in contrast to its position at the previous congress in 1976, when it had "lavished praise on Moscow," this time did not send any representatives, a further indication of the strained relationship between Moscow and Baghdad.[33] Yet a little more than a month later, mindful that Iraq is slated to succeed Cuba in 1982 as the head of the nonaligned movement, that the conflict may drag on for a long time, and that indifference may needlessly alienate Iraq, the Soviet press was ordered to give special attention to the nineteenth anniversary of the signing of the Soviet-Iraqi friendship treaty and to stress the importance of good relations between the two countries and the continuing Soviet friendship. Moscow is hedging its bets.

Moscow has not been able to use the Iraqi-Iranian war to advance its courtship of Iran. This is partly due to Iraq's inability to subdue Iran, which therefore is not pressed to seek significant assistance from another power: Iran's unexpectedly determined resistance rests on the tenacity of the Revolutionary Guards who contest every foot of territory and also on the military infrastructure and production capability bequeathed by the Shah.[34] The current situation on the battlefield has assuredly not helped Moscow's policy of tying Iran more closely to the Soviet Union and has damaged Soviet prospects, not only in Tehran but in Baghdad as well.

THE PRICE OF NATURAL GAS

The period of dislocation attending the fall of the Shah was so short that Moscow anticipated a rapid reestablishement of the extensive economic cooperation that had characterized Soviet-Iranian relations during the years before the end of Pahlavi rule. Iranian oil production had declined in the latter part of 1978 and natural gas shipments had been disrupted, making the winter of 1978-79 a cold one for the Soviet Union's

Armenian and Azerbaijanian republics, but these were regarded as temporary developments, since all the pumping facilities and pipelines remained intact.

Revolutions, however, never follow predictable courses. Within weeks after coming to power, the new régime was accusing the USSR of having profiteered "by buying Iranian gas cheaply and reselling it at three times the price."[35] Soviet sources decried this as "distortion of facts," arguing that "the export of gas to the Soviet Union was profitable for Iran." They expounded the mutually advantageous nature of Soviet-Iranian economic relations, in particular, the sale of natural gas, which otherwise would be burnt off wastefully,[36] and the agreement signed by the USSR, Iran, West Germany, France, and Czechoslovakia for the purchase and sale of gas through a prospective second Iranian Natural Gas Trunkline (IGAT-2), construction of which had begun in 1974 and was due for completion in 1981.[37]

Moscow welcomed the resumption in April 1979 of natural gas shipments from IGAT-1 (which had provided about 10 billion cubic meters of gas annually during most of the 1970-78 period), albeit at levels far below capacity, and hoped that the construction of IGAT-2 could proceed. Despite Iranian hints at a need for new pricing arrangments, for the moment at least, the Soviets were more interested in obtaining assurances on supply than on price. Their uncertainty was heightened by the turnover in Iranian ministries and the inability of officials to make decisions. During his meeting with Vinogradov in June, Khomeini implied that IGAT-2 would not be built. The reason was not merely Soviet policy in Afghanistan, but, perhaps more important in those early heady months of revolutionary change, the Ayatollah's millenarian vision of an Islamic society that was antithetical to modernization and such grandiose industrial projects as IGAT-2.

On July 18, 1979, five days after Khomeini sent a message to Gromyko, the Iranian director of the Planning and Budget Organization announced cancellation of IGAT-2, saying merely that the final decision had been made "a few days ago."[38] The visit in late May by Semyon Skachkov, the head of the USSR's State Committee for Foreign Economic Relations, and Vinogradov's personal intercession with Khomeini in June had failed to save the project that would have knit the Iranian economy closer to the USSR. This disappointment was followed by a formal demand for a higher price for the gas supplied through IGAT-1. Moscow tried to put on a good face by playing up the visit in late July of an Iranian economic delegation—the first since the revolution—that came to discuss plans for completing the expansion of the Soviet-built steel mill in Isfahan; and another that came in October to arrange for a new power station. These interactions were exceptions, however, not the norm. In the fall the flow of natural gas dropped off as a result of the decrease in oil production. Unlike the winter of 1978-79, this time Soviet planners had taken compensatory measures, and there were no shortfalls in the Caucasian republics in 1979-80.

Eager though it was for an expanded economic relationship with Tehran, in March 1980 Moscow rejected Iranian demands for a fivefold increase to bring the price of natural gas to world market levels, from $.76 per 1,000 cubic feet to $3.80—thus prompting a shutdown of deliveries. A high-level Soviet economic mission to Tehran in late April accomplished nothing. Moscow refused to go higher than $2.66 per 1,000 cubic feet, probably for a number of reasons: doubt that Iran could actually deliver the volume of gas stipulated in the existing contract, given the low level of its oil production; belief that the U.S.-Iranian hostage crisis would drag on, thereby increasing Iran's need for good relations with the USSR and readiness to accept the Soviet offer; expectation that economic criteria would prevail and Iran would eventually accept a price that was three times more than under the Shah rather than flare gas indefinitely; and a reluctance to pay more than absolutely necessary. On the other hand, sensitive to Iran's preoccupation with the hostage crisis and internal unrest, the Soviets decoupled the disagreement on gas pricing from other economic and political issues. In order to help circumvent a possible American blockade, they offered transit privileges for Iranian exports and imports, and pressed for completion of the electrification of the 90-mile railroad line from Julfa to Tabriz (a project started under the Shah). Trade prospects were emphasized, as were the USSR's contributions to Iran's economic development, which included the construction of power plants, more than 30 grain storage elevators, the Isfahan steel complex, and the machine-building plant in Arak; and flood control of the Aras, Atrak, and Harirud Rivers. A trade protocol, the first of the post-Shah period, was signed on June 20, 1980; and a transit agreement was concluded in September, at the height of the hostage crisis. Once the crisis was over, however, the transit arrangement and the Soviet broadcasts in Persian stressing its value lost much of their impact.

Moscow has been unable to translate the appeal of the undoubted advantages of economic cooperation into concrete agreements. Trade is modest, the number of Soviet technicians has sharply decreased, and few missions are exchanged. The overall level of economic interaction is low. Far from being able to exploit U.S.-Iranian tensions to expand Soviet-Iranian economic ties and deepen Iran's dependence on the USSR, Moscow has instead angered Tehran with its intransigence and niggardliness on the natural gas issue. There have been no important economic agreements and, with one exception (a proposed power station), no new projects of consequence. Such activities as the Soviet Union is engaged in date back to the days of the Shah. The Soviet-Iranian economic relationship remains a victim of the unresolved domestic struggle for control of the revolution.

SOVIET INTERFERENCE IN IRAN'S INTERNAL AFFAIRS

The periodic allegations of Soviet intriguing in Iran's political, ethnic, and sectarian strife have not precluded a semblance of "normalcy" in Soviet-Iranian relations. Absorbed with their own factional rivalries and more immediate external challenges, competing political groups seem not to view the threat of Soviet subversion as particularly dangerous; indeed, by not making it a critical issue, the men around Khomeini may hope to forestall its becoming an eventuality.

Khomeini's toleration of the Tudeh, as the Iranian Communist Party is called, has undoubtedly contributed to Moscow's forebearance. Under the Shah, the Tudeh, which was declared illegal in 1949, atrophied. During the 1960s and 1970s when rapprochement, not revolution, was the Kremlin's line, much of its membership was disaffected, and it did not play a role in the revolution. Once the Shah's fate was sealed, Moscow purged the Tudeh's leadership, installed Nureddin Kianuri—a rich Tehrani and the son of an Ayatollah martyred in 1907—as first secretary, and ordered the party to support Khomeini.[39] Allowed to operate openly and publish a daily newspaper, *Mardom*, the Tudeh echoed Moscow's approval of Khomeini's antiimperialism (that is, anti-Americanism) and his attempt to create a national coalition of all political forces.[40]

The Tudeh is active, well-organized, and capable of providing tactical leadership. Its current aim is more to sustain anti-Americanism and prevent an opening to the West than to seize power. A short-lived but ominous rift between the Tudeh and Khomeini developed over the former's advocacy of greater autonomy for the ethnic minorities and led to its suppression in August and September 1979, but by October sharp Soviet criticisms persuaded Khomeini to back away from a confrontation and restore the Tudeh's privileges.[41]

Khomeini's "seeming indulgence for the orthodox communists" can be explained by a number of considerations: their support for him when he was in exile, at which time they "regularly broadcast his declarations recorded in Iraq" over Radio Iran Courier, operating out of East Germany; their strident and invidious anti-Americanism; their acceptance of the Islamic Republic; their link to the Soviet Union, for whom he feels ideological antipathy but whose open antagonism he prefers not to trigger; their relative weakness among the leftists, which made it easier to isolate them from other radical groups and enlist their cooperation, witness the Tudeh's acquiescence to Khomeini's decision in early 1980 to close Tehran University, which was traditionally a recruiting ground for communists; and finally, their lack of power, for "unlike the other radical groups, Tudeh maintains no armed military wing which could frighten the regime."[42]

The Tudeh has no doubt infiltrated government ministries, the media, and social institutions. The mayor of Tehran was prompted to resign in late December 1980 because of the IRP's disruptiveness and its inattention to the communist threat.[43] However, Tudeh is not now a critical factor in Iran's internal factional struggles; it was content to watch the collapse of President Bani-Sadr, an open and bitter opponent, and with him the prospects for moderate, centrist, democratically oriented groups; and it awaits the next stage in the dialectical development of the revolution, whose polarization the communists believe will enhance their political fortunes.

The containment of the communists is a secondary concern compared to the ethnic strife that has compounded the military ineffectiveness of the government since the Iraqi invasion. Moscow watches the growing assertiveness of Iran's leading ethnic minorities but refrains from encouraging separatism as it did in 1945 46, when it established puppet Kurdish and Azerbaijanian republics in the areas of northern Iran controlled by the Red Army. (The USSR and Britain had occuped Iran in August 1941 as part of their effort to prevent its becoming a Germany base of operations.) Along the 1,200-mile border between Iran and the Soviet Union, the Kurds, the Azerbaijanis, the Turkomans, and the Baluch are in varying stages of rebellion; as are the Arabs of Khuzistan and the Turkic-speaking Qashqai in the province of Fars in the south. All are seeking greater autonomy, and Tehran fears for the territorial integrity of the Iranian state.

The Soviet government officially denies involvement in the Kurdish uprising that has been going on since the summer of 1979, or in any of the other outbreaks of ethnic unrest, but its insistence that it follows a policy of noninvolvement is difficult to accept, given Moscow's historic interest in dominating northern Iran. The USSR maintains a close watch on events and media coverage of them is extensive. No doubt Iran's ethnic cauldron would be simmering even if there were no Soviet inputs. Weakness at the center has traditionally emboldened autonomist and separatist ambitions among the minorities on the periphery of the Iranian empire. It is also true that if it chose, the Soviet Union could trigger a civil war by shipping large amounts of arms to insurgent groups. That it has not yet done so suggests a desire to preserve a united Iran, at least for the time being. If, as seems likely, modest amounts of arms are being sent covertly, to Kurdistan for example, the purpose may be more to warn the government than to topple it.

Of all the Iranian minorities, the Kurds are portrayed the most sympathetically by Soviet writers who deplore the "artificial separation" of Kurds living in Iran, Iraq, and Turkey, and the hindering of their aspirations for freedom and independence.[44] Moscow criticized the Islamic Council that met in Tehran on August 21, 1979, for banning the Kurdish Democratic Party, which had close ties with the Tudeh; and it reestablished links with the Peshmerga, the forces formerly led by Mustafa Barzani, the Kurdish leader who fought the Iraqi Baathists for many years in a vain attempt to compel Kurdish autonomy. The government in Tehran, unable to maintain effective military control of Kurdistan and unwilling to grant an autonomy acceptable to the Kurds, maintains an uneasy presence, combatting Iraqi efforts to encourage rebellion and endeavoring to discourage greater Soviet interference.

Tehran also has reason to be concerned over the situation in Azerbaijan, where the Muslim People's Republican Party of Ayatollah Mohammad Kazem Shariatmadari, the spiritual head of Iran's Turkic-speaking Azerbaijani minority, has been outlawed by Khomeini. Shariatmadari's acceptance of genteel house detention in Qum has defused the problem, but only temporarily: Khomeini's unwillingness to consider some type of federalism as a solution to the ethnic unrest, when coupled with the widespread sectarian violence, could exacerbate Iran's political disintegration and tempt Moscow to a more venturesome course.

OBSERVATIONS

Soviet influence on the policies of the Khomeini regime has been minimal. With the exception of the restoration of the Tudeh's rights to engage in political activity following the brief crackdown on it in late summer of 1979, on no issue of consequence—political, economic, or diplomatic—has Iran shifted to a position more congenial to the Soviet Union out of an interest in placating its powerful neighbor, even though Iran is now weaker and more vulnerable than at any time since the turn of the century. In a situation of enormous complexity and unpredictability, the Kremlin's restraint is linked to its anticipation that the collapse of Khomeini's Shi'ite millenarianism could well bring communism to Iran, and its wish not to provoke the United States by further Soviet expansion in the area.

Moscow has not sought to Balkanize Iran. Its aims have been to encourage Khomeini's anti-American policy; to seek closer government-

to-government relations, continually emphasizing the utility of cooperation with the USSR;[45] to contain Iran's internal turmoil and the Iraqi-
Iranian conflict; and to allay the suspicions of the Gulf Arabs as to Soviet
objectives in the region. As Brezhnev noted on February 23, 1981, in his
report to the Twenty-sixth Congress of the CPSU, the most salient
consideration shaping Soviet policy toward Iran is Tehran's anti-American
and anti-Western orientation.[46]

With the worsening of Iran's internal condition, Moscow seems
wedded to a watch-and-wait attitude, satisfied to see the hardline Islamic
fundamentalists, operating through the Islamic Republican Party, humble
the moderates of the center. Even though the mullahs are anticommunist,
their dissemination of a virulent anti-Americanism makes them natural
allies of the Soviet-dominated Tudeh Party. Moscow observed with
pleasure as Prime Minister Rajai, the IRP's leading spokesman in the
government, disposed of the nettling Ghotbzadeh in September 1980 and
mounted a campaign that whittled down the prestige and power of
President Bani-Sadr. In June 1981, 18 months after having been elected
by an overwhelming majority of the electorate, Bani-Sadr lost Khomeini's
support and was hounded from office, a victim of religious fanaticism and
the men around Khomeini whose vision of an "Islamic Republic" smacks
of the Inquisition and whose Shi'ite-first outlook sculpted the Constitution
that was ratified in a national referendum held on December 2-3, 1979.[47]
The removal of Bani-Sadr and men like him, known for their secular and
pro-Western outlook, strengthens the counsels of patience and prudence
in the Kremlin.

Viewed in the perspective of the brief period since Khomeini came to
power, the upheaval in Iran, unfinished and erratic, promises to bring yet
additional advantages to the Soviet Union, whose proximity, power, and
compliant proxy in the Tudeh Party seem an irresistible formula for future
political gains. For the moment, Moscow is very much an outsider in
Tehran.

NOTES

1. FBIS/USSR, July 24, 1979, H1.
2. FBIS/USSR, July 6, 1979, H1.
3. P. Demchenko, "Krusheniye absolyutizma" (The collapse of absolutism), *Kommunist*,
no. 3 (February 1979), 83.
4. P. Demchenko, "Iran: stanovleniye respubliki" (Iran: the making of a republic),
Kommunist, no. 9 (June 1979), 116.
5. *Washington Post*, February 16, 1979.
6. New York *Times*, February 26, 1979.
7. *Pravda*, April 4, 1979.
8. FBIS/USSR, April 25, 1979, H6.

9. New York *Times*, June 13, 1979.

10. New York *Times*, September 13, 1979.

11. *Pravda*, April 6, 1979; *Kommunist Tadzhikistana*, August 1, 1979, as quoted in FBIS/USSR, August 14, 1979, H1.

12. FBIS/USSR, February 28, 1980, H4-H5.

13. *Financial Times*, June 13, 1979.

14. *Dawn*, September 20, 1979.

15. New York *Times*, November 22, 1979.

16. *Izvestiia*, November 25, 1979.

17. *The Times* (London), November 25, 1979.

18. *International Herald Tribune*, November 29, 1979.

19. *Pravda*, December 5, 1979.

20. *Pravda*, January 10, 1980.

21. *Daily Telegraph*, April 19, 1980.

22. For example, *Pravda*, June 23, 1980.

23. FBIS/Iran, August 15, 1980, I2–I6; I22.

24. For this insight I am indebted to Miss Michelle Wallace.

25. FBIS/USSR, August 18, 1980, H2.

26. In January 1981 the Soviet media's treatment of attempts to bring the hostage crisis to a satisfactory conclusion was an unmistakeable demonstration of Moscow's inherently unrelenting hostility to U.S. policy and objectives in the Middle East. In the final weeks of Carter's presidency, when he was laboring to fashion a final accord, Moscow accused the U.S. government of "having whipped up an atmosphere of war hysteria," and warned Iranians that "the United States is attempting to increase its pressure on Iran by using the hostage issue, thus terrorizing your country with the threat of military force. The United States has rejected Iranian demands and instead has put forth demands which are insulting to your country and are therefore totally unacceptable." *Pravda*, January 6, 1981, and Vera Lebedeva commentary in Persian to Iran on January 6, 1981, FBIS/USSR, January 8, 1981, H1. See also Bruce Porter, "The USSR and the Hostage: 'Scurrilous Propaganda,'" Radio Liberty Research, RL 29/81, January 19, 1981.

27. FBIS/USSR, September 24, 1980, H3.

28. *Izvestiia*, September 23, 1980.

29. *The Times*, October 6, 1980. Even before the outbreak of Iraqi-Iranian hostilities, Moscow had offered to sell arms to Iran. Baltimore *Sun*, August 23, 1980.

30. New York *Times*, January 16, 1981.

31. FBIS/USSR, January 22, 1981, H 1.

32. New York *Times*, February 4, 1981.

33. Washington *Post*, March 3, 1981.

34. While Iran's aircraft are American and difficult to keep operational because of shortages of spare parts, its Katyushas (40 mm.–barrel rocket artillery), SAMs, armored personnel carriers, and small arms are Soviet. The Shah purchased more than $1 billion worth of weapons and ammunition from the Soviet Union during the 1967-78 period. Dissatisfied with Soviet deliveries and determined to ensure reliable ammunition for his weapons, he built plants to produce the necessary ammunition and spare parts. For example, a factory producing RPG-7 antitank missiles was constructed in the mid-1970s; by 1978 it was operational, turning out thousands of rounds of this type of ammunition. Khomeini's Islamic Republic has been able to defend itself as a result of the Shah's forethought and preparation. Interviews with former Iranian military personnel.

35. Radio Liberty Research, RL 77/79, March 2, 1979, 1.

36. *Pravda*, March 13, 1979. Variations of this theme often appear in Soviet articles.

37. FBIS/USSR, April 26, 1979, H6-H7.

38. New York *Times*, July 19, 1979.

39. *Middle East Intelligence Survey* 8, no. 5 (June 1-15, 1980):39.

40. For example, *Pravda*, March 12, April 24, 25, and 27, 1979.

41. Shahram Chubin, "Leftist Forces in Iran," *Problems of Communism* 29, no. 4 (July-August 1980):9.

42. See Eric Rouleau, "Khomeini's Iran," *Foreign Affairs* 59, no.1 (Fall 1980):18; and Middle East Intelligence Survey, 40.

43. Washington *Star*, December 26, 1980.

44. For example, see the article published by two Georgian scholars in *Tbilisi Kommunisti*, October 1979, as translated in FBIS/USSR, December 28, 1979, H4-H6.

45. For example, *Izvestiia*, February 11, 1981.

46. In Brezhnev's words:

The revolution in Iran, which was a major event on the international scene in recent years, is of a specific nature. However complex and contradictory, it is essentially an anti-imperialist revolution, though reaction at home and abroad is seeking to change this feature. The people of Iran are looking for their own road to freedom and prosperity. We sincerely wish them success in this, and are prepared to develop good relations with Iran on the principles of equality and, of course, reciprocity. *Report of the Central Committee of the CPSU to the 26th Congress of the CPSU*, February 23, 1981 (Moscow), 23.

47. R. K. Ramazani, "Iran's Revolution: Patterns, Problems and Prospects," *International Affairs* 56, no. 3 (Summer 1980):499-53.

6

RUSSIA AND AFGHANISTAN
IN HISTORICAL PERSPECTIVE

The year 1747 is generally accepted as the date that Afghanistan was founded as a distinctive nation-state, though the borders were not completely fixed until the 1890s. Ahmad Shah, an Afghan mercenary in the service of the King of Persia, on learning that his employer had been murdered by the palace guard, returned to his tribal homeland and carved out a kingdom there at the expense of the rudderless Persian Empire and the decrepit Moghul Empire in India that had only recently been sacked by the army of which he had been a part. Though riven by inter-tribal jealousies and feuds, the Afghan tribes accepted him as ruler (1747-73), believing he would be easy to control, in part because he was young (24) and in part because he came from a weak clan, the Saddozai branch of the Popalzais: "He assumed the title Durr-i-Durran, Pearly of Pearls, because, it is said, it pleased him to wear an ear-ring fashioned of pearls. From that time his tribe . . . have been known as the Durranis."[1] His successors clung to the throne, often precariously, until April 1978, when a communist coup ended Durrani rule.

THE EUROPEAN IMPERIAL IMPACT

The arrival in the capital of Kabul in 1809 of the British envoy Mountstuart Elphinstone was the first official contact between the Afghans and an European power. In 1818 the Mohammadzai clan of the Barakzai Durranis assumed power. Dost Muhammad Khan (1826-63), who developed into a stern but just Amir (dropping the more pretentious title of Shah to allay the fears of his factious tribes), ruled during Afghanistan's initial experience with Anglo-Russian imperial rivalry, alternately feeling Russian pressure from the north, and from the southeast that of the Sikhs of the Punjab and, after 1849, their conquerors, the British. As Russia expanded eastward and southeastward, seizing chunks of Persia and absorbing the feudal khanates of Central Asia, and as Britain (the British East India Company officially ruled India until 1857, when the crown assumed direct control) spread its empire northwestward, into the Punjab, Kashmir, Peshawar, Baluchistan, and Sind, the "Great Game" came to a head in Afghanistan. Each sought to buttress its strategic position, by guile and gun, at the expense of Afghan territorial and tribal integrity, but Britain was the primary meddler in Afghan affairs.

Throughout the nineteenth century, British moves against Afghan rulers were precipitated by spasms of Russophobia caused by edginess about the security of India. Thus, the First Anglo–Afghan War (1839-42) was prompted by fears that a Russian–supported Persia was preparing to annex Herat, the western key to control of Afghanistan, and that Russia would then use this as a springboard against India. Britain's attempt to place a puppet on the throne in Kabul ended in disaster and allowed the Afghans several decades of relative quiet. However, the British did seize Peshawar, the southern terminus of the Khyber Pass and principal invasion route of the Indian subcontinent. For the next century, in their efforts to keep the Russians out of Afghanistan, the British alternately advocated making Afghanistan a satellite, a frontier extension of India, or an independent buffer state. Their setbacks stemmed from a combination of British imperial arrogance and insensitivity to the Afghans' fierce determination to remain free; the inability of the Afghan government to prevent volatile tribal incursions into British India; and resentment over British Christian missionary activity.

During this period, Russia's expansion into Central Asia was an amalgam of military, political, and economic considerations. For the small elite around the Czar, the depradations and incessant raids on Russian settlements in the frontier region east of the Caspian Sea were the main reason for pacifying the Kazakh steppe; but there was also the allure of a trade route to India. Foiled in the affair over Herat in 1839-40, Russia moved against the khan of Khiva. Its forces were defeated, as they had been in a previous attempt in 1717 under Peter the Great. By the mid-1840s, however, with superior arms and resources, Russia was not to be denied; it reached the Syr Darya (Jaxartes) River and established positions deep in Turkestan (as the entire area was generally called). Full control of Turkestan, though, was to take three more decades.

Russia's defeat at the hands of Britain, France, and the Ottoman Empire in the Crimean War (1854-56) stimulated its further advance into Central Asia. Russia suspected that the British and the Ottoman Turks were intriguing to sow unrest along its borders in the Caucasus and

Central Asia. When the British war against Persia in 1856 compelled Persia to leave Herat in Afghan hands and induced Dost Muhammad Khan to pursue a policy of friendship with Britain, Moscow saw Afghanistan as having fallen into the British sphere of influence, which was spreading ominously toward Russia's natural line of advance in Central Asia. Simultaneously, in the Far East, the British annexation of Hong Kong and penetration of the Yangtse Valley seemed like a threat to Moscow's growing stake in northern China. The imperial rivalry between Russia and Britain was becoming increasingly global.

In the early 1860s a series of energetic, able ministers and generals obtained the Czar's approval to resume the advance in Central Asia. In November 1864 a memorandum prepared for Czar Alexander II and Russian diplomats by Prince A. M. Gorchakov, the foreign minister, set forth the political-moral-economic premises of Russia's policy:

> The position of Russia in Central Asia is that of all civilized states which come into contact with half-savage, wandering tribes possessing no fixed social organization. It invariably happens in such cases that the interests of security on the frontier, and of commercial relations, compel the more civilized state to exercise a certain ascendancy over neighbors whose turbulence and nomad instincts render them difficult to live with . . .
>
> Thus . . . the Imperial Government finds itself reduced to [a] dilemma: it must allow an anarchy to become chronic which paralyzes all security and all progress, and involves distant and expensive expeditions at frequent intervals [that is, to maintain peace and establish order]; or on the other hand it must enter on a career of conquest and annexation such as [was followed by the United States, France, Holland . . . and] gave England her Indian Empire . . .
>
> [One is thus] inevitably drawn into a course wherein ambition plays a smaller part than imperious necessity, and where the *greatest difficulty is in knowing where to stop* (italics added).[2]

Indeed it was. The following year Russia seized Tashkent, then Kokand, and in 1868 Czarist forces absorbed the khanate of Bukhara, including the city of Samarkand.

Marxist historians stress the economic impetus for this expansion, arguing that with cotton short because of the American Civil War, "Central Asia which had hitherto been regarded primarily as a profitable market now assumed significance as the source of an important raw material."[3] Western analysts, while not denying the "considerable sentiment" among Russian manufacturing and trading interests for raising cotton in Central Asia, believe official policy was overtaken by the military momentum of conquest in the field.[4] Though Gorchakov had been cautious and mindful of the risks of expansion, in his memorandum he did say: "It is a peculiarity of Asiatics to respect nothing but visible and palpable force." When an audacious military commander produced a major victory through a flexible interpretation of orders, there is no gainsaying the readiness of the Czar to add to Russia's empire. The military component of Russia's policy was perhaps best epitomized in a statement by General M. D. Skobelev, one of the swashbuckling commanders who conquered Central Asia: "I hold it as a principle that in Asia the duration of peace is in direct proportion to the slaughter you inflict upon the enemy."[5] One scholar sums the matter up neatly: "Russia was spurred on in Central Asia by a whole complex of motives—the quest for a secure frontier, the provocations offered by unstable neighbors, the fear of being excluded from the area by England, and the temptations of diplomatic leverage, economic profit, and military glory."[6]

Russia's conquest of Bukhara had opened wide the road to Afghanistan. Negotiations between London and Moscow culminated in January 1873 in a "gentleman's agreement" that accepted Afghanistan's northern border as the Oxus (Amu Darya) River, which rises in the Himalayas and flows several thousand miles, eventually emptying into the landlocked Aral Sea. Though not a formal treaty, it forestalled a head-on collision between Russia and Britain. The situation, nevertheless, remained tense, because a few months later Russia added Khiva to its Central Asian conquests, and Britain wondered where it would stop. In 1876-78 the two came close to war when Moscow, flush from victories over the faltering Ottoman Turks, made a drive for the Turkish Straits and sent a strong military mission to Kabul, thus setting off alarm bells in India.

At the Congress of Berlin in 1878, Moscow was kept from the Straits, and it withdrew its mission from Kabul. However, the British Viceroy in India, Lord Lytton, feared the Russians might return and wanted the Afghans to accept a permanent British presence in Kabul. Amir Sher Ali (1863-79) equivocated, and Lytton had the excuse he wanted for an invasion. Britain won the Second Anglo-Afghan War (1878-81) but, in the process, paid a stiff price. Henceforth Britain managed Afghanistan's foreign policy, but permitted it to rule itself internally.

In 1885 war again threatened, this time over the Panjdeh Oasis (a desolate, swampy water-hole 130 miles north of Herat). Russia advanced beyond the city of Merv to a near-confrontation with the Afghans who claimed the area; and Britain backed Amir Abdur Rahman (1881-1901), who at one time it had feared would be pro-Russian, because of the 12 years in exile he had spent in Russia. The crisis subsided, a boundary commission produced a compromise, and in July 1887 the rest of the Russo–Afghan border was established in the northwest, where the Oxus

River turns sharply into Russian territory. Eight years later the two great powers fixed Afghanistan's northeast boundary in the Wakhan area of Pamirs, Afghanistan receiving a sliver of land that insulated British India from direct contact with Russia. These nineteenth-century map-making exercises established the 1,200–mile Russo-Afghan border.

The boundary Britain imposed between Afghanistan and British India—the Durand Line of 1893—though at the time irrelevant to Russian-Afghan relations, proved fateful 60 years later, when it provided the Russians with the opportunity to obtain the major presence in Afghanistan that the British had effectively denied them during the nineteenth century. Sir Mortimer Durand pressured Abdur Rahman to accept a south and southeast border that was a cartographic line of convenience designed to augment the security of India. It was a political and ethnic horror: extending 1,200 miles from Iran to China, it divided the Pashto–speaking Pathan tribes in two and became the lightning rod for Afghan irredentism. The Pathans (also called Pushtuns) have been Afghanistan's ruling ethnic-linguistic group (comprising about 40 to 45 percent of the population), and the Durand Line gave this clan-centered and ruggedly individualistic collection of tribes a symbol around which to unite for anti-British intriguing and fighting (even while Kabul feigned friendship for Britain). After the 1947 partition of India it became the reason for opposing Pakistan, heir to what was originally the North West Frontier of British India, the area containing those Pathans that had been cut off from Afghanistan. The Soviet Union was to emerge as the main source of support for challenging the Durand Line and reuniting the Pathans.

By way of contrast, the Afghans' border with Russia never was a troublesome issue because the tribes and peoples divided by it were Tajiks and Uzbeks, whom the Pathans tend to look down on.

The "Great Game" ended abruptly in 1907, when a worsening strategic position elsewhere impelled Russia to reach an accommodation with Britain. Threatened in the Far East by Japan (by whom it had been defeated in 1904-05) and in Europe by Germany, Russia decided that Afghanistan was not worth its jeopardizing the prospect of friendship with Britain at a time when it desperately needed allies. Uncertainty in Europe mandated stability along the Central Asian rimland. Under the St. Petersburg Convention, Moscow acknowledged Afghanistan as part of the British sphere of influence (infuriating the Afghans, who had not been consulted); and Persia was divided into British and Russian spheres of influence. This carefully designed structure for peace was unhinged by World War I.

OUTCASTS ON THE OXUS

Afghanistan stayed neutral in World War I. Amir Habibullah, who had succeeded to the throne on the death of his father in 1901, resisted strong pressures for belligerency both from the fervent nationalists who saw Britain's absorption in Europe and the Middle East as a heaven-sent opportunity to strike the Raj and from the religious leaders who thought it heresy not to join the *jihad* (Holy War) proclaimed by the Ottoman Caliph against the British infidels. He "stood alone against the nation," trying to reach their shared goals of full independence and recovery of lost lands "peacefully and legally."[7] On February 19, 1919, Habibullah was murdered—the culprit was never caught.

His son, Amanullah, an Anglophobe, succeeded (1919-29) and immediately launched a policy intended to assure his popularity at home and wrest concessions from Britain. The resulting Third Anglo-Afghan War in May 1919 lasted less than a month. Though militarily victorious, Britain was an exhausted power and, leery of further fighting, it agreed in August that Afghanistan should henceforth control its own foreign affairs.

The new era in Afghanistan's foreign policy coincided with momentous changes in its northern neighbor. After the Bolshevik seizure of power and the civil war and Allied intervention that followed, Moscow put a premium on encouraging Afghan independence and an anti-British orientation. A pariah state, Bolshevik Russia wanted to prevent British intrigues and intervention in Central Asia via Afghanistan. Accordingly, it was the first government to enter into diplomatic relations with Afghanistan, recognizing it in May 1919 and concluding a treaty of friendship on February 28, 1921. Soviet recognition, coming as it did during the Afghan war with Britain, was especially welcome in Kabul, as were the rubles, guns, and advisers that Moscow offered in increasing amounts, once its own internal situation was secured. Amanullah wanted the weapons to incite the Pathans in the North West Frontier Province (NWFP) of British India to revolt against the British. The arms link to Russia, though quite modest in the 1920s and virtually nonexistent in the 1930s and 1940s, became significant from the mid-1950s on and had profound consequences in the late 1970s. Moscow was a willing supplier of weapons: The seed had been planted early.

Though Soviet-Afghan relations cooled considerably after the early 1920s (notwithstanding the treaty of neutrality and nonaggression signed in August 1926), Moscow still had reason to be satisfied, since Afghanistan served as an effective buffer against British military power. For his part, Amanullah sought better relations with Britain. Paradoxically, despite three Anglo–Afghan wars, endless campaigns in the NWFP, and Pathan irredentism, he feared Russia more than Britain. First, the Soviet suppression of Muslim separatism in Central Asia in the 1920s and efforts to extirpate religion drove thousands of Tajik and Uzbek refugees to Afghanistan and soured Kabul's attitude toward the communist regime. Indeed, on a number of occasions, Soviet troops pursued rebel Basmachi leaders onto Afghan soil. Second, communist agitation in Afghanistan alerted the leadership to the subversive aims of the Soviet Union. Finally, the Afghan elite had been educated in London, Paris, and Berlin, and their ideas of modernization were Western, not communist.

Amanullah's push for modernization came a-cropper over his decree that women should stop wearing the veil. He was not Ataturk, and Afghanistan was not Turkey. The powerful tradition–bound mullahs, the tribal leaders opposed to social change, and the army disgruntled over back pay, forced his flight into exile in early 1929. Though Amanullah was an ardent nationalist (in 1926 to demonstrate Afghanistan's independence, he had exchanged the title of Amir for that of King), no matter how thin his gruel of liberalism, it was still unpalatable to the Pathan tribal leaders. After a few months they accepted a new king, his cousin Nadir Shah, a national hero because of his generalship in the 1919 war who returned from self-imposed exile in France. When he was assassinated in 1933, his son, Zahir Shah (1933-73) succeeded to the throne.

Throughout the 1930s, Afghanistan, like the Soviet Union, sought to normalize diplomatic relations with its neighbors, while embarking on internal modernization. In 1931 and 1936 the two signed additional treaties, affirming mutual nonintervention in the affairs of the other and abstention from alignments that threatened the other; but relations were not close. The family oligarchy around Zahir Shah looked primarily to Germany for industrial and technical assistance. It stressed Pathan nationalism, and Pashto increasingly replaced Persian as the language of the educated classes and of upward mobility in government and the army. Its special efforts to strengthen the power of the army relative to the tribes were given an unexpected boost by the coming of World War II, which enabled the government "to win tribal compliance with a draft system" that strengthened the royal army and made it superior "to any potential internal opposition."[8] (In 1973 and 1978, ironically, it was military coups that led to the Durranis' undoing.) But the war (during which Afghanistan again remained neutral) seriously undermined the country's halting steps toward economic development, because Britain and the USSR pressured Kabul to terminate all ties with Germany and Italy, its principal sources for assistance.

The end of the war brought Britain's relinquishment of India, the partition of the subcontinent, and the onset of the Cold War. Soon Afghanistan's outlook and policy, especially toward the Soviet Union, underwent a momentous change. Its previous ties to its northern neighbor had on the whole been kept to a minimum, but with the emergence of mutually antagonistic nation-states (India and Pakistan) south of the Khyber Pass and a worldwide mood that extolled progress and change, Kabul increasingly turned to the Soviet Union for economic and military assistance. This policy brought the Bear south of the Oxus, initially by invitation; later by force, with profound consequences for the entire region.

THE PAKHTOONISTAN ISSUE AND REGIONAL POLARIZATION

The establishment of Pakistan as an independent country in August 1947 renewed Afghanistan's interest in the approximately 5 million Pathan tribesmen living in the NWFP. Pakistan accepted the British-imposed Durand Line of 1893 as the border between the two countries; but Afghanistan no longer did. Kabul's intrigues were now directed against a fellow Muslim state. Once it became clear that neither Britain nor Pakistan had any intention of holding a plebiscite to let the Pathans living on the Pakistani side of the border choose whether to stay with Pakistan, to create an independent state of Pakhtoonistan, or to merge with Afghanistan, Kabul started inciting the Pathan tribes to revolt. Ostensibly promoting the principle of national self-determination, it wanted to make certain that Pakistan, like British India, would fail to assimilate the Pathans south of the Durand Line. It is conceivable that Afghanistan's agitation for an independent state of Pakhtoonistan was encouraged by India in the early postpartition days as a way of weakening Pakistan, but Kabul's own ambitions were motivation enough.

The Soviet Union took steps that made it the beneficiary of the mounting tensions. In June 1950, to alleviate the effects of Pakistan's obstruction of Afghan trade with the outside world, which was funneled mostly through the port of Karachi, Moscow signed a transit agreement with Kabul, allowing passage of Afghan goods across the USSR; concluded a four-year trade pact, greatly expanding the heretofore minimal trade; and above all supported Kabul's position on an independent Pakhtoonistan. Pakhtoonistan was the issue from which, for the first time in their history, a close Soviet-Afghan relationship emerged, one the United States inadvertently furthered through its policy of containment and unfortunate polarization of the region's politics.

King Zahir Shah's appointment of his first cousin and brother-in-law Muhammad Daoud Khan as prime minister in September 1953 foreshadowed major shifts in policy: Two decades of cautious and modest reformism gave way to more impatient and ambitious plans for accelerating the country's modernization, and to Daoud's tougher line on the Pakhtoon issue. Daoud declared U.S. military aid to Pakistan was a serious threat, and three months later he abrogated the 1921 treaty with Britain, in which Afghanistan had accepted the Durand Line, contending that a treaty pertaining to British India did not apply to the inheritor of the boundary, Pakistan.

Unlike the older generation, Daoud and the small coterie around him did not believe friendship with the Soviet Union would jeopardize the country's independence. Heretofore, in maneuvering between Britain and Russia to preserve its independence, Afghanistan had operated on the principle that neither country should be permitted a foothold or contacts within its borders:

> Thus, for all the proximity of the Russians and of the British in India and the technical ability of Soviet and British nationals, no more than a few Britons and no Russians had ever been employed by the Afghan government. Both Great Britain and the U.S.S.R. maintained sizable embassies in Kabul, but these, and particularly the Soviet Embassy, were kept out of bounds for most Afghans as though they were nurseries of bubonic plague; and the diplomats and embassy personnel were kept under constant surveillance by the police.[9]

Daoud, however, arrogant and obstinate and convinced that with the British departure from India Moscow had little to gain from undermining or invading Afghanistan—a tough and unripe nut—discarded the previous policy of hiring as technical advisers and teachers only nationals from countries that posed no threat and engaged Russians by the hundreds to develop the nation's infrastructure and industry. Daoud's determination that "the traditional aloofness toward the Soviet Union was no longer necessary" was the first in a series of his tragic misjudgments.[10]

Daoud's interest in closer relations was reciprocated by the Kremlin. The USSR's aim were strategic and political: to prevent Afghanistan from serving as a base for a hostile power and thus encourage its policy of nonalignment; to develop Afghanistan as a showpiece of Soviet developmental assistance and demonstrate to the new nations of the Third World that the USSR was no threat but rather a potential benefactor; to establish a solid presence in Afghanistan and nurture its dependency as a prelude to the exercise of influence over Afghan policy; and ultimately, to neutralize Pakistan and unhinge its alliance with the United States.

PEACEFUL COEXISTENCE

The Kremlin's "new look" was evident in January 1954 with a $3.5 million loan for two grain elevators and a bakery. Taking a leaf from the U.S. aid program, Moscow came with checkbook in hand and lent a receptive ear to requests for a variety of projects. It was in Afghanistan that Moscow ushered in a far–ranging policy designed to reverse Stalin's rigid approach to the new nations of the Afro-Asian world and establish a Soviet presence. In very short order agreements were negotiated for a 60-mile petroleum pipeline (from Termez in the USSR's Uzbek Republic to the Afghan city of Mazar-i-Sharif), a cement factory, roadbuilding equipment, three oil storage tanks, hydroelectric projects, and geologic prospecting. The process of influence–building brought Moscow quick returns, as the Afghan government in deference to Soviet wishes cancelled contracts with Western mining firms who would have been prospecting in the general vicinity of the Soviet border.

Pakistan's decision in early 1955 to merge all the provinces of West Pakistan, including the NWFP, into a single administrative unit precipitated violent demonstrations against its consulates in Afghanistan. In retaliation, the Afghan consulate at Peshawar was attacked, and in July Pakistan abruptly closed the Khyber Pass, blocking landlocked Afghanistan's main artery to the outside world. This near economic strangulation had immediate political consequences. In response to the precarious situation, Prime Minister Daoud quickly accepted the Soviet offer of a five-year transit agreement calling for the free transport of goods over the territory of both countries. Foreign Minister Muhammad Naim exulted: "If one door is slammed shut and another is opened, we will go through it."[11] Even when Pakistan lifted the blockade five months later, Afghanistan routed more and more of its trade through the Soviet Union.

Moscow's support set the stage for the dramatic and highly effective visit in December 1955 of CPSU leader Nikita Khrushchev and Premier Nikolai Bulganin. On the eve of their arrival, Daoud dismissed his minister of defense, who opposed strengthening ties to the Soviet Union.[12] The Khrushchev-Bulganin visit was notable for a number of reasons. First, the treaty of neutrality and nonaggression of June 24, 1931, which had been renewed at five-year intervals, was modified to remain in force for ten years. Second, a major economic agreement, signed on January 28, 1956, extended a long-term credit of $100 million for developing agriculture; building hydroelectric power stations, irrigation installations, and automobile repair shops; and constructing the Bagram airbase (outside of Kabul) and a network of asphalt highways, including a two-mile-long tunnel through the Salang Pass in the Hindu Kush mountain range, which established an all–weather land route from the Soviet border to Kabul. Third, the joint communiqué of December 18, 1955, declared "that those people and nations that are still deprived of freedom and national sovereignty have the right, based on the United Nations Charter, to determine their future fate without pressure and stress from abroad"—a clear allusion to Daoud's call a month earlier for a plebiscite to determine the wishes of the Pathans living in Pakistan. To Daoud's delight, at the formal state banquet, Premier Bulganin was even more specific: "We think the demands of Afghanistan to give the population of bordering 'Pushtunistan' an opportunity of freely expressing their will are justified."[13] Fourth, Afghanistan turned to the Soviet Union for arms. Preliminary discussions led Afghan military missions to visit the Soviet Union and Czechoslovakia during the spring. On August 25, 1956, Daoud confirmed the signing of a military assistance agreement (for about $25 million). In light of Pakistan's accession to SEATO in January 1955 and its arming by the United States (Washington had turned down an Afghan request for arms in 1951), SEATO's upholding of the Durand Line, and Daoud's own Pathan irredentist ambitions, the Soviet offer was too attractive to resist, and from 1956 on Moscow became Afghanistan's sole arms supplier. Henceforth, the 40,000-man army and air force were equipped and trained with modern Soviet weapons; military air fields were built at Mazari-i-Sharif and Bagram; and road construction was pushed. The military infrastructure that was built from 1956 on would one day service a Soviet invasion.

During the next few years high-level exchanges took place, for example, Daoud visited Moscow in October 1956 and May 1959, and King Zahir Shah went in July 1957 and August 1962; Khrushchev returned to Kabul in March 1960, and a delegation from the Supreme Soviet went in October 1961. Soviet projects were to be found throughout the country, ranging from an irrigation canal near Jalalabad to the construction of a river port in Kyzyl-Kala (Qizil Qala) on the Oxus, 250 miles north of Kabul, from apartment houses to a 400-bed military hospital. The growing economic and military dependence on the Soviet Union put *bi-tarafi*, Afghanistan's traditional policy for preserving its independence, in increasing jeopardy.

In 1961 another crisis closed the Afghan-Pakistani border in August and ruptured diplomatic relations, this time for almost two years. A Soviet military mission went to Kabul in October, but Moscow did not offer unequivocal partisanship as it had in 1955: It provided transit privileges and gave economic assistance, but withheld full support on the all-important Pakhtoon issue. Worried over the growing rift with China, Soviet leaders placed a premium on calm borders in Central Asia and intensified their courtship of the rimland states—Turkey, Iran, Afghanistan—and of not only India but Pakistan as well. Moscow appreciated that divisions on the subcontinent benefited China and it determined to keep tensions over Pakhtoonistan from turning into war.

The quarrel between Afghanistan and Pakistan dragged on until March 1963, when, without warning, King Zahir Shah displayed uncharacteristic assertiveness and removed Daoud. Alarmed over the rising dissatisfaction with Daoud's policies, he reckoned that Daoud had brought the country dangerously close to war with Pakistan, become excessively overbearing and insensitive to the pressures from the educated technocracy for democratic reforms, alienated the conservative tribal and religious leaders on whom the monarchy traditionally relied for support with his social and economic policies and lack of consultation, made the army heavily dependent on Soviet arms and training, and failed to make any progress on the issue of Pakhtoonistan.

The new prime minister, Dr. Mohammad Yusuf, wasted no time in putting out a line to Pakistan for a resumption of diplomatic relations: "Afghanistan will continue to support the demand of Pakhtoonistan in a peaceful manner."[14] On May 23, 1963, with the strong assistance of the Shah of Iran and the receptive attitude of Pakistan's ruler, Ayub Khan, diplomatic relations were reestablished and the border was reopened soon thereafter.

Under Daoud, Afghanistan had been pushed onto an uncharted course of rapid internal transformation and high-risk behavior in foreign policy, both of which marked sharp departures from the past. These policies, once set in motion, could be modified but not completely reversed. Their consequences for the future were enormous, and nowhere more than in relations with the Soviet Union.

NOTES

1. Sir Olaf Caroe, *The Pathans: 550 B.C.-A.D. 1957*, 3rd ed. (New York: Oxford University Press, 1967), 256.
2. For a copy of the memorandum, see W. K. Fraser-Tytler, *Afghanistan*, 3rd ed. (London: Oxford University Press, 1967), 333–37.
3. N. A. Khalfin, as translated and condensed by Hubert Evans, *Russia's Policy in Central Asia 1857-1868* (Oxford: St. Anthony's College, Soviet Affairs Study Group, 1964), 50.
4. See Seymour Becker, *Russia's Protectorates in Central Asia: Bukhara and Khiva, 1865-1924* (Cambridge, Mass.: Harvard University Press, 1968), 23.
5. As quoted by Charles Marvin, *The Russian Advance Toward India* (1882), in Charles Miller, *Khyber: British India's North West Frontier* (New York: Macmillan, 1977), 232.
6. Becker, 23.
7. Miller, 312-13.
8. Richard S. Newell, *The Politics of Afghanistan* (Ithaca, N.Y.: Cornell University Press, 1972), 64.
9. Arnold Fletcher, *Afghanistan: Highway of Conquest* (Ithaca, N.Y.: Cornell University Press, 1965), 260.
10. Ibid., 263.
11. *Time*, July 18, 1955, 31.
12. New York *Times*, December 11, 1955.
13. New York *Times*, February 8, 1956.
14. *Dawn*, March 17, 1963.

THE LAST YEARS OF PEACEFUL COEXISTENCE: SOVIET-AFGHAN RELATIONS, 1963-78

During the decade and a half that remained of Afghanistan's existence as an independent nation-state, relations between it and the Soviet Union were excellent. Indeed, from Moscow's perspective, they had never been better. Afghanistan was a showplace for Soviet salesmanship in the Third World. Moscow's courtship had created a stable environment conducive to the promotion of Soviet aims in a strategically important part of Central Asia. Government-to-government exchanges increased, and Afghanistan's heavy dependence on Soviet economic, technical, and military assistance permitted a degree of penetration unmatched anywhere else in the Third World, without seeming to jeopardize its independence. Afghanistan was nonaligned, accepting of the substantial Soviet presence, generally restrained on the Pakhtoonistan question in deference to Moscow's desire that the border between Afghanistan and Pakistan be kept quiet, judicious in refraining from cultivating intimate ties with Peking or exploiting the Sino-Soviet rift, and promisingly receptive to Brezhnev's proposal in June 1969 for an Asian collective security system. In a word, Kabul's foreign policy was as close to Moscow's as that of any nonaligned country.

However, in April 1978 peaceful coexistence was swept aside by a communist revolution, and Soviet military power advanced for the first time in Russian history to the Khyber Pass. This dramatic and permanent change in the Soviet-Afghan relationship, which has had profound regional and international consequences, was the direct outgrowth of the flawed Afghan effort to transform its autocratic monarchical oligarchy into a modern constitutional state with a parliamentary system. Internal developments revolutionized foreign policy relationships.

THE FAILURE OF THE CONSTITUTIONAL EXPERIMENT

King Zahir Shah's experiment in democratization started out well.[1]
After removing Daoud on March 10, 1963, the King appointed a com-
moner, Dr. Mohammad Yusuf, prime minister, thus symbolizing his intention of democratizing the political system. In September 1964, after
almost 18 months of continual activity by a constitutional commission, he
convened a Loya Jirgah or Great Assembly (only the fifth held since
1930), to approve the draft constitution. The members were remarkably
representative of the country's socioeconomic and political diversity. The
Loya Jirgah was a time-honored way for the King to obtain an endorsement by the country's elite for the government's position on a sensitive
issue.

The 1964 Constitution was a liberal document, incorporating, as is the
wont of governments in the second half of the twentieth century,
unassailable principles on equality, freedom, and personal rights. Among
its noteworthy provisions was a prohibition against members of the royal
family serving as cabinet ministers, members of parliament, or justices of
the Supreme Court. (Daoud saw it as directed personally against him; he
took stock, bided his time, and conspired with leftists in the military, which
he had been instrumental in modernizing, to mount a coup nine years
later.)

The elections of October 1965, though bringing a few Marxist,
cryptocommunists such as Babrak Karmal into the parliament, resulted in
a decidedly conservative cast. The new prime minister, the popular
Mohammad Hashim Maiwandwal who had served ably as ambassador to
the United States, found himself confronted with serious student agitation
and a fractious parliament. Despite his best efforts, and those of his
successors, the democratic experiment failed to take root. There were a
number of reasons for this. First, the King never implemented the
legislation calling for the establishment of political parties, with the result
that the prime minister could not institutionalize a necessary base of
political support in the parliament. After fathering a liberal constitution,
the King did little to provide encouragement or leadership. Apparently
that effort marked the limits of his vision and sense of political responsibility. He was reluctant to prod or pressure the parliament; indeed, his
sympathies probably lay with the conservative rural landlords whose
ultratraditionalist and antireformist mentality dominated the legislature.
Moreover, through the royal family, he perpetuated the very nepotism,
corruption, and bureaucratic ineptitude the Constitution was designed to
eradicate. Second, parliament remained a collection of individuals more
preoccupied with local interests than national needs. It spent most of its
time criticizing the government and very little on legislation. This behavior

was even more pronounced after the 1969 elections. The principle of separation of powers, copied slavishly from the U.S. Constitution, was carried to such an extreme that the executive (prime minister appointed by the King) had no leverage or control over the parliament. According to one of the foremost Western specialists on Afghanistan, "the relationships between the executive and the legislative seldom evolved beyond mutual wariness or encroachments into each other's prerogatives, and often erupted into mutual, acrimonious antagonism."[2] Third, the small but highly vocal, energetic, and impatient intelligentsia, frustrated that its demands for immediate and extensive reforms were ignored, became increasingly alienated and disruptive. Modernization thus proceeded fitfully, enough to stimulate their demands for a greater role in policy making but inadequate to satisfy the social groups that it spawned. The conservative tenor of the parliament triggered a counterreaction from the intelligentsia and polarized the 5 percent of the population that was literate and politically engaged.

Dissatisfaction with the King's remoteness spread in the early 1970s, when a severe drought further alienated the left and center from the government, whose indifference and inefficiency contributed to the growing disillusionment with the constitutional experiment. Generous food supplies from the United States alleviated some of the starvation in the 1971-72 period, but politically it may have alarmed pro-Soviet groups more than it galvanized promonarchists or government officials to implement land reforms in the predominately rural and agricultural sector of Afghan society and to curb corruption. When a military coup, led by Prince Muhammad Daoud Khan, toppled the monarchy in July 1973, there were no defenders of the King.

Kabul's policy toward the Soviet Union developed in this general environment. One might more precisely say that preoccupied as it was with domestic affairs, Kabul's foreign policy between 1963 and 1973 (and most of the 1973–78 period as well) basically continued the line of developing close ties to the Soviet Union—the new direction it had taken in the early 1950s (in the wake of the flirtation with Pakhtoon irredentism and Pakistan's temporary disruption of transit privileges). There is no evidence that Daoud (during 1953-63) or King Zahir (1963-73) ever really questioned the wisdom of relying so heavily on Soviet economic assistance or so completely on Soviet military equipment and advisers; or that they became concerned enough over the Soviet penetration of Afghan life to explore other options seriously and expeditiously. Inertia brought ample benefits. Kabul's uncritical economic reliance on Soviet assistance—the easiest course for an inefficient but development-minded elite—helped shape its general accommodation to Soviet preferences in foreign policy.

When, toward the end of Daoud's second period in power (1973-78), he did seek to disengage, return to nonalignment, and diversify sources of aid, it was too late. The earlier lack of discernment proved an invitation to disaster and the end of Mohammadzai Durrani rule.

ECONOMIC DEPENDENCY

By August 1965, when King Zahir visited Moscow and renewed the 1931 treaty of neutrality and mutual nonaggression for ten years, Soviet economic assistance to the First and Second Five Year Plans (FYP) (1956-61 and 1962-67) had begun to transform the Afghan environment: there were, among other projects, the all-weather highway from the Soviet border at Torghundi to Herat and Kandahar (the Kandahar to Kabul highway was built by the United States); the tunnel through the Hindu Kush at the Salang Pass; the network of irrigation and land reclamation projects near Jalalabad; the Kabul Polytechnic; the fertilizer plant in Mazar-i-Sharif; and the exploitation of natural gas wells near Shiberghan and construction of a 125-mile pipeline to the Amu Darya, in accordance with the agreement of July 24, 1965. Though poor and undeveloped, Afghanistan is potentially rich in natural gas and minerals (copper, sulfur, coal, zinc, and iron ore).[3] Soviet leaders, looking ahead, had good reason to expect handsome economic returns, especially in natural gas, which has a ready and natural market in the neighboring Soviet republics of Uzbekistan and Tadzhikistan.

By 1970-71 the Soviet Union had extended credits of about $750 million to Afghanistan's economic development, though actual disbursements, leveling off at between $50 and $75 million a year during the 1967–71 period, were far less than the amounts officially committed. This was enough, however, to make Afghanistan heavily dependent on Soviet assistance for its industrial and infrastructure projects, which were virtually all in the public sector. In the early 1970s, Soviet aid tapered off for a number of reasons: seeing that U.S. aid had dropped to less than $20 million a year and that no other benefactor seemed in the offing, Moscow took Afghanistan for granted; Afghanistan's difficult debt situation, inefficiency, and lack of managerial expertise limited its ability to implement more projects; the Soviet presence was already quite substantial, with advisers attached to the Ministries of Planning, Industry, and Mining, as well as to the army; and Soviet resources could be used more effectively elsewhere in the Third World.

Despite its inordinate dependence on Soviet foreign aid and trade (its main trading partner, and creditor, was the USSR), and the adverse effect of the drought of 1971-72 on exports of cotton and fruit, Afghanistan's balance-of-payments situation and hard currency reserves improved markedly after 1973.[4] Among the key reasons for its international economic turnabout were the increased remittances from Afghans working in Iran and the Arab states of the Gulf; the several moratoriums of debt repayments granted by the Soviet Union; and the increased earnings from natural gas exports to the Soviet Union. From $8 million in 1969, to $14 million in 1971, $35 million in 1975, and $30 million in 1977, natural gas earnings rose, becoming during this period the most important export, providing from 40 to 50 percent of total annual export earnings, and in the process reinforcing the dependence of Afghanistan's economic prospects on good relations with the Soviet Union.

Moscow's willingness to continue to aid Afghanistan, evident in the $120 million credit extended in 1972 for the Fourth FYP (1972-76), was responsive to favorable political developments. On July 17, 1973, Prince Daoud participated in a coup by leftist military officers, exiled the King (his brother-in-law), declared an end to the monarchy, and proclaimed a republic, with himself as president. He categorically denied that any foreign power had been involved in the coup and justified the move on the ground that the former "corrupt and effete" government was no more than "a pseudo–democracy" that had pursued bankrupt economic and social policies.[5] The Soviet Union quickly recognized the new government, and its ambassador assured Daoud that Moscow viewed the events as "a domestic affair of Afghanistan."[6] Soviet aid to Daoud made his previous "premiership look like famine."[7] In rapid succession, Moscow offered

hydroelectric stations; nitric fertilizer factories; a new road; irrigation for Jelalabad province; and—the jewel of the whole complex—a natural gas industry in Mazar-i-Sharif.

Yet each of the projects had its catch—as even the Afghans learned that there is no such thing as a free lunch. The road, for example, linked Kabul with the Soviet border, with a capacity for 80-ton vehicles: there were no such vehicles in Afghanistan, or in the Soviet Union, besides Soviet battle tanks . . . .The Jaraduq Natural Gas Project, a joint venture between Soviet Mitroprom and the optimistically named Afghan National Oil Company, was capitalized at 62.5 million rubles, with the Soviets financing two-thirds of that. According to the agreement, 2 billion cubic metres of gas were to be exported to the Soviet Union each year after 1976. Again, this silver lining had a cloud: the price of gas was fixed in 1975 and remained there long after the world price of natural gas had soared. The Soviets, who had similar agreements with Iran, bought that gas at whatever price the Iranian National Oil Company chose to sell it. The Afghans did not have the kind of clout the Shahanshah enjoyed.[8]

On the eve of a visit to Kabul in December 1975, President Podgorny observed that in the previous two decades more than 80 projects had been completed or were under construction in Afghanistan with Soviet assistance and that 40 more were under active consideration.[9] The Seven Year Plan adopted by Daoud for the 1976-83 period was drafted with the assistance of Soviet specialists; and on April 14, 1977, in Moscow, he signed a twelve-year treaty on extensive economic cooperation that provided for "the development of the gas, oil, petrochemical and chemical industries, agriculture, irrigation and other sectors of the economy, public health and veterinary science," geologic prospecting, the construction of power plants and transportation and communications facilities, and vocational and technical training at all levels.[10] This treaty mortgaged Afghanistan's economic future more completely than ever before to good relations with the Soviet Union.

This domestic situation conditioned Afghanistan's policy on the issues that dominated the Soviet-Afghan relationship in the 1963-78 period: Pakhtoonistan and Afghan relations with Pakistan, Brezhnev's proposal for an Asian collective security system, China, and Afghanistan's Iranian option. None of them was ever a source of serious difficulty between Moscow and Kabul, as will be argued later. Moreover, it must be stressed that Afghanistan's policy of nonalignment, braced as it was by a heavy and growing economic dependence on the USSR, was eminently satisfactory to Moscow. Unlike Turkey or Iran, Afghanistan was not a member of a military pact hostile to the USSR; nor did it harbor any foreign military bases. Furthermore, since the mid-1950s, the Afghan military depended on Soviet weapons, advisers, and training. Afghanistan could not take military action against any country without Moscow's implicit approval. In a word, nonaligned Afghanistan met Moscow's optimal requirements for an ideal noncommunist neighbor.

PAKHTOONISTAN AND PAKISTAN

In the interest of normalization of relations with Pakistan, King Zahir Shah shelved the Pakhtoonistan issue. When USSR President Brezhnev visited Kabul in October 1963 (seven months after Daoud's removal as prime minister), the resulting joint communiqué did not even allude to it. Relations with Pakistan slowly improved, and Kabul stopped its propaganda campaign, though it did not renounce its claims or accept the legality of the Durand Line. At high-level Soviet-Afghan meetings, such as the King's visit to Moscow in September 1971 and President Podgorny's visit to Kabul in May 1973, the only allusion to the Pakhtoonistan matter was reaffirmation by the two leaders of their resolve to adhere to the principles of respect for "national sovereignty and integrity, equality between all states, and renunciation of the use of force and threat of force in solving controversial issues." During the 1965 and 1971 Indo-Pakistani wars, Afghanistan stayed neutral and resisted any temptation to foment unrest in the Northwest Frontier Province among the Pathan tribes, many of whom, interestingly enough, "tried to join the Pakistan armed forces to fight the infidel Hindu enemy"; nor did it, in the immediate post-1971 period, try to exploit the internal tensions in West Pakistan between "the densely populated Punjab and Sind provinces" and the "large, sparsely populated NWFP and Baluchistan" provinces that sought greater autonomy.[11] Moscow, though displeased with Pakistan's military alliances with the United States and its receptivity to China's overtures, counseled restraint in Kabul. It made known its opposition to any Afghan moves against the beleaguered Pakistanis, preferring quiet borders and, at a time of serious Sino-Soviet tensions, better relations with all the governments of the subcontinent. The Soviets wanted the stability of the status quo rather than the uncertainty inherent in a possible breakup of Pakistan.

Daoud's return to power on July 17, 1973, brought renewed tensions to the Afghan-Pakistani border. In his initial proclamation, Daoud declared that Pakistan was the "only nation with which we have differences . . . .Our relations with Pakistan will be based on our permanent efforts for finding a solution for the Pushtunistan [that is, Pakhtoonistan] problem."[12] He revived the Pakhtoonistan issue "at international forums such as the Algiers meeting of nonaligned nations and the Islamic summit held in Lahore" in February 1974; and he openly encouraged the autonomist demands of the national Awami Party of Khan Abdul Wali Khan, who frequently visited Kabul where his father, Khan Abdul Ghaffar Khan, the champion of Pakhtoonistan, lived in self-imposed exile.[13] Daoud's well-known stand on the issue undoubtedly enhanced his appeal for the group of young military officers who had brought him back to power "with the rallying cry of 'Pakhtoonistan.' "[14] To have ignored their mood might have precipitately ended his return to power. On July 19 a clandestine radio station calling itself Radio Pakhtoonistan began broadcasting. Once again, the border brimmed with tension. An interviewer for an Iranian newspaper noted that when questioned on his differences with Pakistan Daoud had a "calmer attitude this time than in the past." Insisting that all he sought was the granting of the right of national self–determination to the Pathans, Daoud blamed "imperialism" for having created the problem between two Muslim nations and stressed his belief that a "knot that can be opened by the hand should not be torn by the teeth."[15]

But he was impatient to reverse the King's conciliatory Pakistan policy. Radio Kabul spoke almost daily of the "occupied" areas of

Pakhtoonistan—"by implication making out a claim for an autonomous state that would embrace half of Pakistan, stretch to the sea, and be closely affiliated to Afghanistan."[16] An unsigned editorial in the August 30, 1974, issue of the Kabul *Times*—once again a government mouthpiece— referred to the "accursed Durand Line" and conveyed the impression that Afghanistan would not allow the situation to drift indefinitely.

On a number of occasions in 1974 and 1975, Pakistan's Prime Minister Bhutto castigated Kabul's indulgence in "provocative attacks," that is, border raids, assassinations, and acts of sabotage.[17] For the most part, he did not respond militarily because of greater absorption with the Baluch insurrection (1973-77). Though aggravated by outsiders (that is, Afghans, Russians, and Iraqis), the Baluch problem was primarily an outgrowth of the Baluch's quest not for independence but for greater autonomy within the existing state of Pakistan.[18] (According to the Afghans, "Pakhtoonistan" includes Baluchistan, the area of northwestern Pakistan contiguous to Afghanistan and extending to the Arabian Sea, with its terminus at the port of Gwadar, the ultimate prize for a landlocked state or an imperial power seeking access to the sea. Though there are interrelationships between Baluch and Pathans, our focus here is on the latter.)

Daoud used the Baluch insurrection to play up the Pakhtoon issue. Despite Pakistan's weakness after its defeat by India in 1971-72, its loss of the eastern part of the country through the secession of Bangladesh, and its domestic turmoil, he insisted that Afghanistan wanted only a peaceful solution of "its political difference" with Pakistan "through unconditional negotiations."[19] His moderation stemmed from military weakness and Soviet opposition. First, Daoud knew that the Pakistani army, notwith- standing its recent defeat, was superior to his own, which was one-quarter its size and not as well equipped for war, and "raids across the border from Pakistan in the summer of 1975 no doubt helped convince Daoud that more than one could play with fire and that Pakistani military capabilities were substantial."[20] Second, Moscow refused to encourage his Pakhtoon passion, and he was realist enough to know that without Soviet backing he lacked the wherewithal for a major struggle. Not even hints that he would support Brezhnev's Asian collective security proposal softened Moscow's opposition. Indeed, a few days after he floated this idea, he retracted it, realizing that the Brezhnev proposal ran counter to his aims and saying, "We like certain things in the doctrine but we do not like its emphasis on the inviolability of frontiers . . . that will mean accepting Pakistan's present frontiers which are the doing of the British."[21] A visit to Moscow in June 1974—the only trip he made abroad during his first year in office—was unproductive. Moscow was evidently keen on playing down the military incidents along the Afghan-Pakistani border. A TASS report of Daoud's luncheon speech carefully omitted a key passage in which he spoke of the "destiny of our Pushtun and Baluch brethren" and attacked Pakistan's leaders.[22] The joint communiqué issued at the end of the visit "expressed the hope that the political dispute between Afghanistan and Pakistan would be settled by peaceful means through negotiations"—a far cry from the support Daoud coveted. Moreover, he acceded to Soviet wishes and put his signature to a formulation on supporting the "creation of a security system by the collective efforts of all Asian peoples"—a modest pay-off for the extensive Soviet investment in his country.

A year after seizing power and surviving several attempted counter-coups from ultramilitants in his camp, Daoud recognized the precarious-ness of his position. The disaffected included many former staunch supporters. Some objected to his slow pace of internal transformation and democratization; others to his go–slow approach on Pakhtoonistan, fearing that he was preparing to sign a no-war pact with Bhutto along the lines of the Indo–Pakistani Simla accord of July 1972. Daoud became withdrawn, rarely appearing in public, secretive, and dependent on his family and a few friends for advice and administration: He reverted to the tribal type.

This combination of internal opposition and Moscow's restraining hand was decisive in the evolution of Daoud's Pakhtoon policy. By 1976 he ended the provocations along the frontier, improved relations with Pakistan, and seemed ready to develop a possible Iranian option that was designed to lessen dependence on the Soviet Union and permit a return to the traditional policy of *bi-tarafi* (literally, "without sides").

Despite Daoud's original preferred policy on the Pakhtoon issue, he was clearly favored over the King in Moscow. Given its penetration of the Afghan military, the Soviet leadership most likely knew of plans for the July 1973 coup, although it was not directly involved in its execution. The fact that Moscow chose not to alert King Zahir Shah strongly suggests that it believed there would be even greater advantages in having a pro Moscow leftist military group headed by Daoud in control in Kabul. Having committed itself to the putschists, Moscow had to allow them to generate the mini-crisis with Pakistan, because once Daoud was in power he could not be prevented, short of an open intervention, from reviving the Pakhtoon issue. While monitoring the situation to prevent undue es-calation, Moscow may even have welcomed the renewed tension and the additional leverage it brought over both Kabul and Islamabad, by showing how dependent Afghanistan had become on Soviet weapons and support, and serving as an unambiguous reminder to Pakistan that too close a relationship with China or the United States might cause an inflamed situation not only in the NWFP but in Baluchistan as well. In early 1975 Bhutto's assessment was that the situation of controlled tension suited Soviet purposes, and that Moscow could bring the bombings and sabotage to an end overnight if it wished, "ungovernable" and unruly though some of the Afghan tribes might be, because Afghanistan was now little more than a Soviet satellite.[23] (Although Bhutto refused to alter his relationship with China or back Brezhnev's collective security proposal, he did mend his fences with Moscow, avoid harsh criticism of Soviet policy, and downgrade relations with the United States—so Soviet expectations were not far off the mark.)

Moscow had another reason for dampening Daoud's irredentist ambitions: détente with the United States. Instigation of an Afghan–Pakistani war would have jeopardized the improving relations with the United States and Iran and created unwanted tensions in a region in which Moscow preferred to preserve the status quo, at least for the time being. Coming so soon after Brezhnev's visit to the United States in June 1973 and the near Soviet-American confrontation in the October 1973 Arab-Israeli War, any deliberate provocation on the subcontinent would have marked the instant end of détente. As one astute Indian journalist noted,

> a leadership which regards the Watergate affair as a plot by diehard elements to undermine President Nixon and his policy of *detente* with the Soviet Union is not likely to want to create problems for him in an area [that is, the Persian Gulf] of supreme importance to the United States and its West European and Japanese allies.[24]

BREZHNEV'S ASIAN COLLECTIVE SECURITY PROPOSAL

By the spring of 1969, relations with China having come close to the flash point of conflict, Moscow sought to isolate China in the world communist movement and in Asia, and to improve relations with key Asian nations in a way that would restrain if not undercut Peking's diplomacy. In late May, during a visit to Kabul, Kosygin had proposed regional economic cooperation among Afghanistan, Pakistan, and India as a step toward creating a peaceful environment in the area. On June 7, at the International Conference of Communist and Workers' Parties held in Moscow, Brezhnev floated a new idea that took Kosygin's proposal into the political and diplomatic realms: "We are of the opinion that the course of events is putting on the agenda the task of creating a system of collective security in Asia." He offered no details at the time, causing foreign observers to regard the move, especially in light of where it had been made, as basically anti-Chinese and an attempt to offer an alternative to the U.S. system of alliances.

However, after a long delay, on March 20, 1972, one month after Nixon's visit to China and the dramatic Sino-American rapprochement, Brezhnev stated:

> Collective security in Asia must, in our view, be based on such principles as renunciation of the use of force in relations between states, respect for sovereignty and the inviolability of borders, noninterference in internal affairs and the broad development of economic and other cooperation on the basis of full equality and mutual advantage.[25]

By stressing the widely supported principle of the inviolability of existing territorial boundaries, he placed the onus for Sino-Soviet border tensions on Peking, which had concluded final border agreements with most of the countries on its periphery, though notably not with the Soviet Union.

The Soviet leadership intensified its quest for adherents to Brezhnev's proposal. Afghanistan was a logical target, but King Zahir Shah took a guarded position. Thus, the joint communiqué issued in September 1971, at the end of his visit to the USSR, first acknowledged Afghanistan's nonaligned status:

> The Soviet side highly assesses the policy of nonalignment consistently pursued by Afghanistan, and considers it an important factor in the struggle of the peoples for their freedom and independence, for strengthening peace and security, for maintaining peace and cooperation with all the peoples.

Only after that did the Afghan side laud the Soviet side for supporting "the struggle of the peoples for their freedom and independence" and acknowledge that "the program for the active defense of peace and for strengthening international security proposed by the Soviet Union merits the support of all peace-loving peoples." King Zahir Shah avoided any commitment either to Brezhnev's proposal, which was vague on specifics, or to a friendship treaty, along the lines of the one between the Soviet Union and India the previous month.

During Podgorny's visit in May 1973, two months after the Shah of Iran had given his general endorsement—the first Asian leader to do so—Moscow could see headway being made with Afghanistan. The communiqué expressed the "great importance" attached by the Soviet Union to Afghanistan's "policy of positive neutrality and nonalignment," and declared that Afghanistan "highly appreciates the Soviet Union's consistent policy of peace"; and it went part of the way toward meeting Moscow's desire on the Brezhnev proposal.

Considering that observance of the principles of peaceful co-existence of states with differing social and political systems is an effective way toward establishing lasting peace both in Asia and in other parts of the world, the USSR and Afghanistan again declare that in order to guarantee security in Asia it is essential for all the countries of this area to make joint efforts in that direction.

On June 9, 1974, when Daoud was in Moscow for the first time since returning to power, he agreed to a formulation in the joint communiqué that more closely corresponded to Soviet statements and wishes:

The Soviet Union and the Republic of Afghanistan are deeply interested in ensuring peace and cooperation in Asia and consider that the creation of a system of security by the collective efforts of all the states of Asia would correspond to the interests of the Asian peoples.[26]

Daoud's acceptance of Brezhnev's proposal reflected a slight shift toward Moscow's position on the Sino-Soviet dispute and a cooling of Kabul's relations with Peking. Podgorny no doubt responded to this at a dinner reception for Daoud, when he not only criticized "aggressive imperialist circles [that is, the United States] who are trying to drag the world back to the times of the cold war," but also lashed out at those (that is, the Chinese) "who for the sake of their hegemonistic plans are striving to supercharge international tension, split peace-loving forces, and create barriers between peoples" that serve the interests of "imperialist reaction."[27]

The above formulation marked the limit of Daoud's accession to Moscow's position on an Asian collective security system. Thus, in the communiqués issued on December 10, 1975, during Podgorny's visit to Kabul, and on April 16, 1977, during what turned out to Daoud's last trip to Moscow, the two leaders briefly mentioned the topic and confirmed the clause on it that had been adopted in June 1974. The seeming constancy belied a strong undercurrent of disagreement and dissatisfaction that emerges from a careful reading of the overall situation. First, during the December 1975 visit, the conversations were not described as having been conducted in a "warm" or "cordial" atmosphere, but in an atmosphere of "frankness." Always a term denoting basic disagreement, this was the first time it was publicly used in their relationship. Second, a comparison of the formal dinner speeches delivered by Podgorny and Daoud were even more revealing of the divergence of priority and attitude than the communiqué. Whereas Podgorny went into a lengthy justification for "the creation of a collective security system on the Asian continent," Daoud ignored the subject, emphasizing instead Afghanistan's "nonattachment to various groupings, free judgment on international questions, active and positive neutrality and peaceful coexistence"; and whereas Podgorny eschewed direct mention of the Pakhtoon issue and strongly upheld "good-neighborly relations and businesslike cooperation among all states and the solution of disputes via talks, and this applies fully to the situation in South Asia and the Middle East," Daoud spoke of "governments which . . . ignore the legitimate demands of the people's masses" and singled out Pakistan and its "different approach to the legal demands and just desires of the Pushtu and Baluchi peoples" for criticism.[28] Moscow had to content itself with the same level of support for its collective security proposal and with the renewal for a further ten years of the 1931 treaty of neutrality and nonaggression, previously extended in 1965.

During Daoud's visit in April 1977, notwithstanding the signing of a treaty on economic development committing Moscow to even greater participation in Afghanistan's modernization program, the communiqué only partially reflected the real situation. In his dinner speech, Daoud conveyed some of the inner tension in the relationship when he said "frankness" was one of the pillars on which Soviet-Afghan relations rested, and when he reaffirmed Afghanistan's policy of nonalignment, amidst unmistakable signs of improved relations between Afghanistan and its Islamic neighbors, Pakistan and Iran.

CHINA

Afghan leaders maintained friendly relations with the People's Republic of China (PRC), but it never loomed prominently in their thinking or was a problem in Soviet-Afghan relations. China was too poor, too weak, and too remote for it to serve as an alternative to the USSR or even as a useful lever to pry more concessions out of Moscow or Washington, even after the road connecting the two countries in the Pamir/Himalayan Mountain range was completed in 1971.

In the 1950s, Sino-Afghan relations had been warm, the PRC providing about $25 million in credits for the First FYP, but they cooled in the mid-1960s, despite the signing in 1960 of a treaty of friendship and mutual nonaggression and the complete demarcation in 1964 of the rugged 46-mile boundary between China's Sinkiang province and Afghanistan's Wakhan corridor. Although in 1968 Peking agreed to build the Parwan hydroelectric project, which included a 30-mile-long canal and an offshoot irrigation system, and was Afghanistan's fourth largest donor of aid after the Federal Republic of Germany, it lacked real leverage. The reasons for this varied: China's growing support for Pakistan, its turbulent Cultural Revolution at home, Afghanistan's unwillingness to align itself with China's hard-line position on Vietnam, and, in light of Kabul's close economic relationship with the USSR, its reluctance to become involved in the Sino-Soviet quarrel.

Even the pro-Maoist group, formed in the mid-1960s, was far weaker among the radical students and intelligentsia than its pro-Soviet counterpart, Parcham, the military wing of Nur Muhammad Taraki's Marxist People's Democratic Party of Afghanistan (PDPA). In 1967 the PDPA split into two groups, Khalq, headed by Taraki, and Parcham, headed by Babrak Karmal, because of "personality conflicts between Babrak and the Khalq leadership; Babrak's desire to form a united front of all coalitions; and Babrak's soft stand on the 'Pushtunistan' issue."[29]

The 1973 coup cast a pall over Sino-Afghan relations. Once Daoud rekindled the Pakhtoon issue his interests ran counter to those of China, which was courting Pakistan, in order to further its principal aim in South Asia, namely, to counter India's close ties to the Soviet Union; but Daoud did not want to alienate China. In December 1974 he sent his brother, Muhammad Naim Khan, as a special presidential envoy to meet with the ailing Chou En-lai to explain that, despite its qualified support for Brezhnev's Asian collective security proposal, Afghanistan would continue to adhere to nonalignment and neutrality on the Sino-Soviet dispute. This produced an immediate improvement in Sino-Afghan relations, reflected in early 1975 by an interest-free long-term Chinese loan of $55 million,[30] and the following year by a protocol on an exchange of goods. Nevertheless, relations were conducted in a minor key and never reached a pitch that could conceivably have jarred Moscow into fearing a threat to the Soviet-Afghan relationship; so Daoud was allowed to play out his Chinese cadenza.

THE IRANIAN OPTION

In the mid-1970s Daoud was groping for a handle on his problems and his power. As is so often the case, domestic factors were crucial in persuading a leader to change his foreign policy. The opposition to Daoud was growing, both from the Muslim Brotherhood on the right, which saw his reforms and secularist bent as communist-inspired, and from the Parcham, which had brought him to power and was increasingly disillusioned by his determination to wield power as an absolute autocrat. Moreover, the ambitious reforms in agriculture, education, and administration, and the nationalization of the banking system, failed to generate development. The economy was in serious trouble:

> Unemployment of the educated was compounded by steep inflation. Both unemployment and inflation were aggravated by an

accelerating tide of migration from countryside to city, especially to Kabul, where the population was pressing close to one million. It was clear that the country was imperiled by its failure to expand the production of food for either subsistence or export earnings.[31]

Overwhelmed by political and economic pressures, Daoud, now in his late sixties, drew on his royal and tribal heritage in an attempt to survive. Domestically, he purged members of the Parcham and replaced them with a coterie of family, friends, and technocrats from previous governments. The need for urgency in implementing the Seven Year Plan (1976-83) that was supposed to have been adopted in March 1976 but was delayed until September took a back seat to political juggling. In January 1977 a hand-picked Loya Jirgah approved a new constitution. ("Naturally," according to Louis Dupree, "the government investigated and approved all the delegates".)[32] There were lively discussions and many amendments, but the final document provided for a one-party system that was very much Daoud's creation and creature. "So single-mindedly" did Daoud concentrate "on the political problems of consolidating power that economic and social issues were left unattended or in confusion," with the result that he alienated natural allies among those who had supported the King's efforts to develop a constitutional monarchy.[33]

In foreign policy Daoud hesitantly veered to an approximation of the policy that had traditionally been used to preserve independence—*bi-tarafi*, the balancing of external influences. *Bi-tarafi* might, he reasoned, bring him the time and additional assistance he needed to entrench himself internally and he took three steps toward realizing it.

The first step was to defuse the Pakhtoon issue and normalize relations with Pakistan. Pakhtoonistan was no longer the unifying issue it had seemed in 1973, and the new "old guard" Mohammadzais close to him counseled disengagement from a policy that had led to less than cordial relations with key Muslim nations in the area, namely, Iran, Saudi Arabia, and Kuwait. Not incidentally, these countries were now all enormously wealthy (thanks to the leapfrogging OPEC oil prices) and were potentially important sources of economic support to tide over Afghanistan's ailing economy. Daoud and his advisers finally accepted the fact that it was not in Afghanistan's power to dismember Pakistan and that by pressing the Pakhtoon issue they "played into Soviet hands by increasing Afghan dependence on Soviet aid."[34]

The Afghan-Pakistani rapprochement went slowly, despite frequent meliorative efforts by the Shah of Iran. Bhutto's unexpected remark in January 1976 that he was prepared to fly to Kabul without any pre-conditions went unanswered. The breakthrough came four months later, when the Pakistan government offered relief supplies for the flood–stricken areas of southern Afghanistan. An initial rejection by the Afghan foreign ministry was countermanded by Daoud, who accepted the offer and thanked Pakistan for its good-neighborly gesture. Shortly thereafter he invited the Pakistani president to Kabul.[35] Bhutto's visit in early June was a success: In the joint communiqué, which Daoud insisted on, there was a call for Afghan-Pakistani friendship on the basis of the principles of coexistence accepted by all members of the nonaligned movement, including acceptance of existing boundaries and noninterference in the internal affairs of member states. In August Daoud returned the visit, which later occasioned reports of a far-reaching draft agreement having been reached calling for provincial autonomy for the NWFP and Baluchistan in exchange for "simultaneous recognition by Afghanistan of the Durand Line as the permanent border between the two countries."[36] Speaking to the Loya Jirgah on January 30, 1977, he said that as a result of "these direct contacts and the exchange of views, which took place in an atmosphere of cordiality and understanding, a climate has developed that makes us hopeful of reaching an honorable solution to our political dispute, to enable the two countries to live together as friends". He added that whether or not a final settlement was reached, the agreement to end "hostile propaganda" against each other was representative of the desire of both sides and urged "that this main dispute be ended."[37]

The search for a solution continued. General Zia-ul-Haq, who deposed Bhutto in July 1977, visited Kabul in October and Daoud returned to Pakistan in early March 1978, and in return for an amnesty "for Pathan and Baluch rebels in Pakistan . . . is said to have agreed to the repatriation of Baluch and Pushtun political refugees from Afghan soil— forcibly if necessary."[38] The next step might have been the long-elusive acceptance of the Durand Line as the legal boundary between Afghanistan and Pakistan; but in late April he ran out of time.

The second and most important of the three steps Daoud took in quest of bi-tarafi was the opening to Iran.[39] The Shah had long been concerned over the dispute between Afghanistan and Pakistan and had played a key role in their resumption of diplomatic relations in 1963. After Pakistan's defeat in 1971, Iraq's attempt to turn the unrest in Baluchistan against Iran convinced him of the need to improve Iranian-Afghan and Afghan-Pakistani relations. On March 13, 1973, Afghanistan and Iran signed an agreement in Kabul ending their lingering dispute over the apportionment of the waters of the lower Helmand River.[40] After the coup in July, Daoud sent his brother to Tehran to reassure the Shah of his intention of abiding by the terms of the treaty. In fact, however, he was very slow to implement the key provisions, in part because of a serious clash at the Afghan-Iranian border in Sistan in October 1973 and in part to enhance his bargaining position for Iranian loans.

During Daoud's revival of the Pakhtoon issue, the Shah repeatedly assured Pakistan of his support against any attempts to destabilize Pakistan, a clear warning to Daoud not to stir up tribal unrest. In August 1974 Iran's foreign minister visited Kabul, and in September and October senior colleagues went to Kabul and Islamabad; all failed to persuade either party to accept Iran's mediation of their dispute.

On innumerable occasions after 1963 the Shah had broached the possibility of placing Iran's port facilities at the disposal of Afghanistan, thereby offering an alternative to the transit of Afghan goods through either the Soviet Union or Pakistan, but to no avail. Later, the Shah's persistence—and new oil wealth—suited Daoud's changing mood. During a visit to Tehran in April 1975, he accepted the offer of a $2 billion credit, of which $300 million was earmarked for Afghanistan's Seven Year Plan, then under preparation, making Iran the second most important donor after the Soviet Union,[41] while about $1.7 billion was to go toward construction of an 800-mile railroad from the Iranian port of Bandar Abbas on the Strait of Hormuz, north to Kerman, then east to the border town of Zahidan and on to Herat and Kandahar and eventually to Kabul. An ambitious ten-year project, feasible because of Iran's burgeoning oil wealth, it held out the allure of an end to Afghan dependence on the USSR. A more immediate consequence was Daoud's intervention the following month to overrule his foreign minister and accept Bhutto's offer of relief assistance, thus ushering in the reconciliation between Afghanistan and Pakistan, and encouraging the Shah to broaden his plan for Regional Cooperation for Development, an organization established in 1964 to promote closer economic and cultural ties among Turkey, Pakistan, and Iran.

The Shah's diplomacy seemed on the threshold of a stunning triumph, but fickle history would have it otherwise. Daoud had the financial commitments he needed not only from Iran but also Saudi Arabia and Kuwait—to implement his domestic programs and lessen his dependence on Moscow; but deeply rooted political predilections and personality, always an important and so much unknown variable in foreign policy decisionmaking, intruded. Whereas the Shah urged speedy implementation of their agreements, dismissing the assessments of SAVAK, his secret police, which said Daoud was controlled by Moscow, Daoud dawdled. He was slow to respond to the Shah's concessions and commitments; he refused, for example, to implement the Helmand River treaty until June 1977, and delayed the start of surveying for the projected railroad. He regarded with suspicion the Shiite Iranians, whom the Sunni Pathans traditionally held to be weak, untrustworthy, and decadent, whereas the Shah had transcended an equally traditional Iranian view of the Afghans as primitive, ruthless, and unsophisticated, as inferiors, not equals. In the end, nothing was done, not on Helmand River water-sharing, and not on the railroad, which never moved beyond the paper stage. Very few of Iran's much-publicized economic commitments ever became actual projects.

The Soviet role in all of this must, in the absence of suitable evidence, remain conjectural. Moscow never commented on the moves toward amity between Kabul and Tehran or Kabul and Islamabad, but it could not have been pleased: If Daoud's reconciliations took hold they would inevitably lessen Afghanistan's dependence on the Soviet Union. From Moscow's point of view, intimacy between Afghanistan and its Islamic neighbors was as much to be prevented as open conflict: no peace, no war was preferable. Soviet leaders were in a predicament: how to forestall Daoud's Iranian option and keep him dependent without jeopardizing their budding economic and diplomatic relationship with the Shah. Ever since the mid-1960s, Soviet-Iranian relations had improved significantly. They were important enough not to disrupt. Yet the possibility of a Tehran-Kabul-Islamabad coalition could not be ruled out; such a grouping would, Moscow felt, be intrinsically anticommunist, with a pro-U.S. tilt, and a setback for Soviet aims in the area. It would strengthen three countries, who, taken individually, were relatively weak, more vulnerable to manipulation, and to some degree dependent on Soviet good will. At the very least it would weaken Soviet influence in Kabul.

Moscow could not directly pressure Afghanistan to refrain from improving relations with Iran, but it could outbid the Shah by offering additional credits, as Podgorny did during his visit in December 1975; and it could commit Daoud to a long–term economic treaty, as it did during his visit in April 1977, by providing additional assurances, which had the effect of perpetuating Daoud's dilatoriness in dealing with the Shah. It also brought the Khalq and Parcham together again in July 1977 after a ten-year split, the better to undermine Daoud from within, an opportunity that may have eventuated sooner than they expected.

The third step in Daoud's search for *bi-tarafi* was a return to an active policy of nonalignment. The least important politically, it nonetheless had symbolic importance. In the period from 1976 to 1978, Daoud made frequent trips abroad, everywhere conveying Afghanistan's interest in closer ties with other nonaligned countries. In early 1978, in what was to be a final flurry of diplomatic activity, he visited Yugoslavia, Egypt, and India—the three leading members of the movement—and associated Afghanistan with their efforts to keep nonalignment on a moderate course and Castro from being elected to head it for a three-year period, starting in September 1979. In addition, in an unmistakable indication of his desire to resume a more prominently nonaligned stand, "Daoud began to send Afghan military personnel for training in India and Egypt and expanded the number being trained in the United States, clearly in an attempt to lessen Afghan dependence on Soviet military training."[42]

The three steps—reconciliation with Pakistan, reliance on Iran economically, and active affiliation with the nonaligned movement—might, with more time and if fully implemented, have kept Afghanistan independent and the Soviet Union north of the Oxus River.

THE DOWNFALL OF THE MOHAMMADZAI DURRANIS

The story is told that when Daoud visited Moscow in April 1977 and Brezhnev berated him for failing to implement land reforms, support his Asian collective security proposal, show appreciation for Soviet aid, and keep communists in the government, Daoud icily replied, "I am the president of an independent country and not a member of your East European bloc." As he stalked out, Daoud's aide whispered, "You've just signed your death warrant."

Daoud was being assertive in foreign policy at the very moment that he had lost control of the domestic situation, in which were sowed the seeds of destruction. The end came suddenly.

On April 17, 1978, a well-known Parcham labor leader and ideologue, Mir Akbar Khyber, was murdered, assailants unknown, though among the various explanations is one suggesting that the Soviet KGB masterminded the incident in order to generate enough social unrest and confusion to screen the thrust against Daoud, who had outlived his usefulness. Two days later, the PDPA (composed of the re-formed Khalq and Parcham communist factions) organized mass demonstrations. Protest rallies sprouted across the capital. Shortly after midnight, on April 26, Daoud arrested the leading communists, including Nur Muhammad Taraki and Babrak Karmal. Inexplicably, however, Hafizullah Amin was only placed under house arrest until 10:45 A.M. According to Khalqi hagiography, before he was taken off to prison, Amin had enough time to send instructions through his children to communist cells in the military ordering them to carry out previously laid plans for the coup.

On the morning of April 27, as Daoud and his cabinet were meeting in the presidential palace to consider further measures, armored units of the army attacked, seizing the radio station and other key installations. Thirty-six hours later, after fierce resistance by Daoud's 2,000-man elite force, the putschists were victorious. The turning point was probably the precision bombings of loyalist positions that were carried out "with amazing competence," leading some observers to suggest "that Soviet pilots were flying the Afghan planes."[43] Daoud was killed, as were most of his family and close associates, and with him ended 160 years of Mohammadzai Durrani rule.

The victors proclaimed a Democratic Republic of Afghanistan (DRA) and promised policies that would be based on Islamic principles, Afghan nationalism, economic and social justice, and nonalignment in foreign affairs.

Although there is no documentary evidence that Moscow ordered the coup, this time, unlike July 1973, the inferences of its complicity are compelling.[44] First of all, it had the motive and the timing was right. Daoud was unpopular, the economy was suffering from inflation and unemployment, and the anticipated benefits from Iran and the oil-rich Arab states had not yet arrived. To have delayed would have enabled him to use subsidies to consolidate his position and regain a measure of support, in addition to widening his purge of communists and pro–Soviet leftists from the military.

Second, the PDPA (Khalq-Parcham) was undeniably communist, with intimate links to Moscow, though for several months after the coup prominent specialists such as Louis Dupree and journalists such as Simon Winchester of *The Times* (London) persisted in contrary assessments, accepting at face value Taraki's self-description of nationalist and revolutionary.[45] Third, Taraki's government was recognized by Moscow almost immediately, even before other foreign embassies could establish telephone contact with the new regime, suggesting foreknowledge of the events.[46] Finally, the speed and scale of Soviet efforts to buttress the new regime "speaks volumes":

> Immediately twenty-five agreements with Comecon countries were signed by the new regime; an unusual burst of diplomacy on the part of a government scarcely secure in its own capital. While street-fighting went on in Kabul, the government began contracting for Bulgarian television and East German printing equipment, together with an additional 22 million dollars from the Soviet Union to exploit natural gas. Fidel Castro paid a brief visit shortly after the revolution, presumably to assure the new government that it is possible to run a small country entirely on Soviet aid for years.[47]

Dupree, who does not believe the Soviets were "directly involved" (although he says "Soviet military personnel may have played an advisory role during the fighting which followed the start of the coup"), dismisses the significance of the above:

> It is true that the USSR was the first state to recognize the DRA, but it had also been the first to recognize the Daoud regime in 1973. It is true that within in a month of the coup the Soviets signed more than 30

aid agreements with the DRA, but most of these had been initiated during the Daoud period. And it is true that large numbers of Soviet technicians and their families swarmed into the country after April 1978 but they had after the Daoud coup as well.[48]

For him "the reality is that the DRA regime acts in ways it *assumes* the USSR wants it to act because it *assumes* the USSR will never abandon it." This does not explain why the DRA made such assumptions, but let that pass.

Beyond the formal similarities, there are significant differences between the two revolutions. In the three months after the April coup the two governments exchanged nine missions (none previously scheduled, as far as I know), whereas in 1973, in a comparable period, only three had been exchanged. There were more missions—20—exchanged in the eight remaining months of 1978 than in any calendar year since the Soviet courtship had begun in the 1950s. Unlike 1973, the Soviet press covered Afghanistan like a tent. No political, economic, educational, juridical, or agrarian development went unreported. Moscow evinced an intensity of interest (in early July it organized the first-ever exhibition of Afghan export staples) that suggests it perceived something unusual had happened. Unlike 1973, the number-two man in the government visited Moscow three weeks after the coup. True, this visit of Hafizullah Amin on May 18 was a stopover enroute to a meeting in Havana of the Coordinating Bureau of the nonaligned countries, but the attention given it suggests that it had been arranged with a definite political purpose in mind, namely, to convey abroad the symbiotic relationship and "all-round cooperation" between the Democratic Republic of Afghanistan and the Soviet Union and their "unbreakable bonds of friendship." The publicity accorded the visit showed the ideological character of the regime and of the new Soviet-Afghan relationship, and was intended as a warning to outside powers to keep "hands off." Like Daoud, Taraki wrapped himself in republican cloth; but he was a communist bent on radical changes, not a conservative seeking reform within a basically traditional framework, and his embrace of Moscow showed that he was not taking any chances.

OBSERVATIONS

For most of the period under consideration, Afghanistan's foreign policy was highly satisfactory to Moscow. The leadership's options on the key issues that dominated the Soviet-Afghan relationship were limited and narrowly confined by internal and external determinants. Examination of the issues suggests that, overall, Afghanistan adapted its preferences to fit the parameters set by Soviet wishes and warnings.

Afghanistan's enormous economic and military dependence and relative geographic isolation meant Moscow's counsels carried extraordinary weight, far more than in the case of Turkey or Iran. On no issue of consequence to it did Kabul's preferences take precedence over Moscow's. With one exception, Kabul was constrained, both under the King and under Daoud, from striking out on its own; and that exception, Daoud's search for an Iranian option, may have been one of the causes of his demise. In the 1973–78 period, the pervasive penetration of the military by pro-Soviet elements was an ever-present reminder to Daoud of the possibility of a Soviet-inspired coup or of a direct intervention. The vulnerable common border lent special credence to these possibilities and shaped the general context within which he tried to maneuver. In retrospect, we see that Afghanistan's high degree of dependence bred a Soviet influence and an environment in which it was felt even when not exercised; it was an influence that transcended the general accord and seeming equality of relations that emerged on most issues from a consideration of the wording of the joint communiqué and near symmetry in the exchange of missions. The pattern of Afghanistan's starkly circumscribed options (and their inexorable conclusion) was recognized by a few astute observers, for example, the "quite clairvoyant minister" who told U.S. Ambassador Theodore Eliot in 1973: "I give Mohammad Daoud six years before the Communist decide to dispense with him."[49]

The "hard" data—missions, communiqués, editorials, speeches, statistics—did not reveal the essence of the Soviet-Afghan relationship, but they did provide vital glimpses and insights into its true nature. If they only hinted at the differences that existed, the reasons are fairly clear: For the most part, the differences were not serious, and when they were, neither party had an interest in highlighting them. For Moscow, Afghanistan was the showpiece of peaceful coexistence and a demonstration of the value of Soviet foreign aid in all its aspects. The determination to preserve this positive image—made easy because Afghan policies seldom contravened Soviet interests—induced Moscow to be supportive, sympathetic, or forebearing, depending on the issue and circumstance. For Kabul, the Soviet Union was a prime benefactor, from whom little could be gained by public disagreements and, indeed, much could be lost.

The hypotheses tested were essentially confirmed. For example, heightened Soviet interaction with Afghanistan did contribute to increased Soviet influence, especially as a consequence of the extensive military relationship and the steady stream of Afghan officers sent to the USSR for training—and recruitment; the greater Soviet presence brought greater influence, not so much directly as in the ways that it reinforced Kabul's dependence, which, in turn, elicited special sensitivity to Soviet wishes; and the Soviet Union's role as sole arms supplier was more important than the level of sophistication of the weapons, which were generally older models. This monopoly position aided the Soviet penetration of the military and the recruitment of agents for the 1973 and 1978 coups. (It may well be that the Soviet monopoly position was not as critical as the dissatisfaction and disaffection of many young officers who were motivated by a desire to modernize their country.)

The Afghan leadership began to lose its way—and ultimately its independence—when it lost its perspective, when irredentist ambitions distorted the proper sense of history and geography and led it to Moscow for aid against Pakistan; and when the desire to modernize led to immoderate impatience with the leadership's inefficiency and corruption. Still, the country might have surmounted the erratic and often frustrating lurch toward modernity and survived the dependence on the Soviet Union, the army honeycombed with leftist, vaguely Marxist officers, and the painful process of seeking greater economic development, social justice, and political participation for the new breed of educated technocrat. What it could not survive was betrayal.

Daoud's coup against the King was the first and most serious betrayal. By toppling the monarchy, he shredded the carefully patterned fabric that had bound the disparate tribes together and had offered a promising political framework for creating a consitutional monarchy suited to Afghan culture and ethnic diversity. Without Daoud's participation, there might never have been a successful, or even an attempted, coup. His prestige and connivance lent legitimacy to the ill-intended venture. The second, and final, betrayal was perpetrated by the impatient leftist officers who, whether through idealism or ideology, allowed themselves to be used by the communists, hungry for power, manipulated by Moscow, and obsessed by their own millenarian vision of the future. They destroyed Daoud in April 1978, and in the aftermath of this very same process, most of them ended up as diposable pawns, swept aside by internecine communist infighting at the top and by the onrushing tide of myrmidons from the Soviet Union.

One final comment. The Soviet Union may well have decided to destroy Daoud. If so, it was Brezhnev's covetousness and not the Shah of Iran's "ambitious effort to roll back Soviet influence in surrounding countries and create a modern version of the ancient Persian empire," as postulated by one writer, who in his argument: exaggerates the Shah's influence over Daoud and subservience to the United States; mistakes the Shah's commitment to build a rail and highway network with the hoped-for political consequences that might have developed after its completion at the end of the 1980s; acknowledges "it is difficult to believe that there was no Russian involvement [in the April coup], given the extent of the

Soviet military and intelligence presence in Kabul" and the probable involvement of Soviet pilots during the critical moments of the fighting, but yet uncritically accepts the questionable assumption that Daoud, and not the KGB, murdered Mir Akbar Khyber; and finally, ignores Daoud's desire to regain a measure of Afghan flexibility in foreign policy, attaches to this effort the politically dubious label of a move "again toward a pro-Western stance" (as if Daoud had ever been in the Western camp), and contends this was what provoked the Russians.[50]

Daoud's Iranian option was no serious threat to the Soviet-Afghan relationship. True, it might eventually have attenuated Soviet-Afghan economic ties (though not until considerably later, since the USSR was Afghanistan's principal donor for the Seven Year Plan, adopted in 1976, and was the only market for its increasingly important exports of natural gas); but Moscow had no cause whatsoever to be concerned over its security or legitimate vital interests. Daoud did not threaten the Soviet position in the region, and neither the United States nor China was in a position to benefit directly from his attempted shift to a more genuine and open nonaligned policy. In trying to reemphasize Afghanistan's non-aligned status, Daoud was not about to join any military pact of any Shah-sponsored security grouping or to permit Afghanistan to become a base for a foreign power.

What Moscow may have feared was diminished ability to intrigue in Afghanistan's political and military system. Hence, when an opportunity arose in April 1978 to unseat Daoud, its behavior was shaped by imperial ambition, not national security.

NOTES

1. The most comprehensive and authoritative account of King Zahir Shah's domestic policies in the years from 1963 to 1973 is Louis Dupree, *Afghanistan*, rev. ed. (Princeton, N.J.: Princeton University Press, 1980), Chapter 24.

2. Ibid., 754.

3. The iron ore deposits are near the surface, but remote from any feasible railway link; and Afghanistan has yet to build its first railroad. During a visit to Pakistan in 1970 I was told that Moscow had suggested to Afghanistan and Pakistan that the three countries develop an integrated transportation-economic relationship that would exploit Afghan iron ore and promote Pakistan's steel production. However, political suspicions and economic costs precluded serious exploration of such a plan. The vision of a railroad connecting Soviet Central Asia with Kabul, Karachi, and New Delhi, with branch lines to exploit mineral deposits, must add considerable economic weight to Moscow's strategic and political calculations.

4. Dupree, 765-66. For a more detailed treatment, see Dupree's "Afghanistan 1977: Does Trade Plus Aid Guarantee Development?" *American Universities Field Service Reports* (hereafter *AUFS Reports*), (Asia Series) 21, no. 3, (1977).

5. *The Times of India*, July 26, 1973.

6. *Dawn*, July 20, 1973.

7. David Chaffetz, "Afghanistan in Turmoil," *International Affairs* 56, no. 1 (January 1980):17-18.

8. Ibid., 18.

9. *Izvestiia*, December 8, 1975.

10. *Pravda*, April 15, 1977.

11. Stephen Oren, "The Afghani Coup and the Peace of the Northern Tier," *The World Today* 30, no. 1 (January 1974):28-29.

12. FBIS/Middle East, July 18, 1973, M1.

13. Shirin Tahir-Kheli, "The Foreign Policy of 'New' Pakistan," *Orbis* 20, no. 3 (Fall 1976):747.

14. Ibid., 749.

15. FBIS/Middle East, August 6, 1973, M1.

16. *Financial Times*, July 17, 1974.

17. For example, FBIS/Pakistan, July 17, 1974, T1.

18. Selig S. Harrison, "Nightmare in Baluchistan," *Foreign Policy*, no. 32 (Fall 1978), 136-60.

19. *Kabul Times*, October 28, 1974

20. Theodore L. Eliot, Jr., "Afghanistan after the 1978 Revolution," *Strategic Review* 7, no. 2 (Spring 1980):59.

21. Quoted in A. G. Noorani, "Soviet Ambitions in South Asia," *International Security* 4, no. 3 (Winter 1979/80):41. Noorani's chronology on this incident, however, is not clear.

22. FBIS/USSR, June 7, 1974, J1.

23. *The Times*, March 8, 1975.

24. Girilal Jain, *The Times of India*, July 25, 1973.

25. *Pravda*, March 21, 1972.

26. FBIS/USSR, June 10, 1974, J4.

27. FBIS/USSR, June 12, 1974, J2.

28. FBIS/USSR, December 12, 1975, J2-J5.

29. Dupree, *Afghanistan*, 771.

30. *Kabul Times*, January 2, 1975.

31. Nancy Peabody Newell and Richard S. Newell, *The Struggle for Afghanistan* (Ithaca, N.Y.: Cornell University Press, 1981), 48.

32. Dupree, *Afghanistan*, 763.

33. Newell and Newell, 47.

34. Eliot, 59.

35. Salamat Ali, "Kabul Warns to an Old Enemy," *Far Eastern Economic Review* 93, no. 31 (July 30, 1976):11.

36. Michael Richardson, "Breaking the Territorial Ice," *Far Eastern Economic Review* 101, no. 39 (September 29, 1978):31. A detailed assessment of the Bhutto-Daoud reconciliation and their effort to defuse the Pakhtoon issue is to be found in Louis Dupree, "Toward Representative Government in Afghanistan, Part I: The First Five Steps," *AUFS Reports* (Asia) 1 (1978) 7–9. Dupree, *Afghanistan*, 767.

37. FBIS/South Asia, February 3, 1977, S1.

38. Lawrence Lifschultz, "Accounting for the Past in Pakistan," *Far Eastern Economic Review* 100, no. 25 (June 23, 1978):32.

39. Compare James Ross, "Before the Deluge: The Soviet-Afghan Influence Relationship from 1973 to 1978," unpublished manuscript, 1981.

40. A. H. H. Abidi, "Irano-Afghan Dispute over the Helmand Waters," *International Studies* 16, no. 3 (July-September 1977):370-75. An insightful and persuasive piecing together of evidence suggesting Soviet complicity is to be found in Anthony Arnold, *Afghanistan: The Soviet Invasion of Afghanistan* (Stanford, Calif.: Hoover Institution Press,

1981), 68-72. Arnold observes, among other things, that Moscow's recognition of the new government came on Sunday, April 30, "in the middle of the long weekend celebrations for May Day"; that "the triggering catalyst for the coup—Khyber's assassination"—was virtually ignored, once Taraki seized power; and that Amin's courier for transmitting instructions used photocopies that were made at a friendly (Soviet?) diplomatic compound, since it is always difficult to obtain photocopies commercially in Kabul, "much less in the dawn hours."

41. *Middle East Economic Digest* 21, no. 11 (March 18, 1977):3.

42. Eliot, 59.

43. Hannah Negaran, "The Afghan Coup of April 1978: Revolution and International Security," *Orbis* 23, no. 1 (Spring 1979):101.

44. For a skillful but (in this writer's judgment) flawed interpretation of the relationship between Daoud and the Shah and of the Soviet role in the coup as "a secondary one," see Selig S. Harrison, "Dateline Afghanistan: Exit Through Finland?" *Foreign Policy*, no. 41 (Winter 1980-81), 163-87.

45. See Louis Dupree, New York *Times*, May 20, 1978; and Simon Winchester, Washington *Post*, May 8, 1978. The U.S. government was "from the outset . . . under no illusions . . . that the coup was a communist takeover." Theodore L. Eliot, Jr. (who was American ambassador in Kabul at the time), *Survival* 22, no. 6 (November/December 1980):263-64.

46. Salamat Ali, "Daoud's Day of Reckoning," *Far Eastern Economic Review*, 100, no. 21 (May 26, 1978):28.

47. Chaffetz, 20.

48. Louis Dupree, "Afghanistan Under the Khalq," *Problems of Communism* 28, no. 4 (July-August 1979):46-48.

49. Chaffetz, 17.

50. Selig S. Harrison, "The Shah, Not Kremlin, Touched Off Afghan Coup," Washington *Post*, May 13, 1979.

8

EMBRACED BY THE BEAR:
THE SOVIETIZATION OF AFGHANISTAN

After the old regime was toppled in a bloody military coup that claimed about 2,000 lives (the exact number is unknown), the new government set out to construct a society on the lines of the one they imagined to exist in the Soviet Union. Unmistakably pro-Soviet and Marxist-Leninist, the People's Democratic Party of Afghanistan, headed by Nur Muhammad Taraki, was assisted by an influx of hundreds of Soviet advisers and technicians. Though refusing to identify themselves as Marxist (most likely to forestall the reflex opposition of religious and tribal groups and the alienation of other Muslim states), the PDPA propagandists tipped their bent when they issued a pamphlet entitled "A Short Information about People's Democratic Party of Afghanistan," printed in Kabul in 1978, in which the party was described as the "vanguard of the working class of the country" (a standard communist phrase for the party) and "Comrade Taraki" was identified as an experienced Marxist-Leninist" who had spread "Marxism-Leninism" throughout the country ever since the party was established on January 1, 1965. They also acknowledged that plans for the coup had been made in 1976, but Comrade Taraki, with the close collaboration of comrade Hafizullah Amin, had held off until "all the possibilities for assuming political power were at hand."[1]

The leadership, a Khalq-dominated coalition with Parcham, was announced on May 2, 1978: Taraki was head of state (chairman of the Revolutionary Council), prime minister, and secretary-general of the PDPA; Hafizullah Amin (Khalq) was appointed deputy prime minister and foreign minister; Babrak Karmal (Parcham), vice-president and deputy prime minister; and General Abdul Qadir (Parcham), the air force officer whose initiative had swung the course of the revolution at a critical moment, defense minister. The honeymoon lasted until July, when Taraki

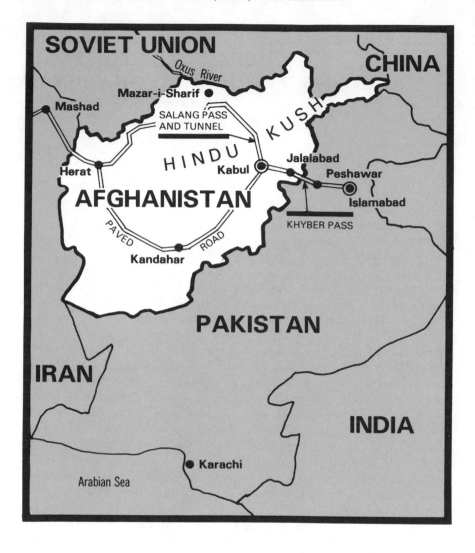

purged Karmal, Qadir, and other Parchamis, posting some abroad as ambassadors, arresting others, and soon afterward declaring them traitors. (Those assigned to embassies found refuge in Eastern Europe, as Moscow refused to hand them over, and later returned with the invading Soviet troops in December 1979.) No mention of Karmal's fall appeared in the Soviet media, suggesting that Moscow considered him reliable and was safeguarding him for future use.

Taraki pushed changes with undue haste. He overhauled the ministries of interior, planning, justice, and information, and rid the civil service of Mohammadzais and Western-trained administrators, in the process creating a severe shortage of trained personnel. With ideological zeal and indifference to the character of the society he wanted to transform, he pressed economic and social reforms, alienating rural tribal groups, religious leaders, and the urban middle class. The poorly implemented reforms incurred resentment and eroded support for the government: They trampled on religious practices by banning dowries and arranged marriages, introduced a system of land redistribution that threatened tribal patterns of authority, and though decreeing an end to usury offered no satisfactory method of providing credit in rural areas. In October, Taraki committed a gross stupidity. He changed the flag, replacing the traditional Islamic green with a red flag similar to that used by union republics of the Soviet Union. He was "dizzy with success" (a term Stalin used disingenuously in 1931 to denounce those who pushed forced collectivization without regard for local conditions or consequences) in his efforts to accelerate revolutionary transformation. Soviet military advisers poured into the country, assuming "command positions down to brigade level within the armed forces" to ensure the irreversibility of the communist coup.[2] To encourage Pakistani quiescence, Taraki remained silent on his intentions concerning the Pakhtoon and Baluch questions, for the moment declining to take a position on the agreement reached between Pakistan and the Daoud regime.

Taraki was eulogized as the "Great Leader" and the "Beloved Leader." Determined to create a new society quickly and lacking any governmental experience, he looked to the Soviet Union for a model and guidance. Moscow did not try to temper his policies, possibly remembering its disappointment with Daoud's failure to press socialist reforms after coming to power in 1973; possibly having Ethiopia in mind as an example of a revolution that can be ruthlessly and effectively imposed on a feudal people and structure; or possibly considering its own transformation of Central Asia. Moreover, more than a century of familiarity with Afghan primitiveness, backwardness, corruption, inefficiency, and parochialism, plus the traditional Russian contempt for the Afghans (and all colored peoples, who are disparagingly referred to as *chornetsi*—the colloquial Russian word for "black"), may have led Moscow to reason—as did Macbeth when he was contemplating murder—"If it were done when 'tis done, then 'twere well It were done quickly." If so, Soviet leaders ignored Shakespeare's sequent "But here, upon this bank and shoal of time . . . We still have judgement."

Taraki was a poet, an ideologue, a romantic revolutionary. Like Abolhassan Bani-Sadr in Iran two years later, he did not have the slightest idea of how to institutionalize his power and transform society. He pinned his hopes on Moscow.

TYING THE KNOT

Taraki's visit to Moscow in early December led to a treaty that bound Afghanistan even more closely to the Soviet Union and that later provided the juridical justification for the Kremlin's military intervention and occupation.

On December 5, 1978, a 20-year Treaty of Friendship, Neighborliness and Cooperation between the USSR and the Democratic Republic of Afghanistan was signed by Brezhnev and Taraki.[3] Reaffirming "the aims and principles" of the 1921 and 1931 treaties, it declared "their determination to strengthen and deepen" their "inviolable friendship . . . and . . . develop all-around cooperation." Of special importance was Article 4 (subsequently cited by Moscow to justify its invasion a year later), calling on the two parties to "consult each other and take by agreement appropriate measures to ensure the security, independence, and territorial integrity of the two countries," and stating that in the interest of strengthening their "defense capacity" they "shall continue to develop cooperation in the military field on the basis of appropriate agreements concluded between them." This provision gave Taraki confidence that Moscow would back him to the hilt. Article 8, which called on the two countries to facilitate "the creation of an effective security system in Asia" (the proposal Brezhnev had been promoting since 1969), tilted Afghanistan to the Soviet side of the Sino-Soviet dispute. Article 14 was unusual in that it allowed either party to give six months' notice, instead of the customary one year, for termination of the treaty.

For the first time, Moscow had achieved ideological congruence and de facto alliance with its strategically situated neighbor. In his effusive speech at the banquet held in the Great Kremlin Palace that night, Taraki said the treaty "is a resolute reply to the common enemies of the country of the October Revolution—the Soviet Union—and the country of the April Revolution—Afghanistan." As expanded quantities of arms, aid, and advisers poured into Afghanistan, the treaty wove a protective cocoon that, within a year, required for its defense the despatch of a Soviet army. The joint communiqué issued on December 7 added one point to the treaty: an admonition to the "forces of aggression" not to interfere in the internal affairs of Iran, "which directly borders both on the USSR and the DRA." The warning, a follow-up of Brezhnev's of November 19, came as the crisis in Iran was reaching its climax and the Shah was on the verge of losing his throne.

On February 14, 1979, U.S. Ambassador Adolph Dubs was kidnapped in downtown Kabul by a group of terrorists seeking the release of three prisoners (whose names were never divulged by Afghan authorities) and was killed four hours later by Afghan security police with four Russian advisers in attendance, in a purported rescue attempt. Whether through inexperience or preoccupation with eliminating its opponents, the Afghan government's indifference to U.S. appeals for caution reflected its general disdain for friendly ties with Washington. The Afghans' "callousness included the fact that not only was the Foreign Minister himself unavailable to the American Embassy during the crisis after the kidnapping and before the shoot-out, but he also did not appear at the Embassy to sign the condolence book nor at the airport ceremony when Ambassador Dubs' body departed Kabul."[4] The Soviet government denied having anything to do with the decisions of the Afghan police and stated that "Soviet representatives had arrived at the place of the incident with the aim of protecting the life of Soviet citizens, whom the terrorists were also threatening."[5] There is no evidence to substantiate the putative threat to Soviet nationals, and a report issued by the U.S. State Department a year later stops just short of charging Soviet culpability.[6] As a result of the Dubs incident, the United States terminated its small economic aid program, further reducing its presence and leaving the Soviet Union even more definitely the sole Afghan creditor.

Reports of tribal unrest had begun to filter out of Afghanistan in late summer of 1978. By the following spring, fierce resistance was openly challenging the regime and making a mockery of Taraki's assurance to an army group on February 1, 1979, that "there is now complete security and tranquility throughout the country."[7] A general rebellion spread from the remote province of Nuristan in the extreme east to all 28 of the country's provinces. On March 18 Pravda gave prominent attention to Kabul's (false) charge that Iran had sent several thousand Iranian soldiers, disguised as Afghans, across the border to trigger an uprising. The following day, the Kremlin's first authoritative commentary on the "bands of saboteurs and terrorists" who are calling for a " 'holy war' against the legal government" was published in Pravda, under the pseudonymous byline of I. Aleksandrov, who stressed the religious causes of the unrest and repeated Kabul's accusation against Iran.[8]

A revolt in Herat (400 miles west of Kabul) in mid-March elicited Soviet admission of the spreading spectre of counterrevolution. No longer did the media label Western reports of armed clashes "slanderous" and "absurd . . . propaganda sorties."[9] The unrest in Herat was blamed on "imperialism," on provocations from abroad, from "enemies of the revolution . . . testing the strength" of the borders to determine whether "brazen aggressive provocations and attacks on Afghanistan" could undermine or inhibit the revolution;[10] some commentators alleged the cause was Muslim "fanaticism" and compared the "bandits" to the Basmachis (a Turkic-language word meaning marauder or raider), a loosely linked grouping of Turkic-speaking Muslims who fought against the reimposition of Great Russian rule in Central Asia in the 1920s.

The insurrection was serious and, in early April, Moscow was worried enough to send General Aleksei A. Epishev, the head of the Main Political Directorate of the Soviet army and a hardliner who had strongly advocated the Soviet invasion of Czechoslovakia in August 1968, to assess the situation faced by Soviet advisers helping the Afghan army suppress the rebels; and also to make recommendations for tightening political control and discipline in the Afghan military, which was beginning to experience large-scale desertions. The USSR's military assistance—tanks, artillery, helicopter gunships, small arms, and ammunition—grew, and of necessity so did its direct involvement.

In May, as a follow-up to the Epishev visit, Moscow assigned Vassily Safronchuk, a veteran diplomat, to its embassy in Kabul. Though officially listed as minister-counselor, he was generally considered the one responsible for devising a political strategy for countering the mounting Afghan resistance, in practice relegating Ambassador Alexander Puzanov, who had served in Kabul since 1973, to a secondary role.[11] However, Moscow's attempt to find a political formula fell afoul of Afghan party infighting. Although completely dependent on Soviet support for their survival, Taraki and Amin (who had become prime minister in March) rejected out of hand the suggestion that they effect a reconciliation with Parcham and, instead, intensified their purge of its known adherents. The military position continued to deteriorate, and in August a large Soviet military delegation, headed by General Ivan Pavlovskii, a deputy defense minister, came to study the situation, remaining until October, when it allegedly returned with a grim assessment that may have been instrumental in the Kremlin's decision to invade.[12] Faced with guerrilla attacks and growing mutinies in the Afghan army, Soviet forces took over the Bagram airbase north of Kabul, the better to supply Soviet troops and establish a secure stronghold for possible expansion of Soviet activities.

In late summer the Soviet leadership had a number of options: to withdraw and permit the communist government to fall; to continue to back the Afghan regime, while at the same time pressuring it to follow a less rigid political strategy that might fragment the opposition; in addition to the search for a political solution, to destroy the resistance by an intensive use of air power and artillery, focusing attacks on villages suspected of aiding the opponents of the regime; to engineer a coup that would install a leadership more compliant with Soviet wishes; and to invade and assume the main responsibility for pacifying and transforming the country.

Meanwhile, Soviet relations with the United States were adversely affected by the situation. After the Carter-Brezhnev meeting in Vienna in June 1979, Moscow expected that President Carter would present the SALT II treaty to the Senate for ratification. It could not have been unaware of the possible political fallout from its greater involvement in Afghanistan. But so low was the U.S. credibility after it had allowed the Shah to fall, that Soviet leaders paid little heed to the Carter administration's stern warnings in March and again August, when Zbigniew Brzezinski, assistant to the president for national security affairs, stated that since the United States had shown "prudent" restraint during the crisis that toppled the Shah, "we expect others similarly to abstain from intervention and from efforts to impose alien doctrines on deeply religious and nationally conscious peoples."[13] The Kremlin's arrogance and/or ignorance of American domestic politics was such that it refused to make even some token concession during the mini-Cuban crisis that was spawned in July 1979 by the White House's "revelations" (aired by Senator Frank Church, who was running for reelection) concerning the Soviet combat brigade in Cuba, the net effect of which was to strengthen the anti-SALT and antidétente forces in the U.S. Senate.

A number of Afghan resistance groups were operating at this time, some based in Pakistan, some in Iran, but "most of the fighting in Afghanistan was undertaken by various localized ethnic, tribal, and sectarian groups without direct links" with organizations abroad.[14] The fragmentation of efforts minimized their political impact abroad and enabled the regime, reeling though it was, to retain control of the cities and main towns. The behavior of the Afghan resistance groups

is more reminiscent of the warlords of the Chinese Civil War than of the more coordinated Islamic Revolution of Iran. The fragile mosaic of social groups in Afghanistan underscores this segmenting effect. The rebel bands are isolated by their mountains, like the Hazaras; by linguistic and cultural identity, like the Nuristanis; or by bitter memories of political rivalries, like the Pathan Khans of Pakistan's North–West Frontier Province. It should not be forgotten that the Khalqis are all Ghilzai Pathans, long-time rivals of the Durrani Pathans, including the former royal family and many of the present rebel clans.[15]

Tragically for the Afghan freedom-fighters, their shared hatred of the Russians and communist rule has yet to congeal into a concrete political action program capable of unifying the diverse resistance groups; indeed, so deep-rooted and bitter are the personal and sectarian quarrels that they have not even been able to establish an umbrella organization (an equivalent, for example, of the Palestine Liberation Organization) under which all groups can be accommodated to present a common front against the Russians.[16]

FROM BETRAYAL TO BETRAYAL

Developments in Kabul soon narrowed Soviet options. On September 10, Taraki stopped in Moscow on his journey home from Havana where he had attended a nonaligned summit conference. According to TASS, in his meeting with Brezhnev and Gromyko, he received assurances that in its "just struggle" to build a new society, "the friendly Afghan people can further count on the Soviet Union's all-round and unselfish aid"; and the conversation was described as having been passed "in a heartfelt, comradely atmosphere."[17] However, the following day at the airport Taraki said merely that the meeting was held in "a *frank*, fraternal atmosphere" (italics added); and the Brezhnev-Taraki statement failed to declare "a complete unity of views" on bilateral issues, as it did with respect to international ones.[18]

On September 14, in circumstances that remain obscure, there was a shoot-out between Taraki and Amin, in which the latter survived a botched attempt to oust him. Two days later Radio Kabul announced that Taraki had resigned his government and party posts for "reasons of health" (an official statement issued on October 9 announced his having "succumbed to a grave disease he was ill with for some time"). The Soviet media reported the announcement without comment.

From available evidence, by no means conclusive, it appears that the chain of events was unleashed by the Kremlin's intriguing with Taraki to remove Amin and to introduce a more cautious policy: The Soviet leadership had given Taraki "an especially high-level reception in Moscow" and presumably would not have done so had they "been planning to get rid of him in a few days"; initial Soviet reactions were hesitant; Kosygin who returned to the Soviet Union "from India a few days later overflew Afghanistan but did not make a stop in Kabul, something that would have been expected had relations with Amin been correct"; and Ambassador Puzanov was replaced in November, at Amin's request.[19] Furthermore, since Taraki was already only a figurehead, Amin, who held the reins of power in the military and party, would have had little cause to act against him unless he saw an immediate threat to his own status or survival.

On September 17, evidently not enthusiastic but unabashed, the Kremlin sent formal congratulations: "We express confidence that fraternal relations between the Soviet Union and revolutionary Afghanistan will be further developed successfully on the basis of the treaty of friendship, good neighbor relations and cooperation." It congratulated Amin on his "election" to the posts of general secretary of the PDPA, chairman of the Revolutionary Council, and prime minister. Moscow even swallowed his accusations in early October of Soviet complicity in the bungled September coup.[20] For the moment, it had no viable alternative to support for Amin, and so went along with his harsh and varied attempts to stamp out the spreading rebellion.

Amin launched a series of local offensives, arrested thousands of Taraki supporters, removed the omnipresent portraits of Taraki and set about building up his own personality cult, established organizations such as the National Organization for the Defense of the Revolution in an effort to mobilize and control the population, created a constitutional commission, and regularly spoke of Soviet assistance and Afghanistan's unity with the socialist camp and the USSR.

The Soviet Union provided economic and military support, and Soviet commentators reported that "the Khalqi order is well established" and that Amin was building a society based on the dictatorship of the proletariat and the interests of the working class.[21] In Moscow, in late October, the first session of the Soviet-Afghan Intergovernmental Standing Commission for Economic Cooperation mapped out a program designed to expand Soviet involvement in the Afghan economy, especially in the exploration and extraction of natural gas, oil, and minerals.[22]

Amin pressed his relentless campaign against rebellious tribes in the northern and eastern provinces of Badakshan and Kunar, confident of and eager for increased Soviet military support. This uncritical confidence was his undoing and belies subsequent Western speculations that he was a Tito-in-the making:[23] He was difficult to deal with but completely pro-Soviet. Amin ignored the old adage: To sup with the Devil you need a long spoon.

By early December, when Lt. General Viktor Paputin, the first deputy minister of interior, arrived in Kabul, ostensibly to tighten security and coordinate plans for counterinsurgency operations, Soviet military personnel in Afghanistan numbered 3,500 to 4,000, at a minimum.[24] Security at the key airbase at Bagram, 31 miles north of Kabul, which had been assigned to Soviet troops since September, was strengthened with the arrival of additional combat troops. Transport aircraft flew in growing quantities of military equipment and supplies, with Amin's knowledge and apparent approval. On the diplomatic front, the presentation of credentials by the new Soviet ambassador on December 1 and the exchange of comradely messages between Brezhnev and Amin on December 5 (the first anniversary of the Soviet–Afghan treaty) suggested that Moscow had reconciled itself to working closely with him. Politically, the Soviet media approved Amin's establishment of the National Organization for the Defense of the Revolution—a umbrella organization to mobilize the masses against "the remnants of the feudal class, leftwing extremists, reactionary clergy and nationalists."[25] Criticism of alleged CIA interference grew. On December 13 Paputin left Kabul.[26] A week later Kabul radio announced that the offices of Amin's Revolutionary Council had been moved to the Darulalam Palace, on the outskirts of Kabul, near the Soviet Embassy. Not even reports of a large-scale buildup of Soviet troops on the Afghan border occasioned any second thoughts in Amin. The ruthless intriguer was cooperating fully in his own downfall. Moscow's grand deception was almost complete.

INVASION

On December 23, 1979, an article by A. Maslennikov in *Pravda* began with the following information printed in bold type:

WESTERN, AND PARTICULARLY AMERICAN, MASS MEDIA HAVE RECENTLY BEEN DISSEMINATING DELIBERATELY INSPIRED RUMORS ABOUT SOME SORT OF SOVIET "INTERFERENCE" IN AFGHANISTAN'S INTERNAL AFFAIRS. THINGS HAVE EVEN GOTTEN AS FAR AS ALLEGATIONS THAT SOVIET "COMBAT UNITS" HAVE BEEN INTRODUCED IN AFGHAN TERRITORY.

The next day the truth of these "rumors" and "transparent fabrications" was revealed, as Soviet transport planes, landing and taking off at 15-minute intervals, airlifted about 5,000 troops during the next three days. On December 27 the Soviet minister of communications, who had arrived in Kabul on December 24, paid a courtesy call on Amin and left in early afternoon. Up to the very end, Moscow feigned support of the sorely beset Amin.

At about 7 P.M. local time on December 27, Soviet troops seized the Ministry of Interior in the center of Kabul. Shortly thereafter the radio station, hitherto guarded by Afghan soldiers, was attacked. Soviet advisers had cleverly disarmed two key Afghan armored divisions "by persuading officers to turn over their ammunition for inventory and their tank batteries for winterizing,"[27] and Soviet troops poured across the border.

The first announcement of the coup was broadcast by Babrak Karmal from the Soviet Union in early evening of December 27. Shortly past midnight, on December 28, TASS transmitted the text of his message, announcing that "the torture machine of Amin . . . has been broken."[28] Three hours later Kabul radio reported a list of the members of the new Revolutionary Council, headed by Babrak Karmal, who was described as secretary-general of the PDPA and president of the Revolutionary Council; the execution of Hafizullah Amin by a "revolutionary tribunal"; and, in accordance with the 1978 treaty, a request from the government of the Democratic Republic of Afghanistan for Soviet military, political, economic, and moral assistance, to which the Soviet government agreed. Babrak Karmal, who was not in the country at the time, did not make his first public appearance until January 1, 1980, when he spoke on Kabul television.

Moscow justified its military invasion on the grounds that it had acceded to the "urgent request" of the DRA's government under Article 4 of the 1978 treaty for help in repelling "outside armed intervention" and that the "invitation" had come on December 28.[29] It is impossible to take this explanation at face value, because there is no evidence of any U.S., Chinese, or Pakistani "armed intervention" and because by that date Soviet troops had already invaded the country and occupied Kabul. Equally difficult to take seriously is the USSR's contention that its intervention was a response to previous requests. "In 1978-1979, the Afghan Government turned repeatedly to the Soviet union with requests for support, including military assistance, in response to armed interference by imperialist forces."[30] Left unanswered in this line of justification is the question: Why had the Kremlin acted to help Hafizullah Amin if he was the tyrant and stooge of American imperialism that he subsequently was alleged to have been all along? The explanation that Amin was in danger of being overthrown is specious: He was encountering strong resistance to his radical measures and harsh repression, but he was not threatened by the "clear and present danger" that would have warranted a full Soviet intervention. The Mujahedeen (Afghan freedom-fighters) were just not strong enough to wrest Kabul from the Moscow-backed regime.

Speculations based on the fragmentary evidence are endless, but Moscow's Jesuitical justifications need not preoccupy us. It is enough to know that Soviet troops did invade in force, killed Amin, and installed Karmal, the very same Karmal (a Parchamite) who had been purged by Nur Taraki (a Khalqi), whom Moscow regarded as having been the "lawful" president when killed by Amin in September 1979. What we may reasonably conclude from the information at our disposal is that Moscow used the treaty and the various requests of assistance as a *pretext* for its invasion.

Nor is it necessary, given the focus of this study on the influence relationship between the Soviet Union and Afghanistan, to examine the growing body of work that seeks to shed light on the considerations that prompted the Soviet leadership to invade.[31] Suffice it to say that the explanations vary greatly, each analysis being shaped by a priori and implicit (rarely explicit) assumptions about Soviet foreign policy in the Third World in general. Briefly, the Soviet decision to intervene is variously assessed as: a defensive reaction arising from growing concern that the instability might possibly spill over into the bordering Soviet Uzbek and Tadjik union republics; an underestimation of the costs of suppressing Afghan tribal resistance and installing a more compliant Soviet satrap; a fear that China and the United States would exploit a Soviet setback in Afghanistan and acquire increased influence in the Muslim world; a response to a target of opportunity that was especially attractive given U.S. preoccupation with the Iranian hostage crisis, and exploitation of which would inevitably in time vastly improve the USSR's geopolitical position vis-a-vis Iran, Pakistan, and India and a possible future drive to the Gulf; a shedding of restraint occasioned by the deterioration in relations with the United States and the belief that the SALT II treaty was dead; a manifestation of traditional Russian imperialism, which has always sought to acquire additional territory along its periphery; a necessary step toward eventual acquisition of warm–water ports on the Indian Ocean that also served to warn nations of the region to normalize relations with the Soviet Union and to avoid too heavy a reliance on the United States; and, finally, a determination argued forcefully in the Politburo by ideologues such as Mikhail Suslov not to abandon a progressive movement to reactionaries or allow it to fall victim to its own ultraleftist excesses. Whatever the controlling consideration(s) for the Kremlin, we can accept Brezhnev's word (in a statement on January 12, 1980) that "it was no simple decision."

The Soviet invasion was widely condemned abroad. On January 7, 1980, a UN Security Council resolution deploring the "armed intervention" and calling for the "immediate and unconditional withdrawal of foreign troops" was vetoed by the Soviet representative. Meeting in emergency session a week later, the General Assembly, by a vote of 104 to 18, with 18 abstentions, called for an immediate end to foreign intervention and the right of the Afghan people "to determine their own form of government and choose their economic, political and social systems free from outside intervention, subversion, coercion or constraint of any kind whatsoever." Conferences of Islamic countries have denounced (though not unanimously, because radical Arab states and movements, eager for Soviet support and weapons, prefer not to antagonize Moscow) the Soviet invasion. All to no avail.

On April 4, 1980, Moscow announced the ratification of a Treaty on the Temporary Stay of the Limited Soviet Military Contingent on Afghan Soil, the first indication the outside world had that a treaty institution-alizing a Soviet military presence was being negotiated. It is assumed that this treaty grants Soviet forces and their dependents extraterritorial privileges and immunities from local laws, like those in the Soviet-Czechoslovak treaty of October 1968, which legalized the presence of Soviet troops in Czechoslovakia after the Soviet military intervention the previous August. All evidence indicates that the Soviet army is planning for a long stay in Afghanistan: the Soviets are constructing permanent underground fuel and ammunition storage facilities, and are taking over the better-equipped Afghan bases; Soviet engineers have resurrected the long-discussed plan to build a railroad connecting the Soviet Union with Kabul, the only link at present being a small spur between the USSR and Afghanistan crossing the border near the Soviet city of Kushka; they are building two permanent bridges across the Oxus River, and upgrading key airfields to handle the growing volume of military traffic; and all kinds of new Soviet equipment are being used, and tested under combat conditions, for example,

> new armored personnel carriers and variants of known models, new models of multiple-rocket-launcher systems, new automatic mortars, new fixed-wing and helicopter aircraft, new assault rifles, a new battle-management computer system, self-propelled artillery, antipersonnel artillery shells, armored mine-laying vehicles, sophisticated mine-clearing equipment, and automatic grenade launchers.[32]

Despite economic and political pressure from the United States (though hardly of a consistent or sustained character, witness the Reagan administration's lifting in April 1981 of the grain embargo that the Carter administration had imposed in January 1980), and despite the general opprobrium of most Muslim countries, Moscow has shown no signs of being willing to ease its grip on Afghanistan. Probably typical of the Kremlin's attitude is the view expressed shortly after the intervention in an unsigned article in the foreign affairs journal New Times. Rebuking "some Communist parties" for adopting an ambivalent position and even expressing "doubts regarding the expediency and legitimacy" of the Soviet Union's military action, the article says:

> The experience of the revolutionary liberation struggle of the peoples shows that at critical moments solidarity with a victorious revolution calls not only for moral support but also for material assistance, including, under definite circumstances, military assistance. To deny support to the Afghan revolution, to leave it face to face with the forces of imperialist

reaction and aggression would have been to doom it to defeat, which would have been a serious blow to the entire Communist and national liberation movement.[33]

Highly reminiscent of the "Brezhnev Doctrine," enunciated in *Pravda* on September 26, 1968, in order to justify the invasion of Czechoslovakia, the article continued:

Today, when there exists a system of socialist states, it would be simply ridiculous to question the right to such assistance. In cases when such an extreme necessity arises, the Soviet Union acts fully in keeping with the norms of peaceful coexistence written into international acts. To refuse to use the possibilities at the disposal of the socialist countries would signify virtually evading performance of the internationalist duty and returning the world to the times when imperialism could throttle at will any revolutionary movement. In the given instance, not to come to Afghanistan's aid would signify leaving the Afghan revolution and people prey to the class enemies, to imperialism and feudal reaction and at the same time objectively helping imperialism to extend and make even more dangerous the seat of international tension in that region of the world.[34]

The Soviet leadership had decided, irrespective of possible short–term or residual difficulties, to do whatever was necessary to keep a pro-Soviet Communist party in power in Afghanistan.

CONSEQUENCES

The implications of the Soviet occupation of Afghanistan have yet to be fully absorbed by policy makers in affected countries. That landmark development will have profound consequences for the politics of South and Southwest Asia in the decades ahead.

Perhaps the most significance inheres in the advance of Moscow's military power to the Khyber Pass for the first time in its long imperial history. The USSR's domains now border directly on the Indian subcontinent, and as a result its diplomatic options and political leverage have been enormously increased. Whereas control of the Wakhan corridor contributes only marginally to the USSR's policy of outflanking China and heightening its sense of vulnerability, the frontal advance to the long and exposed Pakistani border unquestionably establishes the USSR as a force to be feared, even more than in the 1960s and 1970s, in the foreign policy evaluations of Islamabad and New Delhi. The era is largely past when Pakistan and India (and of course Afghanistan) could contemplate exploiting the U.S.-Soviet global rivalry to extract regional advantages.

Henceforth, the threat of intrusive and potentially disruptive Soviet power and subversion must condition the policies of the regional actors; for example, the issue of Baluch separatism, more than ever before, is susceptible to Soviet manipulation. The Persian Gulf states, too, now that Soviet power is less than 300 miles from the Strait of Hormuz, are on notice that in the future Moscow's interests and attitude will have to be considered more carefully than in the past. Time will tell how the "demonstration effect" translates into increments of Soviet influence on the politics of the region.[35]

Second, the Soviet move, coming as it did on the heels of the revolution in Iran with all that is implied therein for the spread of unrest and instability to the Arabian Peninsula, marks a new and dangerous step in the ongoing Soviet-American rivalry and a blow to prospects for the détente that the two superpowers tried to fashion in the early 1970s. Time and again, Moscow has acted in the Middle East to advance its objectives, regardless of the effects of its actions on its relations with Washington: It has fueled Middle East arms races, opposed U.S. efforts to reduce the likelihood of another Arab-Israeli war, and lavishly subsidized and supported anti-U.S. regimes and movements. With extension of Soviet control over Afghanistan, Moscow has, willy-nilly, signalled the primacy of its regional geostrategic ambitions over global concerns for stabilizing U.S.-Soviet relations. Whatever short-term difficulties Moscow faces in pacifying Afghanistan are overshadowed by the advantages that may redound to a Soviet Union entrenched on Afghan territory, and none more ominous, as far as U.S.-Soviet relations are concerned, than the enhanced options for undermining U.S. interests in the Persian Gulf-Arabian Peninsula region.

Finally, and of special relevance to our assessment of influence, the relationship between the Soviet Union and Afghanistan has been transformed, and permanently. No longer is it that of a powerful neighbor and patron interacting with an economically backward but politically independent client; it is now a relationship of ruler to ruled, of occupier to occupied, of invader to invaded. Afghanistan, which was never before in its history in the Russian sphere of influence, has lost its nonaligned and independent character. The "fraternal assistance," to use a Soviet phrase, being extended by Moscow may be costly, involve shedding blood, and have "negative" as well as "positive" aspects, but its aims are completely different from any that preceded the invasion of December 1979. Moscow's aim is no longer to exercise influence over an independent Third World country, but to incorporate Afghanistan into the USSR's imperial system.

Moscow wants the future Soviet-Afghan relationship to approximate that between the USSR and the People's Republic of Mongolia. In the early 1920s it installed a compliant Communist Party in power in Mongolia and granted that nation formal independence and a substantial measure of internal autonomy, while retaining full strategic control. In the 1930s Mongolia served as a defensive buffer against an aggressive and powerful Japan and provided defense in depth for a beleaguered Soviet Union. However, since the 1960s, when the USSR emerged as a superpower, Mongolia has been a base from which to threaten China. In accordance with what Owen Lattimore once called "the doctrine of irreversible minimum," the Soviet leadership considers its control over Mongolia permanent. Afghanistan seems likely to experience a similar fate.

EPILOGUE TO AN INFLUENCE RELATIONSHIP

With the KGB and the Soviet army functioning as judge and jury, subordination not asymmetry now characterizes the Soviet-Afghan relationship. The previously relevant data, such as joint communiqués and exchanges of missions (which have, incidentally, soared since April 1978—see Appendix 3), which presupposed the interaction of independent governments, can shed no light on the nature of the new political situation. As long as Soviet forces remain in the country and dispose of officials as so many pawns in the game of Sovietizing Afghanistan, the ability of the Afghans to bargain over issues or policies is severely circumscribed—if it exists at all. As Soviet surrogates, the Afghan communists have a long and difficult road to travel before they approach the autonomy enjoyed by Mongolia or the countries of Eastern Europe.

Afghanistan is a distinctive case in the USSR's quest for influence in the Third World, not because of Soviet readiness to use its military power outside of the Soviet bloc (since at various times the Soviet Union has deployed combat units in Cuba, Egypt, Ethiopia, Syria, and Iraq) but because this marks the first time in a Third World setting that Soviet troops have been used to replace one domestic faction with another; and because, notwithstanding the risk of international opprobrium, Moscow set greater store on institutionalizing ultimate Soviet authority through direct interference in the internal affairs of a friendly government than on continuing support for a communist client whose policies it deemed detrimental to long–term Soviet interests in the area. Contiguity was also a crucial catalyst, and it could occasion a similar Soviet response in Iran, if that revolution were to veer to the pro-Soviet left and then be threatened with destabilization and counterrevolution. However, the massive Soviet military intervention in Afghanistan is an improbable model for predicting Soviet policy in the Third World lying beyond the borders of Afghanistan and Iran.

For the foreseeable future, Moscow's aim is pacification. Through a combination of subsidies to tribal leaders, concessions, and coercion, Moscow seeks to break the back of serious resistance and gain acceptance for its PDPA puppet. The process may be lengthy, but the costs are not intolerable, and Moscow is patient. Estimates of the financial burden (economic and military) on the USSR vary greatly, but without trying to fix any actual dollar figure, most analysts believe that in the short run at least the burden is manageable. What no doubt helps ease the economic drain is the USSR's exploitation of Afghanistan's natural gas resources. In 1979 Afghanistan exported about 2.1 billion cubic meters of natural gas to Soviet Central Asia (97 percent of its total output).[36] This is about 15 percent of the amount that the USSR imported annually from Iran in the years preceding the Shah's fall. The Soviets do not publish the prices paid the Afghans, but it is reasonable to assume, based on information that we have of the prices paid to Iran and Afghanistan under the Shah and Daoud, respectively, that Moscow pays far below the world market rate and that this arrangement is highly profitable.

Shortly after being installed in office by the Red Army, Karmal adopted a number of measures to win popular support: he dropped the harsher impositions on the rural population, offered pardons for those who "repented," and changed the flag and emblem of the DRA from the red variant of a Soviet union republic adopted by Taraki to a less offensive tricolor that is supposed to symbolize "national and *religious* traditions" (italics added).[37] His repeated calls for reconciliation have, however, gone unheeded. He has failed to heal the rift with the Khalq, which resents the replacement of its adherents in the military and government by Parcha-mites, Parcham's stranglehold on PDPA membership, and Parcham's subordination to the Russians. He has also been unable to stop the hemorrhaging of the army, which through desertions has shrunk to less than half its former size and remains demoralized and unreliable. His problem of recruiting cadres can be seen in the year-long delay to find a suitable ambassador to send to Moscow.

While Babrak Karmal struggles to patch together a functioning regime, the Soviet army wars on "bandits" and "enemies" of the people, as Moscow calls the Mujahedeen. It engages in search-and-destroy missions that utilize helicopter gunships, artillery, and tanks in order to keep casualties to a minimum. Having found the resistance far stiffer than expected, the Soviets rely heavily on their monopoly of air power, strafing and napalming villages, interdicting communications and isolating resistance groups, preventing any concentration of enemy forces, and launching frequent, sharp strikes against points of resistance, particularly in the provinces bordering on Pakistan. In waging counterinsurgency operations, they even use, according to recurrent reports from Afghan refugees, lethal chemical agents to spread terror and fear among the local population.[38] For the moment, the Soviet strategy seems to seek control mainly of the urban centers (where the Parcham draws its support) and lines of communications and to depopulate the rural areas that offer resistance to occupation. The latter objective bears all the hallmarks of a conscious policy of selective genocide, that is, the systematic destruction of as much of Afghan tribal society as is necessary to ensure Soviet control over the country. The statistics provide some measurement of the scale of the Soviet drive to rid troublesome parts of Afghanistan of Afghans; they cannot convey the brutality and ruthlessness with which that drive is conducted: 100,000 refugees in the late spring of 1979 (after Taraki began his campaign to cow the tribal leaders into submission); 200,000 refugees in Pakistan by late 1979, and about 100,000 in Iran; the UN High Commissioner for Refugees (UNHCR) reported that on December 31, 1980, there were 1.4 million refugees in Pakistan and 400,000 in Iran; in the fall of 1981 the number in Pakistan had swelled to 2.4 million. By the end of 1981 almost 3 million Afghans—approximately 20 percent of the total population—had been driven from their homes and made refugees, and the number continues to grow. For the first time in their 2,500-year history, the tribesmen, who had always fought invaders, are being driven from their ancestral lands by an invader whose military power is a thousandfold greater than their own.

The most likely long-term Soviet aim is the institutionalization of rule by a compliant communist leadership, and not, as has been suggested by some Western officials and scholars, neutralization or a return to the nonalignment practiced by Afghanistan prior to the Saur Revolution (April 1978). The lack of success to date has occasioned a far-reaching effort to restructure political, military, juridical, social, educational, labor, and cultural institutions and to staff them with loyal, suitably indoctrinated cadres. "Socialist transformation" is being undertaken concurrent with counter-insurgency. This process of sovietization succeeded in Mongolia[39] and in the Muslim union republics of the USSR.[40] Because of the circumstances that brought the communists to power, Afghanistan should prove more difficult and more costly, but Moscow does not seem deterred or discouraged by the challenge.

Illustrative of the attention to institution-building was Babrak Karmal's announcement on December 27, 1980, the first anniversary of the Soviet military occupation, of the creation of a National Fatherland Front (NFF) that is intended to encompass a broad spectrum of nonparty and tribal representatives; enlist the participation of the Afghan people "in the building of a new society, a flourishing Afghanistan, with due consideration for the directives of the sacred religion of Islam, and the historical traditions of our society"; and "explain, publicize and propagate the policy of the Revolutionary Council and the government." On June 15,

1981, at the founding congress in Kabul, Saleh Mohammad Ziray (a Parchamite), member of the PDPA's Politburo and Central Committee and the DRA's Revolution Council, was appointed chairman. Soviet advisers and experts, who permeate every level of the government and make key decisions, are in the wings, offering guidance and shaping personnel shifts (what the Russians call *nomenklatura*). A few days earlier, the Revolutionary Council, the top organ of government, appointed Soltan Ali Keshtmand (a Parchamite and close associate of Karmal's) as prime minister (that is, the chairman of the DRA's Council of Ministers). Babrak Karmal, who relinquished the post, continues to be head of state (that is, president of the Revolutionary Council) and General Secretary of the party. Moscow, disappointed with Babrak Karmal's failure to reconcile the Kahlq and mobilize popular support for the regime, may be casting about for a successor and a suitable political formula for curbing the unrest and consolidating the newest addition to Moscow's imperium. But reliable satraps have always been hard to secure in Afghanistan, however. Among Moscow's options are: withdrawal, neutralization, conditional nonalignment, annexation, sovietization, and continued occupation with a low-level counterinsurgency effort. The following joke is told about the least likely scenario: Babrak Karmal, fearful for his life and eager to stay in power, goes to the country's leading religious figure to ask his help in getting the Russians to pull out and allow him to run the country. "Do you want me to use natural or supernatural means?" asks the Imam. Being a Marxist and a believer in the materialist explanation of political phenomena, Karmal asks what the use of natural means would entail. "I would call on the Prophet Mohammad to hurl down bolts of fire and visit innumerable plagues on the Russians till they left," explains the Imam. Amazed at this response, Karmal asks what the supernatural means would be, to which the reply is, "The Russians will leave voluntarily."

NOTES

1. I am indebted to Robin Knight, then bureau chief in Moscow for *U.S. News & World Report*, for bringing to my attention the pamphlet he had obtained from the Afghan Embassy. During a visit to Kabul in November 1978 he was told by Hafizullah Amin that the pamphlet was "out of date," thus prompting the speculation that it may have been intended for distribution in communist circles only. *International Herald Tribune*, March 17-18, 1979.

2. *The Daily Telegraph*, August 7, 1978.

3. For the text, see FBIS/USSR, December 6, 1978, J10-J13.

4. Theodore L. Eliot, Jr., "Afghanistan After the 1978 Revolution," *Strategic Review* 7, no. 2 (Spring 1979):61.

5. TASS statement in FBIS/USSR, February 22, 1979, J1.

6. "The Kidnapping and Death of Ambassador Adolph Dubs, February 14, 1979, Kabul, Afghanistan," Summary of Report of Investigation, prepared by the Special Assignments

Staff, Office of Security, Department of State, n.d. The report concludes with a note, both ironic and frustrating, that precludes our ever knowing the Afghan side of the incident:

Three of the principal Afghan officials involved in the Afghan Government's actions on February 14 have been subsequently killed. Sayed Daoud TAROON, who was the Commandant of Police and directed the action of the police from his office in the Interior Ministry, was killed in an intra-party power struggle at the People's Palace in Kabul on September 14, 1979. Lal MOHAMMAD, who was the Kabul Police Chief in charge of police at the hotel and who led the forced entry into Room 117, was killed in the countryside outside Kabul by insurgents about the same time. Hafizullah AMIN, who was the Foreign Minister/Deputy Prime Minister and later the President, was killed in Kabul on December 27, 1979 during a Soviet invasion of Afghanistan.

Dr. Steve R. Pieczenik, a former deputy assistant secretary of state, who resigned in November 1979 over the handling of the Iranian hostage crisis, alleges that the Dubs tragedy occurred because an official (unnamed) in the operations room of the State Department, when asked by the embassy in Kabul whether Afghan troops should attack,

"said yes—assault. As he hung up, a dispute broke out in the operations room. They *can't* attack, said another official. Dubs is likely to be killed . . . An urgent message was flashed immediately to our people in Kabul: *Under no circumstances—repeat no circumstances—should the room be assaulted.* But it was too late. The Afghans had gone in. Ambassador Dubs was dead."

Washington *Post*, February 15, 1981. The State Department denied Dr. Pieczenik's account. Washington *Post*, February 18, 1981. If his account is accurate, one must wonder why the Afghan authorities have never mentioned that they had been given a green light by the U.S. Embassy for the assault.

7. FBIS/USSR, February 2, 1979, J2.

8. I. Aleksandrov has been the pseudonym generally used for far–ranging criticisms of China. The narrow focus on Afghanistan was atypical of an Aleksandrov piece and was more in the style of *Pravda's* "Observer" articles. FBIS Trends in Communist Media, March 21, 1979, 1.

9. Moscow TASS in English January 15, 1979, in FBIS/USSR, January 18, 1979, J1.

10. For one such view, see *Krasnaia zvezda*, April 10, 1979, as quoted in FBIS/USSR, April 11, 1979, D1.

11. Salamat Ali, "Accepting the Limits of Aid," *Far Eastern Economic Review*, August 31, 1979.

12. Jiri Valenta, "From Prague to Kabul," *International Security* 5, no. 2 (Fall 1980):125–26.

13. New York *Times*, August 3, 1979.

14. Zalmay Khalilzad, "The Struggle for Afghanistan," *Survey* 25, no. 2 (Spring 1980):204.

15. David Chaffetz, "Afghanistan in Turmoil," *International Affairs* 56, no. 1 (January 1980):26.

16. At the meeting of Islamic foreign ministers held in Islamabad in late May 1980, the leaders of the different Afghan resistance groups were told that they "must make a greater show of unity to attract outside aid." New York *Times*, May 26, 1980.

17. FBIS/USSR, September 12, 1979, D1.

18. Ibid., D4.

19. Fred Halliday, "War in Afghanistan," *New Left Review*, no. 119 (January-February 1980), 34-35.

20. Ibid., pp. 35-36.

21. For example, Igor Savchenko, FBIS/USSR, October 15, 1979, D1.

22. *Pravda*, November 4, 1979.

23. See Selig S. Harrison, New York *Times*, January 13, 1980; December 22, 1980. His analogy does not take into consideration that Tito never relied on Soviet military advisers or faced an open rebellion; and that Yugoslavia, unlike Afghanistan, does not share a border with the Soviet Union, and had a strong Communist party organization.

24. Baltimore *Sun*, December 5, 1979.

25. FBIS/USSR, December 11, 1979, D1.

26. On January 3, 1980, *Pravda* reported Paputin's "untimely death" at the age of 53. According to well-informed Yugoslavs, he committed suicide. Other versions contend that he botched the assignment of persuading Amin to accept greater Soviet control and was shot by Amin's men; though if such were the case, Paputin would probably have received a prominent obituary instead of the minor notice on the back page. New York *Times*, February 3, 1980.

27. Los Angeles *Times*, January 10, 1980.

28. FBIS/USSR, December 28, 1979, D1.

29. *Izvestiia*, January 1, 1980.

30. An article signed by Alexei Petrov (a pseudonym) in *Pravda*, December 31, 1979.

31. For example, Selig S. Harrison, "Dateline Afghanistan: Exit Through Finland?" *Foreign Policy*, no. 41 (Winter 1980-81), 163-87; Mark Heller, "The Soviet Invasion of Afghanistan," *Washington Quarterly* 3, no. 3 (Summer 1980):36-59; Richard S. Newell, "Soviet Intervention in Afghanistan," *The World Today* 36, no. 7 (July 1980):250-58; Jiri Valenta, "From Prague to Kabul," *International Security* 5, no. 2 (Fall 1980):114-41; Jiri Valenta, "The Soviet Invasion of Afghanistan: The Difficulty of Knowing Where to Stop," *Orbis* 24, no. 2 (Summer 1980):201-18; B. Vivekanandan, "Afghanistan Invasion Viewed From India," *Asia Pacific Community*, Summer 1980, 63-82; Geoffrey Warhurst, "Afghanistan—A Dissenting Appraisal," *RUSI: Journal of the Royal United Services Institute for Defence Studies*, 125, no. 3 (September 1980):26-36; and Robert Weinland, "An (the?) Explanation of the Soviet Invasion of Afghanistan" (Washington, D.C.: Center for Naval Analyses, Professional Paper 309/May 1981).

32. Eliza Van Hollen, "Soviet Dilemmas in Afghanistan" (Washington, D.C.: Department of State, Bureau of Intelligence and Research, Special Report No. 72, June 1980), 3.

33. "World Communist Solidarity with the Afghan Revolution," *New Times*, no. 3 (January 18, 1980), 9.

34. Ibid.

35. A glimmer of what may be expected in the years ahead can be detected in the Soviet report of an interview granted a Paris published Arabic language weekly by Shaykh Zaid Ibn Sultan al Nuhayyan, the head of state of the United Arab Emirates, in which he criticized Western accounts of the Soviet military involvement in Afghanistan and, according to *Krasnaia zvezda*, "rejected allegations that the presence of a limited Soviet military contingent" in Afghanistan "poses any threat to the states situated in the Persian Gulf region." FBIS/USSR, June 15, 1981, H4.

36. FBIS/USSR, April 1, 1980, D5.

37. FBIS/USSR, April 28, 1980, D1.

38. See Sterling Seagrave, *Yellow Rain: A Journey Through the Terror of Chemical Warfare*. New York: Evans, 1981.

39. For example, see C. R. Bawden, *The Modern History of Mongolia* (New York: Praeger, 1968); Henry S. Bradsher, "The Sovietization of Mongolia," *Foreign Affairs* 50, no. 3 (April 1972): 545-54; and Robert Rupen, *Mongols in the Twentieth Century* (Paris: Mouton, 1964).

40. For example, see Alexandre Benningsen, "Soviet Muslims and the World of Islam," *Problems of Communism* 29, no. 2 (March-April 1980):38-51; Alexandre A. Benningsen and

S. Enders Wimbush, *Muslim National Communism in the Soviet Union* (Chicago: University of Chicago Press, 1979); Alexandre Benningsen and Chantal Lemercier-Quelquejay, *Islam in the Soviet Union* (New York: Praeger, 1967); Sir Olaf Caroe, *Soviet Empire: The Turks of Central Asia and Stalinism* (London: Macmillan, 1953); and Geoffrey Wheeler, *The Modern History of Soviet Central Asia* (New York: Praeger, 1964).

9

THE DYNAMICS OF INFLUENCE

The Soviet Union has achieved its greatest strategic-political triumph in the Third World in the changed policies of Turkey, Iran, and Afghanistan. Since the late 1950s and early 1960s, when its courtship shifted into high gear, the regional environment has altered in ways that have made Moscow the prime beneficiary. Its successes have amply repaid all Soviet efforts of the past two decades.

Moscow's interest in fostering better relations accorded with the desire of its three non-Arab Muslim neighbors for assistance and quiet borders. It normalized diplomatic relations, extended economic assistance, and eased military pressures. Notwithstanding inevitable disagreements and difficulties, there were no abrupt cancellations of aid, no suspensions of agreements, and no strong-arm tactics. Moscow was a persevering suitor—patient, flexible, and prudent. The effect of the overall Soviet courtship was that the deep-rooted fears of traditional Russian imperial ambitions were allayed sufficiently to permit these countries to redirect their priorities to domestic problems and other regional matters. Each side deferred to the other on issues they did not deem essential; asymmetries of aims and priorities kept disagreements minimal and allowed for an improvement in relations. Toward the end of the 1970s the pattern of bilateral interactions and the range of activities between the Soviet Union and the three countries had become impressive.

The relaxation of tensions with the Soviet Union occurred against a background of deteriorating relations with the United States. Moscow's consistency contrasted with Washington's vacillations and contributed to disenchantment with the United States. That Turkey, Iran, and Afghanistan would want to normalize relations with their powerful neighbor to the north was geopolitically natural, but the USSR's success in cultivating a benign image and the U.S. move toward détente with the USSR disposed them to venturesome regional policies that were beyond their capabilities and that inadvertently redounded to the USSR's advantage.

The success of Soviet policy inhered in its differentiated, gradualist and permissive character. In return for assistance, Moscow required only what was easy for it to obtain, namely, the normalization of relations. Its concern primarily with bilateral connections meant that it could respond quickly and cater to the desires of the courted country. Moscow did not set conditons, such as the legalization of local communist parties or changes in a client's alliances. It accommodated to the domestic and regional priorities established by the Turkish, Iranian, and Afghan leaderships. By way of contrast, America's policy of containment in the area was conceptually flawed, because it ignored the diverse and often divergent interests of the countries it sought to ally. Washington stressed the Soviet threat long after the regional actors had discounted its immediacy and directed their primary efforts elsewhere. Moreover, where the U.S. embrace was often overbearing, the Soviet Union's was relatively unobtrusive. Soviet policy was directed toward optimizing improvement in the short term; its ultimate goals were left deliberately ambiguous, in order not to interfere with the process of diplomatic normalization and expanding interactions.

A series of dramatic events in the late 1970s so altered the situation in this crucial sector of the Third World that by the beginning of the 1980s Soviet policy was operating in a completely different, and more promising, setting. All the changes cannot be attributed to mere happenstance.As with any reversal of outlook or alignment, the causes were multiple and complex, but in great measure the behavior of the Soviet Union itself prepared the way. The Soviet presence was important, so that once domestic developments unhinged the general regional configuration that had held sway in the Iranian-Afghan sector since the Bolshevik Revolution and the end of World War I, and in the Turkish sector since World War II, the Soviet Union was able to exercise its power and leverage to fashion a strategic environment conducive to the promotion of its ambitions. Just as in the early part of the twentieth century internal troubles in Russia stymied imperial expansion, so in the late 1970s and 1980s domestic instability in the tier states has faciliated Moscow's hegemonial ambitions and the advancement of its long-term objective of bringing about the dealignment of the entire rimland region from Greece to Afghanistan. Looked at in historical perspective, the Soviet Union's strategic situation in the area has never been better.

Our aim was to examine three important bilateral relationships, to concentrate on the key issues that dominated them. As always in evaluating influence, it is necessary to consider three levels for analysis: (1) the domestic system of the target country, (2) the government-to-government relationship, and (3) the regional subsystem in which the two countries are interacting. In a policy-oriented study of bilateral relationships, inevitably, the focus is on the second, but where appropriate, commentary is made on the first and third. For most of the period covered in this study the evidence showed that the USSR's policy did not shape, in any significant way, domestic institutions or policies (for Afghanistan, 1978 was, of course, a watershed in this respect). It also became clear that at the government-to-government level, under conditions of internal cohesion and strength, small states were not only able to resist the imposition of a superpower's will but also to use the relationship for their own limited and local interests. Thus, on narrow issues, the weaker party was often able to exact concessions from the stronger, for two basic reasons. First, the courting power did not want the courted to look elsewhere, lest its options be decreased; second, it considered the give-and-take and the achievements and disappointments on specific issues within a broader strategic context, that is to say, within a multilateral arena.

If we wish to understand and evaluate properly the reasons for the commitments and behavior of a superpower patron toward a Third World country, it is necessary that we assess the superpower's policy in the regional and global context that impels its overall foreign policy. For even if a superpower is unable to impose its preference on the domestic or foreign policy behavior of a client, it may nonetheless be quite satisfied with the bilateral relationship because of the accretion of regional and global advantages that stem from encouragement of a client's general policy orientation. In short, strategic context is intrinsic to any assessment of an influence relationship. Looked at in this way, Soviet diplomacy toward Turkey, Iran, and Afghanistan in the period since the early 1960s must be judged to have been remarkably skillful and successful; some might add lucky.

Another conclusion derived from the case studies is the impermanence of influence in the Third World, where regimes generally lack a popular base and hence are vulnerable to sudden deposal. Drastic changes in domestic leadership, outlook, and policy provided Moscow with its opportunities for sudden political gains. To be positioned for these diplomatic windfalls that can transform the strategic environment is— even more than the desire for concessions on the normal run of day-to-day issues—possibly a superpower's major reason for nurturing an influence relationship. This is why, in other words, a superpower feels it should court Third World countries.

As it looks ahead, the Soviet Union has cause for confidence. The Straits are accessible as never before, and Moscow anticipates no major problem in using them to promote its forward policy in Africa and the Arab East. Iran is in chaos. As in the nineteenth century, it is once again a target of opportunity for Russian encroachment; moreover, unlike a century ago, there is no countervailing great power effectively situated to thwart Moscow's expansion. Afghanistan appears to have fallen permanently into the Soviet sphere of influence. For the first time in Moscow's long imperialistic tradition, the Khyber Pass, not the Oxus (Amu Darya) River, marks the farthest line of advance. Barring a most unlikely diplomatic offensive from the Muslim world, the Soviet army of occupation will remain, operating on the principle expressed by Czar Nicholas II in 1850, when he was informed that a Russian officer had exceeded instructions and seized some Chinese territory: "Where the Russian flag has once been hoisted it must not be lowered."

The Soviet Union has fashioned new relationships with the Muslim lands on its southern border. Its influence over them in the years ahead will significantly affect the politics and prospects for peace in the region and the nature of the U.S.-Soviet adversarial relationship.

APPENDIXES

APPENDIX 1. Soviet-Turkish Exchange of Missions

Year	Political		Economic		Military		Cultural/Scientific	
	to Turkey	to the USSR	to Turkey	to the USSR	to Turkey	to the USSR	to Turkey	to the USSR
1970	1	1	1	0	0	0	0	0
1971°	0	0	0	0	0	0	0	0
1972	1	0	0	0	0	0	0	0
1973°	0	0	0	0	0	0	0	0
1974	1	1	1	0	0	0	0	0
1975	1	3	5	2	0	1	0	2
1976	1	3	1	2	0	0	0	2
1977	1	1	1	2	0	0	2	0
1978	2	3	2	4	1	0	4	6
1979	2	4	3	5	0	0	0	1
1980	1	4	2	2	0	0	0	0
1981	0	0	2	1	0	0	1	0

°Possibly incomplete data.
Source: Compiled by the author.

APPENDIX 2. Soviet-Iranian Exchange of Missions

Year	Political		Economic		Military		Cultural/Scientific	
	to Iran	to the USSR	to Iran	to the USSR	to Iran	to the USSR	to Iran	to the USSR
1968	2	2	2	6	1	0	1	2
1969	1	2	1	4	0	0	0	3
1970	4	4	2	1	0	0	1	2
1971°	1	0	0	1	0	0	0	0
1972	0	1	0	1	0	0	0	0
1973	1	1	10	2	0	1	1	4
1974	0	4	4	3	0	0	4	4
1975	1	2	3	6	0	0	0	2
1976	0	2	4	1	0	0	1	0
1977	0	0	3	4	0	0	0	0
1978	0	0	2	1	0	0	2	1
1979	0	0	1	2	0	0	0	0
1980	0	0	1	2	0	0	1	0
1981	0	1	2	3	0	0	0	1

°Incomplete data.
Source: Compiled by the author.

APPENDIX 3. Soviet-Afghan Exchange of Missions

Year	Political to Afghanistan	Political to the USSR	Economic to Afghanistan	Economic to the USSR	Military to Afghanistan	Military to the USSR	Cultural/Scientific to Afghanistan	Cultural/Scientific to the USSR
1964	3	4	1	0	0	1	0	3
1965°	2	2	0	0	0	0	0	2
1966	3	3	0	1	0	1	1	2
1967	2	1	0	0	0	1	1	1
1968	1	2	1	1	0	0	1	5
1969	2	2	0	1	2	1	1	2
1970	0	3	2	4	0	2	1	1
1971°	1	2	1	0	0	2	0	0
1972°	2	1	1	2	2	2	0	0
1973	2	2	2	1	1	0	0	0
1974	0	1	3	2	0	1	0	1
1975	1	1	4	1	0	1	0	1
1976	0	2	4	2	0	0	1	0
1977	1	2	1	2	0	0	1	0
1978	2	3	4	4	0	0	4	3
1979	4	3	4	5	2	0	1	2
1980	3	11	2	8	0	3	3	7
1981	0	13	1	5	2	2	4	7

°Possibly incomplete data.
Source: Compiled by the author.

SELECTED BIBLIOGRAPHY

SOVIET-TURKISH RELATIONS

Anderson, M. S. *The Eastern Question, 1774-1923*. New York: St. Martin's Press, 1966.

Carr, Edward H *The Bolshevik Revolution 1917-1923*, Vol. III. New York: Macmillan, 1953

Erkin, Feridun Cemal. *Les Relations turco-soviétiques et la question des Détroits*. Ankara: Basnur Matbaasi, 1968.

Gürkan, Ihsan. *NATO, Turkey and the Southern Flank: A Mideastern Perspective*. New York: National Strategy Information Center, 1980.

Harris, George S. *The Origins of Communism in Turkey*. Stanford, Calif.: The Hoover Institution, 1967.

_____. *Troubled Alliance: Turkish-American Problems in Historical Perspective 1945-1971*. Washington, D.C.: American Enterprise Institute, 1972.

Hostler, Charles W *Turkism and the Soviets*, New York: Praeger, 1957.

Hurewitz, J. C., ed *The Middle East and North Africa in World Politics: A Documentary Record*, 2d ed., Vol. II, *British-French Supremacy, 1914-1945*. New Haven, Conn.: Yale University Press, 1979.

Kapur, Harish. *Soviet Russia and Asia, 1917-1927: A Study of Soviet Policy Towards Turkey, Iran and Afghanistan*. Geneva: Michael Joseph, 1966.

Karpat, Kemal H. *Turkey's Politics*. Princeton, N.J.: Princeton University Press, 1959.

Kilic, Altemur. *Turkey and the World*. Washington, D.C.: Public Affairs Press, 1959.

Kinross, Lord. *Ataturk: A Biography of Mustafa Kemal*. New York: William Morrow, 1965.

Kirk, George. *Survey of International Affairs: The Middle East in the War*. London: Oxford University Press, 1952.

Kuniholm, Bruce R. *The Origins of the Cold War in the Near East: Great Power Conflict and Diplomacy in Iran, Turkey, and Greece*. Princeton, N.J.: Princeton University Press, 1980.

Landau, Jacob M. *Radical Politics in Modern Turkey*. Leiden: E. J. Brill, 1974.

Mango, Andrew. *Turkey: A Delicately Poised Ally*. Beverly Hills, Calif.: Sage Publications, 1975.

Robinson, Richard D. *The First Turkish Republic: A Case Study in National Development*. Cambridge, Mass.: Harvard University Press, 1963.

Sezer, Duygu Bazoğlu. *Turkey's Security Policies*. London: International Institute for Strategic Studies, 1981.

Shaw, Stanford J. and E. K. Shaw. *History of the Ottoman Empire and Modern Turkey*, Vol. II. Cambridge: Cambridge University Press, 1977.

Váli, Ferenc A. *Bridge Across the Bosporus: The Foreign Policy of Turkey*. Baltimore: Johns Hopkins University Press, 1971.

_____. *The Turkish Straits and NATO*. Stanford, Calif.: Hoover Institution Press, 1972.

Weber, Frank G. *The Evasive Neutral: Germany, Britain and the Quest for a Turkish Alliance in the Second World War*. Columbia: University of Missouri Press, 1979.

Weiker, Walter F. *The Modernization of Turkey, 1923-1979*. New York: Holmes and Meier, 1979.

Weisband, Edward. *Turkish Foreign Policy 1943-1945: Small State Diplomacy and Great Power Politics*. Princeton, N.J.: Princton University Press, 1973.

SOVIET-IRANIAN RELATIONS

Amirsadeghi, Hossein, ed. *Twentieth-Century Iran*. New York: Holmes and Meier, 1977.

Atkins, Muriel. *Russia and Iran, 1780-1828*. Minneapolis: University of Minnesota Press, 1980.

Browne, Edward G. *The Persian Revolution of 1905-1909*. Cambridge: Cambridge University Press, 1910.

Chubin, Shahram. *Soviet Policy Towards Iran and the Gulf*. London: International Institute for Strategic Studies, Adelphi Paper 157, 1980.

Cottam, Richard W. *Nationalism in Iran*, rev. ed. Pittsburgh: University of Pittsburgh Press, 1979.

Curzon, George N. *Persia and the Persian Question*, 2 vols. London: Longmans, Green, 1892.

_____. *Russia in Central Asia in 1889 and the Anglo-Russian Question*. London: Longmans, Green, 1889.

Eagleton, William Jr. *The Kurdish Republic of 1946*. New York: Oxford University Press, 1963.

Entner, Marvin L. *Russo-Persian Commercial Relations, 1828-1914*. Gainsville: University of Florida Press, 1965.

Fatemi, Faramarz S. *The U.S.S.R. in Iran*. Cranbury, N.J.: A. S. Barnes, 1980.

Fatemi, Nasrollah S. *Diplomatic History of Persia 1917-23*. New York: R. F. Moore, 1952.

Frye, Richard N. *Iran*. New York: Henry Holt, 1953.

Graham, Robert. *Iran: The Illusion of Power*. New York: St. Martin's Press, 1978.

Hamzavi, Abdol H. *Persia and the Powers*. London: Hutchinson, 1950.

Kazemzadeh, Firuz. *Russia and Britain in Persia, 1864-1914; A Study in Imperialism*. New Haven, Conn.: Yale University Press, 1968.

Keddie, Nikki R. *Roots of Revolution: An Interpretive History of Modern Iran*. New Haven, Conn.: Yale University Press, 1981.

Lenczowski, George. *Russia and the West in Iran, 1918-1948*. Ithaca, N.Y.: Cornell University Press, 1949.

_____. ed. *Iran Under the Pahlavis*. Stanford, Calif.: Hoover Institution Press, 1978.

Mohammad Reza Pahlavi, the Shah of Iran. *Mission For My Country*. New York: McGraw-Hill, 1961.

_____. *Answer to History*. Briarcliff Manor, N.Y.: Stein and Day, 1980.

Nollau, Gunther and Hans Wiehe. *Russia's South Flank: Soviet Operations in Iran, Turkey, and Afghanistan*. New York: Praeger, 1963.

Pierce, Richard A. *Russian Central Asia 1867-1917*. Berkeley: University of California Press, 1960.

Ramazani, Rouhollah K. *The Foreign Policy of Iran, 1500-1941*. Charlottesville: University Press of Virginia, 1966.

_____. *Iran's Foreign Policy 1941-1973*. Charlottesville: University Press of Virginia, 1975.

Rezun, Miron. *The Soviet Union and Iran: Soviet Policy in Iran from the Beginnings of the Pahlavi Dynasty until the Soviet Invasion in 1941*. Leiden: Sijthoff, 1981.

Saikal, Amin. *The Rise and Fall of the Shah*. Princeton, N.J.: Princeton University Press, 1980.

Sykes, Sir Percy M. *A History of Persia*, 2 vols. London: Macmillan, 1915.

Thomas, Lewis and Richard N. Frye. *The United States and Turkey and Iran*. Cambridge, Mass.: Harvard University Press, 1952.

Vambery, Arminius. *Central Asia and the Anglo-Russian Frontier Question*. London: Smith, Elder & Co., 1874.

Wilbur, Donald N. *Iran: Past and Present*. 7th ed. Princeton, N.J.: Princeton University Press, 1975.

_____. *Riza Shah Pahlavi: The Resurrection and Reconstruction of Iran 1878-1944*. Hicksville, N.Y.: Exposition Press, 1975.

Zabih, Sepehr. *The Communist Movement in Iran*. Berkeley: University of California Press, 1966.

SOVIET-AFGHAN RELATIONS

Adamec, Ludwig W. *Afghanistan's Foreign Affairs to the Mid-Twentieth Century: Relations with the USSR, Germany, and Britain*. Tucson: University of Arizona Press, 1974.

_____. *Afghanistan 1900-1923*. Los Angeles: University of California Press, 1967.

Arnold, Anthony. *Afghanistan: The Soviet Invasion in Perspective*. Stanford, Calif.: Hoover Institution Press, 1981.

Becker, Seymour. *Russia's Protectorates in Central Asia: Bukhara and Khiva, 1865-1924* Cambridge, Mass.: Harvard University Press, 1968.

Caroe, Olaf. *The Pathans: 550 B.C.–A.D. 1957*, 3rd ed. New York: Oxford University Press, 1967.

_____. *Soviet Empire: The Turks of Central Asia and Stalinism*. London: Macmillan, 1953.

Chakravarty, Suhash. *From Khyber to Oxus*. New Delhi: Orient Longman Ltd, 1976.

Curzon, George N. *Russia in Central Asia*. London: Longmans, Green, 1889.

Dupree, Louis. *The First Russo-Afghan War*. Bloomington: Indiana University Press, 1982.

_____. *Afghanistan*. 2nd Printing, Princeton, N.J.: Princeton University Press, 1980.

Fletcher, Arnold. *Afghanistan: Highway of Conquest*. Ithaca, N.Y.: Cornell University Press, 1965.

Fraser-Tytler, W. K.. *Afghanistan*, 3d ed. London: Oxford University Press, 1967.

Gregorian, Vartan. *The Emergence of Modern Afghanistan: Politics of Reform and Modernization, 1880-1946*. Stanford, Calif.: Stanford University Press, 1969.

Griffiths, John C. *Afghanistan: Key to a Continent* Boulder, Colo.: Westview Press, 1981

Harrison, Selig S. *In Afghanistan's Shadow: Baluch Nationalism and Soviet Temptations*. Washington, D.C.: Carnegie Endowment for International Peace, 1981.

Hobberton, William. *Anglo-Russian Relations Concerning Afghanistan, 1837-1907*. Urbana: University of Illinois Press, 1937.

House of Commons. Fifth Report from the Foreign Affairs Committee 1979/1980 Session on "Afghanistan: The Soviet Invasion and Its Consequences for Britain." London: Her Majesty's Stationery Office, 1980.

Hussain, Syed Shabbir, Abdul Hamid Alvi, and Absar Hussain Rizvi. *Afghanistan under Soviet Occupation*. Islamabad: World Affairs Publications, 1980.

Keay, John. *The Gilgit Game*. London: Archon, 1979.

Miller, Charles. *Khyber: British India's North West Frontier*. New York: Macmillan, 1977.

Misra, K. P., ed. *Afghanistan in Crisis*. New Delhi: Vikas, 1981.

Monks, Alfred L. *The Soviet Intervention in Afghanistan, 1979-1980*. Washington, D.C.: American Enterprise Institute, 1981.

Morgan, Gerald. *Anglo-Russian Rivalry in Central Asia 1810-1895*. London: Frank Cass, 1981.

Newell, Nancy Peabody and Richard S. Newell. *The Struggle for Afghanistan*. Ithaca, N.Y.: Cornell University Press, 1981.

Newell, Richard S. *The Politics of Afghanistan*. Ithaca, N.Y.: Cornell University Press, 1972.

Poullada, Leon B. *Reform and Rebellion in Afghanistan 1919-1929: King Amanullah's Failure to Modernize a Tribal Society*. Ithaca, N.Y.: Cornell University Press, 1973.

Rawlinson, Major General Sir Henry. *England and Russia in the East*. London: John Murray, 1875.

Sykes, Sir Percy. *A History of Afghanistan*, Vol. II. London: Macmillan, 1940.

Teplinskii, L. B. *50 Let sovetsko-afghanskikh otnosheniia 1919-1969*. Moscow: Nauka, 1971.

Wolpert, Stanley. *Roots of Confrontation in South Asia: Afghanistan, Pakistan, India, and the superpowers*. New York: Oxford University Press, 1982.

Yapp, M. E. *Strategies of British India: Britain, Iran and Afghanistan, 1798-1850*. Oxford: Clarendon Press, 1980.

ABOUT THE AUTHOR

ALVIN Z. RUBINSTEIN is Professor of Political Science at the University of Pennsylvania, and Senior Fellow of the Foreign Policy Research Institute.

He has written widely on Soviet and communist policies toward the Third World. In addition to numerous articles, his publications include: *Soviet Foreign Policy Since World War II: Imperial and Global*, *Red Star on the Nile: The Soviet-Egyptian Influence Relationship Since the June War*, *Yugoslavia and the Nonaligned World*, and *The Soviets in International Organizations*.

Dr. Rubinstein has received fellowships from the Ford Foundation, the Rockefeller Foundation, the Earhart Foundation, and the John Simon Guggenheim Memorial Foundation.